Applying the Wisdom of the Word

# Applying the Wisdom of the Word

## A Golden Treasury of Quotations for Everyday Life from Matthew Henry's *Commentary On The Whole Bible*

Selected and Thematically Arranged by Dave G. Becher

Copyright © 2017, Dave G. Becher

All rights reserved. No part of this book may be reproduced, scanned, or distributed in any printed or electronic form without permission.

Unless otherwise indicated, Scripture quotations in this publication are from The Authorized (King James) Version.

This Edition: 2017

ISBN: 978-0-9988812-3-2

Book Design and Typesetting by Great Writing Publications
Cover Concept and Design by Great Writing Publications
www.greatwriting.org
Taylors, SC, USA

For my granddaughter, Jordan

Having you in my life has let me know
what it feels like to be kissed by God.

# Contents

Acknowledgments ......................................................................... 9
Textual Note ................................................................................ 11
Preface .......................................................................................... 13

Part I: Folly (Damnation) ............................................................ 15
1. Disbelief .................................................................................. 16
2. Willful Disobedience ............................................................. 30
3. Scorners ................................................................................... 40
4. Corruption .............................................................................. 52
5. Pride, Vanity, Misplaced Faith in Man .............................. 62
6. Judges, Politicians, National Sins ....................................... 72
7. Pharisees ................................................................................. 84
8. Hypocrisy ............................................................................... 96
9. Carnality and Idolatry ........................................................ 108
10. Flattery, Lies, Deception .................................................... 120
11. Judgment and Retribution ................................................ 132

Part II: Wisdom (Salvation) ...................................................... 147
1. Repentance and Forgiveness ............................................. 148
2. Pardon and Redemption .................................................... 160
3. Mercy and Grace ................................................................. 172
4. Patience and Faith ............................................................... 186
5. Obedience and Perseverance ............................................ 200
6. Communion and Prayer .................................................... 214
7. Humility ............................................................................... 228
8. Backsliding and Discipline ................................................ 240
9. Rewards and Blessings ...................................................... 250
10. Service .................................................................................. 262
11. Ministers .............................................................................. 280
12. Prophecy .............................................................................. 296

Thematic Subtopic Index .......................................................... 308

# Acknowledgements

I thank Graham Hind of Evangelical Press for putting me into contact with Jim Holmes of Great Writing Publications, www.greatwriting.org. Without Jim's invaluable direction, this book would never have come to publication.

# Textual Note

All quotes are taken from

MATTHEW HENRY'S COMMENTARY ON THE WHOLE BIBLE
New Modern Edition
Complete and Unabridged in Six Volumes
Copyright 1991 by Hendrickson Publishers, Inc.
ISBN: 0-943575-51-6
Third Printing—September 1994

Original spellings from Matthew Henry have been retained in the body text of this book.

# Preface

## The Whole Duty of Man

> [9] And moreover, because the Preacher was wise, he still taught the people knowledge; yes, he pondered and sought out *and* set in order many proverbs. [10] The Preacher sought to find acceptable words; and *what was* written *was* upright-words of truth. [11] The words of the wise are like goads, and the words of scholars are like well-driven nails, given by one Shepherd. [12] And further, my son, be admonished by these. Of making many books *there is* no end, and much study *is* wearisome to the flesh.
> [13] Let us hear the conclusion of the whole matter: Fear God and keep His commandments, For this is man's all. [14] For God will bring every work into judgment, Including every secret thing, Whether good or evil. —Ecclesiastes 12:9-13.

As I read and studied Matthew Henry's inspired *"Commentary On The Whole Bible,"* I began to mark in the backs of the books the page numbers of those notes of his that I found instructive, and which had enlightened me in some way. After many years of compiling these page number references (through multiple readings of his work), I realized that the numbers themselves were useless without the actual quotations. Thus began the lengthy process of looking up each of the thousands of numerical references I had made, and transferring them all to paper, to *"set in order"* the material so as to make the most sense of its broad range.

The chapters herein are of my own construction and represent an attempt at creating some order out of that random chaos. Many of the quotes are overlapping in subject content, and could be placed under other chapter headings. One hundred people tasked with organizing this material would, no doubt, come up with one hundred differing arrangements. I placed them to the best of my ability, guided by the Spirit, in an attempt to maintain the continuity of thought within each chapter. The notes within, ministerial and proverbial in nature, are all Matthew Henry's Spirit-inspired observations of biblical Scripture, and are presented here as a

## Preface

quick summary of deeper issues—so as not to become *"wearisome to the flesh"* in study. The over-six thousand pages of fine print in the original work have taken me years just to read through and study, once. I have now read through this complete work four times.

I feel that this summary of key elements of his wisdom, organized into handy reference chapters, is a good way for people to be introduced to this monumental work, since the sheer volume of it is daunting to most. Though each quote was written in regard to a specific biblical incident, I have placed them under general headings for a more universal application in our own lives (while acknowledging the specific book, chapter, and verse on which Matthew Henry was expounding).

It is presented in two parts, *Folly* and *Wisdom*, because "Words of conviction must be followed with words of comfort, for he that has torn will heal us." It is my fervent prayer that they enlighten you as they did me.

"We must not bury our talent, though it be but one, but, as we have received the gift, so minister the same, if it be but to collect what others have written." Matthew Henry

*Dave. G. Becher, July 2017*

# Part I

## Folly (Damnation)

# -1-

# Disbelief

Disbelief is a sin by which men greatly dishonour and displease God, and deprive themselves of the favours he designed for them.

Matthew Henry
on 2 Kings 7:2

Disbelief is a sin by which men greatly dishonour and displease God, and deprive themselves of the favours he designed for them. (2 Kings 7:2)

Those that live in unbelief are forever undone if they die in unbelief. (John 8:24)

Our unbelief and distrust are a great offence to the God of heaven. He justly takes it ill to have the objections of sense set up in contradiction to his promise. (Genesis 18:13-14)

Nothing is more offensive to God than disbelief of his promise and despair of the performance of it because of some difficulties that seem to lie in the way. (Psalm 95:8-11)

Rejecters of the gospel and opposers of it are really tormentors to themselves. Enmity to God is a heart-cutting thing; faith and love are heart-healing. (Acts 7:54)

Miserable is the case of those to whom the light of divine truth is become a torment. (John 8:47)

But this is our comfort, that, when the time appointed comes, it will appear that the unbelief of man has not made the promise of God of no effect. (Luke 18:8)

The workman is known by his work. The variety, multitude, order, beauty, harmony, different nature, and excellent contrivance, of the things that are made, the direction of them to certain ends, and the concurrence of all the parts to the good and beauty of the whole, do abundantly prove a Creator and his eternal power and Godhead. Thus did the light shine in the darkness. And *this from the creation of the world.* (Romans 1:20)

[T]here is an infinite Being who is the fountain of all being.... Those that are ignorant of this are willingly ignorant; the light shines in their faces, but they shut their eyes against it. (Isaiah 40:21-26)

Christ is the light of the world, and good Christians are lights in the world. When God raises up a good man in any place, he sets up a light in that place. (Philippians 2:15)

The gospel light and sound open the faculties, and enlarge the capacities of all that see and hear it, either to receive the riches of *divine grace,* or (if that grace be slighted) to take in the more plentiful effusions of *divine wrath.* (Matthew 11:22)

God is willing more abundantly to show the truth of his word, and is not sparing in his proofs; the multitude and variety of the miracles corroborate the evidence.... Unbelief shall be left inexcusable, and convicted of a wilfull obstinacy. (Exodus 4:6-7)

[R]eligion has so much self-evident reason and righteousness on its side that it may safely be referred to every man that allows himself a free thought either to choose or refuse it;

# 1 Disbelief

for the merits of the cause are so plain that no considerate man can do otherwise but choose it. The case is so clear that it determines itself. (Joshua 24:15-23)

Yet ... the most sensible proofs will not of themselves conquer an obstinate infidelity. (Exodus 34:30-32)

It is hard to persuade men to believe what they are not willing to find true; they are ignorant, in many cases, because they are willing to be ignorant, and they do not know because they do not care to know. (2 Peter 3:3-7)

The method of proof is such as gives abundant satisfaction to those who are piously disposed to receive the doctrine and law of Christ, and yet leaves room for those to object who are willingly ignorant and obstinate in their unbelief. And this is a fair trial, suited to the case of those who are probationers. (John 20:1-10)

Many that have reason enough to be comforted go mourning from day to day, because they do not see the reason they have for comfort. There is a well of water by them in the covenant of grace, but they are not aware of it; they have not the benefit of it, till the same God that opened their eyes to see their wound opens them to see their remedy, John 16:6, 7. (Genesis 21:17-20)

What is it that lies at the bottom of all our uneasiness, but our unsteadiness in religion? (2 Thessalonians 2:16-17)

It is owing to the weakness of our faith that we are so much wanting in joy and peace. (Romans 15:13)

Many have the heavens opened to receive them but they do not see it. (Mark 1:10)

Many remain ignorant because they are ashamed to enquire. (Mark 9:31-32)

The goodness of some, who have less helps and advantages for their souls, will aggravate the badness of those who have much greater. Those who by the twilight discover *the things that belong to their peace,* will shame those who grope at noon-day. (Matthew 12:41)

Thus the plainest things are riddles and parables to those who are resolved to hold fast their prejudices; day and night are alike to the blind. (John 8:27)

Those that rebel against the light can expect no other than to perish in the dark.... Ignorance is so far from being the mother of devotion that it is the mother of destruction; lack of knowledge is ruining to any person or people. (Hosea 4:6)

They who do not *come to the light* thereby evidence a secret *hatred* of the light. If they had not an antipathy to *saving knowledge,* they would not sit down so contentedly in *damning ignorance.* (John 3:20)

The eyes that have been wilfully shut against the grace of God shall be opened to see his destruction. (Job 21:20)

Justly is the light taken from those that either play by it, or rebel against it. (Matthew 15:21)

Wilfull hardness is commonly punished with judicial hardness. If men shut their eyes against the light, it is just with God to close their eyes. Let us dread this as the sorest judgment a man can be under on this side hell. (Exodus 9:12)

Take away the talent from him that buried it; those that *will not see, shall not see.* (Matthew 21:27)

Those that bury the knowledge they have are justly denied further knowledge. (Luke 20:4-8)

Men's rejecting the knowledge of God will not secure them from his knowledge of them; and when he contends with them he will prove their sins upon them by his own knowledge, so that it will be in vain to plead *Not guilty.* (Hosea 5:1)

The word of God, if it be not received now as a testimony to us, will be received another day as a testimony against us, and will judge us. (Ezra 5:1)

A practical disbelief of God's omniscience is at the bottom of all the wickedness of the wicked.... Half the pains that many take to damn their souls would serve to save them. (Psalm 64:5-6)

Sinners that are resolved to go on in sin are well enough pleased with gods that *neither see, nor hear, nor know,* for then they may sin securely; but they will find, to their confusion, that though those are the gods they choose those are not the gods they must be judged by, but one to whom *all things are naked and open.* (Daniel 5:22-23)

A practical disbelief of God's omniscience is at the bottom of our treacherous departures from him. (Ezekiel 8:12)

Those that leave God wander endlessly, and a vagrant lust is insatiable. (Jeremiah 2:20)

Those that want the gospel walk in darkness, and know not what they do nor whither they go; and they dwell in the land of the shadow of death, in thick darkness, and in the utmost danger. (Isaiah 9:2)

A sinful state is a *wilderness*, remote from communion with God, barren and dry, and in which there is no true comfort; it is a wandering, wanting state. (Song of Solomon 8:5)

Those who will not be cultivated as fields and vineyards shall be rejected as barren rocks and deserts, Heb. 6:7, 8. (Amos 7:11-12)

Those that by their unbelief oppose Christ thereby set themselves as *briers and thorns* before a *devouring fire,* Isa. 27:4. (Malachi 4:1)

There is no shaking off God's dominion; rule he will, either with the golden sceptre or with the iron rod; and those

# 1 Disbelief

that will not yield to the power of his grace shall be made to sink under the power of his wrath. (Ezekiel 20:33)

If God load us daily with his benefits, and we, notwithstanding that, load him with our sins, how can we expect any other than that he should load us with his judgments? (Amos 2:13-16)

Christ gives the means of grace to many he knows will not make a good use of those means, puts many a price into the hands of fools to get wisdom, who not only have no heart to it, but have their hearts turned against it. Thus he will magnify his own grace, justify his own judgment, leave them inexcusable, and make their condemnation more intolerable. (Ezekiel 2:3-5)

The fair warning given to a careless world, if it be not taken, will aggravate its condemnation another day. The lion roared, and they were not moved with fear to prepare an ark. O the amazing stupidity of an unbelieving world, that will not be wrought upon, no, not by the *terrors of the Lord!* (Amos 3:8)

The destruction of impenitent sinners is a thing which shall surely be; it is not mere talk, to frighten them, but it is an irrevocable sentence. And it is a mercy to us that it is *made known* to us, that we have timely warning given us of it, that we may *flee from the wrath to come.* (Hosea 5:9)

The *day of the Lord* will be a dark, dismal, gloomy day to all impenitent sinners; the *day of judgment* will be so; and sometimes the day of their present trouble. And, when God makes a day dark, all the world cannot make it light. (Amos 5:20)

There is a day coming when God will *deal with sinners,* a day of visitation. He deals with some to bring them to repentance, and there is no resisting the force of convictions when he sets them on; he deals with others to bring them to ruin. (Ezekiel 22:14)

Be it observed here, to the honour of God's wisdom, that he made nothing in vain, but intended every thing for some end and fitted it to answer the intention. If any man prove to have been made in vain, it is his own fault. (Isaiah 45:18)

Strong convictions often come short of a sound conversion. Many a pang have owned the absurdity and dangerousness of sin, and yet have gone on in it. (Daniel 3:1-2)

Many will commend the wit of a sermon, that will not be commanded by the divine laws of a sermon. (Mark 12:17)

Many that cannot but wonder at the works of Christ, yet do not, as they ought, *wonder after him.* (Mark 5:20)

Those that begin well and promise fair, but do not perform and persevere, will justly be upbraided with their hopeful and promising beginnings.... Thus they began in the Spirit, and God puts them in mind of it, that they might be ashamed of ending *in the flesh*. (Jeremiah 2:2-5)

Many, that seem to be affected and pleased with the gospel at first, afterwards despise and reject it; it is common for forward and noisy professors to cool and fall off. (John 5:35)

How soon do unsanctified hearts lose the good impressions which their convictions have made upon them and return with the dog to their vomit! (1 Samuel 26:2)

The confusion of sinners is owing to their own contrivance. God's counsels would have saved them, but their own counsels ruined them. (Hosea 11:6)

Many have such an opinion of their own capacity as to think that that cannot be *proved* which they cannot *believe*; by *wisdom* they *knew* not Christ. (John 3:9)

Those that resolve to be their own masters, let them expect no other comfort and happiness than what their own hands can furnish them with, and a miserable portion it will prove. (Ezekiel 22:15-16)

The children of this world have their all in hand, and nothing in hope (Luke 16:25); while the children of God have their all in hope, and next to nothing in hand. (Genesis 36:43)

Those will soon come to make nothing of God that will not be content to make him their all. (2 Kings 16:12-14)

The great folly of sinners, and that which ruins them, is being content to have *their portion in hand*, now in this lifetime to *receive their good things*. They look only at the things that are seen, that are temporal, and covet only a present gratification, but have no care for a future felicity, when that is spent and gone. (Luke 15:12)

Those are very much strangers to their own interest who prefer the conveniences and ornaments of the temporal life before the absolute necessities of the spiritual life, who are full of care to enrich their own houses, while God's temple in their heart lies waste, and nothing is done for it or in it. (Haggai 1:4)

[T]his is at the bottom of our apostasy from him; men forsake their duty to God because they stand in no awe of him, nor have any dread of his displeasure. (Jeremiah 2:17)

These two commonly go together: those that fear not God regard not man; and then every mouth speaks folly, falsehood, and reproach, both against God and man; *for out of the abundance of the heart the mouth speaks*. (Isaiah 9:17)

Those who lay not the word of God and his providences to their hearts do thereby show that they have not the fear of God before their eyes. And multitudes are ruined by fearlessness, forgetfulness, and mere carelessness.... (Isaiah 57:11)

# 1 Disbelief

Multitudes perish eternally through mere carelessness, who have not any direct aversion, but a prevailing indifference, to the matters of their souls, and an unconcernedness about them. (Matthew 22:3)

The God of our salvation is the rock of our strength; and our forgetfulness and unmindfulness of him are at the bottom of all sin. *Therefore have we perverted our way, because we have forgotten the Lord our God*, and so we undo ourselves. (Isaiah 17:10)

Sinners may be convicted of folly by the plainest and most self-evident truths, which they cannot deny, but will not believe. (Isaiah 31:3)

[M]any people are kept from the ways of religion by the unreasonable prejudices they have conceived against religion, upon the account of some foreign circumstances which do not at all touch the merits of the case. (John 1:46)

If men's prejudices be not conquered by the evidence of truth, they are but confirmed; and if the corruptions of the heart be not subdued by faithful reproofs, they are but enraged and exasperated. (Mark 12:12)

[A]theists are the greatest fools in nature; for they see there is a world that could not make itself, and yet they will not own there is a God that made it. (Genesis 1:1)

Those that have no religion commonly speak with disdain of those that are religious, and look upon them as mad …. The highest wisdom is thus represented as folly, and those that best understand themselves are looked upon as beside themselves. (2 Kings 9:11)

Believers are branded as fools by atheists, and infidels, and free-thinkers, and their most holy faith is censured as a fond credulity; but Christ tells us that those are *fools* who are *slow of heart to believe*, and are kept from it by prejudices never impartially examined. (Luke 24:25)

The doctrine of Christ may safely appeal to all that know it, and has so much right and reason on its side that those who will judge impartially cannot but witness to it. (John 18:20-21)

If the gospel of Christ had not been of God, it could not have made its way, for it had both the learning and power of the world against it, both the colleges of the scribes and the courts of the elders. (Acts 4:5-6)

The most sensible evidence will not convince men, without the concurring operation of the Holy Spirit. (Matthew 28:11-15)

The Spirit convinces of the fact of sin, that we have done so and so; of the fault of sin, that we have done ill in doing so; of the folly of sin, that we have acted against right reason, and our true interest; of the filth of sin, that by it we are become odious to God; of the fountain of sin, the corrupt nature;

and lastly, of the fruit of sin, that the end thereof is death. (John 16:8-9)

The labour of ministers is all lost labour, unless the grace of God make it effectual. Men do not understand that which is made most *plain*, nor believe that which is made most *evident*, unless it be given them from heaven to understand and believe it. (John 3:27)

Those who *receive the Holy Ghost* are thereby *endued with a power from on high*, a supernatural power, a power above any of their own; it is *from on high*, and therefore draws the soul upward, and makes it to *aim high*. Christ's apostles could never have planted his gospel, and set up his kingdom in the world, as they did, if they had not been endued with such a power; and their admirable achievements prove that there was an excellency of power going along with them. (Luke 24:49)

Those whose hearts are hardened against conviction are justly deprived of the means of conviction. Why should not the reprovers be dumb, if, after long trials, it be found that the reproved resolve to be deaf? (Ezekiel 3:26)

It is common for sinners, under convictions, to endeavour to shake them off, by shifting off the prosecution of them to other persons … or to another *more convenient season*…. (Jeremiah 36:19)

Those have a great deal to answer for who, by telling sinners that they shall have peace though they go on, harden their hearts in a contempt of the reproofs and admonitions of the word, and the means and methods God takes to bring them to repentance. (Jeremiah 28:16)

As confidence in God is a hopeful presage of approaching deliverance, so security in sin is a sad omen of approaching destruction. (Jeremiah 34:22)

Those who regard not the threatenings of the word when they are preached will be made to remember them when they are executed. (Ezekiel 24:24)

Those that will not *hear the word of the Lord* giving them their direction shall be made to hear the word of the Lord reading them their doom. (Ezekiel 34:7-9)

The word of God will be the death either of the sin or of the sinner, a savour either of life unto life or of death unto death. (Hosea 6:5)

The writing of the scripture is by divine appointment. (Jeremiah 36:1-2)

The divinity of the scriptures must be known and acknowledged in the first place, before men can profitably use them, before they can give good heed to them. (2 Peter 1:19-21)

[W]hat is written to us by the finger of God is legible to all; whoever will may read the mind of God in the scriptures. (Daniel 5:7)

We must not in all cases adhere to the express words of scripture, but study

# 1 Disbelief

the sense and meaning of them, otherwise we shall be led into blasphemous errors and absurdities: we must not imagine that God hath eyes, and ears, and face, though these are the express words of the scripture. (1 Peter 3:12)

The great design of the gospel is to instruct the ignorant, and to rectify the mistakes of those who are in error, that things may be set and seen in a true light. (Acts 26:18)

In all controversies in religion this must be our question, *What saith the scripture?* It is not what this great man, and the other good man, say, but What saith the scripture? (Romans 4:3)

[F]or *whatsoever things were written aforetime were written for our learning.* (Romans 15:4)

Nothing in scripture is written in vain. God had wise and gracious purposes towards us in leaving the Jewish history upon record; and it is our wisdom and duty to receive instruction from it. (1 Corinthians 10:11)

What is handed down by tradition is easily mistaken and liable to corruption; but what is written is reduced to a certainty, and preserved safe and pure. (Habakkuk 2:2)

What is written in the Bible, and what is preached by the ministers of Christ according to what is written there, must be heard and received, not as the word of dying men, which we may be judges of, but as the word of the living God, which we must be judged by, for so it is. (Micah 1:1)

God in Christ reconciling a sinful world to himself, and shedding abroad the riches of his grace on a reconciled world, is the sum and substance of the gospel. (1 Corinthians 3:22-23)

Those that are sure of an interest in the promised seed will see no reason to doubt of a title to the promised land. If Christ is ours, heaven is ours. (Genesis 15:7)

Disbelief of the promise is a forfeiture of the benefit of it. Those that despise the pleasant land shall be shut out of it. (Numbers 14:23)

Those who would understand the things of God must consider them, must apply their minds to them, ponder upon them, and compare spiritual things with spiritual. The reason why we are so much in the dark concerning the revealed will of God, and mistake concerning it, is want of consideration. This vision both requires and deserves consideration. (Daniel 9:23)

Thoughts ripened into resolves by serious consideration are likely to be kept always in the imagination of the heart, whereas what is soon ripe is soon rotten. (Ruth 1:8)

Though the attempts of hell against the word of God are very daring, yet not one iota or tittle of it shall fall to the ground, nor shall the unbelief of man

## Part I: Folly (Damnation)

make the word of God of no effect. Enemies may prevail to burn many a Bible, but they cannot abolish the word of God, can neither extirpate it nor defeat the accomplishment of it. (Jeremiah 36:27-28)

While we are in this world we are in a state of probation; the time of trial lasts as long as the time of life, and according as we are found at last will be with us to eternity .... The reason why sinners go on in their evil ways is because they do not consider what will be *in the end thereof*. (Ezekiel 18:21-28)

It [death] is a final period to our state of probation and preparation, and an awful entrance upon a state of recompense and retribution. To the wicked man it is the end of all joys; to a godly man it is the end of all griefs. (Psalm 39:4)

The children of men are easy, and think themselves safe, in their sinful ways, only because they never think of death, and judgment, and their future state. (Isaiah 47:8-9)

[Unbelieving sinners should not] put off their repentance to their death bed, or to hope that then they shall find mercy; for, though it is certain that true repentance is never too late, it is as certain that late repentance is seldom true. None can be sure that they shall have time to repent at death.... (Luke 23:39-43)

Unbelieving hearts, and unpurified unpacified consciences, need no more to make them miserable than to have their own fears brought upon them. (Isaiah 66:4)

Those that cast off the fear of God expose themselves to the fear of everything else, Prov. 28:1. (Leviticus 26:36)

Those that will not fear the eternal God, he can make afraid of a shadow. (1 Samuel 14:15)

It is common for those that have fretful uneasy spirits industriously to create inconveniences themselves, that, resolving to complain, they may still have something to complain of .... It is just that those who love to complain should never be left without something to complain of, that their folly may be manifested and corrected, and, if possible, cured. (Jonah 4:5-11)

Anger is a sin that is its own punishment. Fretful passionate people tear and torment themselves. (Job 18:1-4)

Those that are of a fretful discontented spirit will always find something or other to quarrel with, though the circumstances of their outward condition be ever so favourable .... Though God graciously gives us leave to complain to him when there is cause (Ps. 142:2), yet he is justly provoked, and takes it very ill, if we complain of him when there is no cause: such conduct in our inferiors provokes us .... When we complain without cause, it is just with God to give us cause to complain. (Numbers 11:1)

# 1 Disbelief

It is best to be content with such things as we have, since changes made by discontent often prove for the worse. The uneasiness we know is commonly better, though we are apt to think it worse, than that which we do not know. (Deuteronomy 24:1-4)

A murmuring complaining temper, indulged and expressed, lays men under a very bad character; such are very weak at least, and for the most part very wicked. They murmur against God and his providence, against men and their conduct; they are angry at everything that happens, and never pleased with their own state and condition in the world, as not thinking it good enough for them. (Jude 16)

By indulging ourselves in discontent and fretfulness, we deprive ourselves of the comfort we might have both from God's word and from his providence, and must thank ourselves if we go comfortless. (Exodus 6:8-9)

Those that are of a fretful spirit, and are apt to lay provocations too much to heart, are enemies to themselves, and strip themselves very much of the comforts both of life and godliness. (1 Samuel 1:7)

Those that might be very happy often make themselves very miserable by their discontents. (Numbers 11:4-6)

[D]iscontent magnifies what is past, and vilifies what is present, without regard to truth or reason. None talk more absurdly than murmurers. (Exodus 16:2)

Indeed to be careless is a fault; a wise concern about worldly interests is a duty; but to be careful, full of care, to have an anxious and perplexing care about them, is a sin. All that care which disquiets the mind, and distracts it in the worship of God, is evil; for God must *be attended without distraction.* (1 Corinthians 7:35)

God is acquainted with the secret frettings and murmurings of the heart, though they are industriously concealed from men. (Numbers 11:1)

It is absurd to *fear continually every day,* to put ourselves upon a constant rack, so as never to be easy, nor to have any enjoyment of ourselves. Now and then a danger may be imminent and threatening, and it may be prudent to fear it; but to always be in a toss, and to tremble at the shaking of every leaf, is to make ourselves all our lifetime *subject to bondage* .... A timorous spirit is thus apt to make the worst of every thing, and to apprehend the danger greater and nearer than really it is. (Isaiah 51:13)

Thus even good men, when things go against them a little, are too apt to fear the worst, and make harder conclusions than there is reason for. (Joshua 7:9)

We often perplex ourselves with imaginary troubles. We fancy things worse than they are, and then afflict ourselves more than we need. Sometimes there needs no more to comfort us than to undeceive us: it is good to hope the best. (Genesis 37:35)

Let us think as bad as we can of sin, provided we do not think it unpardonable; let us despair of help in ourselves, but not of help in God. He that thinks to ease his conscience by destroying his life, doth, in effect, dare God Almighty to do his worst. And self-murder, though prescribed by some of the heathen moralists, is certainly a remedy worse than the disease, how bad soever the disease may be. Let us watch against the beginnings of melancholy, and pray, Lord, *lead us not into temptation*. (Matthew 27:3-5)

*A broken spirit*, sunk by the burden of afflictions, and especially a conscience wounded with the sense of guilt and fear of wrath, *dries the bones*, wastes the radical moisture, exhausts the very marrow, and makes the body a mere skeleton. We should therefore watch and pray against all melancholy dispositions, for they lead us into trouble as well as into temptation. (Proverbs 17:22)

Nothing is more contrary to natural conscience than blaspheming God, nor to natural sense than self-murder; therefore the suggestion of either of these may well be suspected to come immediately from Satan. Lord, *lead us not into temptation*, not into such, not into any temptation, but *deliver us from the evil one*. (Job 2:9)

Business is a good antidote against melancholy. Let the mind have something without to fasten on and employ itself about, and it will be the less in danger of preying upon itself. (1 Samuel 17:1-2)

How uneasy soever the soul's confinement in the body may be, it must by no means break prison, but wait for a fair discharge. (Job 6:89)

To give assistance to any in murdering themselves, directly or indirectly, if done wittingly, incurs the guilt of blood.... (2 Samuel 1:14-16)

Death will not always come just when we call for it, whether in a passion of sorrow or in a passion of joy. Our times are in God's hand, and not in our own; we must die just when God pleases, and not either just when we are surfeited with the pleasures of life or just when we are overwhelmed with its griefs. (Genesis 46:30)

[T]hough our heavenly Father's house above be ever so desirable ... yet we must stay on earth till our warfare be accomplished, wait for a due discharge, and not anticipate the time of our removal. (Joshua 22:1-9)

Death is a departure, the souls' departure out of the body, from the world of sense to the world of spirits. We must not depart till God gives us our discharge, for we are his *servants* and must not quit his service till we have accomplished our time. (Luke 2:29)

Those greatly profane and pollute

God's name who despise the business of religion, though it is very honourable, as not worth taking pains in, and the advantages of religion, though highly valuable, as not worth taking pains for. (Malachi 1:12-13)

What a pity it is that such rich grace [as religion] should be received in vain, that precious souls should perish at the pool's side because they will not step in and be healed! (Isaiah 53:1)

# -2-

# Willful Disobedience

[Jesus said] *"If I wash thee not, thou hast no part with me"* ... as a severe caution against disobedience: *"If I wash thee not,* if thou continue refractory, and wilt not comply with thy Master's will in so small a matter, thou shall not be owned as one of my disciples, but be justly discarded and cashiered for not observing orders" ... for *to obey is better than sacrifice.*

Matthew Henry
on John 13:8

[Jesus said] *"If I wash thee not, thou hast no part with me"* ... as a severe caution against disobedience: *"If I wash thee not, if thou continue refractory, and wilt not comply with thy Master's will in so small a matter, thou shall not be owned as one of my disciples, but be justly discarded and cashiered for not observing orders"* ... for *to obey is better than sacrifice.* (John 13:8)

[A]s disobedience in a small matter shows a very great contempt of the law, so obedience in a small matter shows a very great regard to it. (Deuteronomy 22:6-7)

Those that go contrary to their duty go contrary to their interest; they will not obey, will not come to Christ, that they may have life, John 5:40. And it is therefore just that those who will not live and flourish as they might in their obedience should die and perish in their disobedience. (Ezekiel 20:21)

Those are ripening apace for ruin whose hearts are unhumbled under humbling providences; for God will walk contrary to those who thus walk contrary to him and provoke him to jealousy, as if they were stronger than he. (Isaiah 9:9-11)

Those are ripe for ruin, and there is little hope of their repentance, who have made themselves believe that they shall have peace though they go on in a sinful way. (Deuteronomy 29:19)

Some that are really rich would be thought to be poor, and are thought to be so, because they sordidly and meanly live below what [talent] God has given them, and choose rather to bury it, than to use it.... In this there is an ingratitude to God, injustice to the family and neighbourhood, and uncharitableness to the poor.... Grace is the riches of the soul; it is true riches; but men commonly misrepresent themselves, either designedly or through mistake and ignorance of themselves. (Proverbs 13:7)

Many wish for larger possessions who do not cultivate and make the best of what they have, think they should have more talents given them who do not trade with those with which they are entrusted. Most people's poverty is the effect of their idleness; would they dig, they need not beg. (Joshua 17:15)

If men bring themselves into straits by their own folly, yet they are to be pitied and helped, not trampled upon and starved. (1 Samuel 25:10-11)

The talents we are entrusted with must not be laid up, but laid out; not hid in a napkin, but traded with. What have we all our gifts for, but to do good with them? (Exodus 36:1)

The rule is that whatever gift, ordinary or extraordinary, whatever power, ability, or capacity of doing good is given to us, we should minister, or do service, with the same *one to another*, accounting ourselves not masters, but only *stewards of the manifold grace,* or the various gifts, of God. (1 Peter 4:11)

## 2: Willful Disobedience

Burying a talent is the betraying of a trust, and amounts to a forfeiture; and gifts and graces *rust* for want of *wearing*. (Mark 4:25)

An unwilling mind will take up with a sorry excuse rather than none, and is willing to devolve those services upon others that have anything of difficulty or danger in them. (Exodus 4:13)

Thus many of God's gifts are received in vain, because they are buried; make them to appear, and they become serviceable. (Genesis 1:11)

That is our true character; we are bent to backslide from God, but altogether unable of ourselves to return to him. This is mentioned not only as our infelicity (that we go astray from the green pastures and expose ourselves to the beasts of prey), but as our iniquity. We affront God in going astray from him, for we turn aside every one to his own way, and thereby set up ourselves, and our own will, in competition with God and his will, which is the malignity of sin. Instead of walking obediently in God's way, we have turned wilfully and stubbornly to our own way, the way of our own heart, the way that our own corrupt appetites and passions lead us to. We have set up for ourselves, to be our own masters, our own carvers, to do what we will and have what we will. (Isaiah 53:6)

God's commands must not be disputed, but obeyed; we must not consult with flesh and blood about them (Gal. 1:15, 16), but with a gracious obstinacy persist in our obedience to them. (Genesis 22:9-10)

Disobedience, even in a small matter, is very provoking. (Exodus 16:28)

God has a clearer title to a dominion over us than the potter has over the clay.... One turn of the hand, one turn of the wheel, quite alters the shape of the clay, makes it a vessel, unmakes it, new-makes it. Thus are our times in God's hand, and not in our own, and it is in vain for us to strive with him. (Jeremiah 18:6)

Wicked people, however in other things they may be wits and politicians, in their greatest concerns are of no understanding; and their ignorance, being wilful, shall not only be their excuse, but it shall be the ground of their condemnation; for therefore *he that made them*, that gave them their being, *will not have mercy on them*, nor save them from the ruin they bring upon themselves; and *he that formed them* into a people, formed them for himself, to show forth his praise, seeing they do not answer the end of their formation, but hate to be reformed, to be new-formed, will reject them and *show them no favour* .... Sinners flatter themselves with hopes of impunity, at least that they shall not be dealt with so severely as their ministers tell them, because God is merciful and because he is their Maker. But here we see how weak and insufficient those pleas will be. (Isaiah 27:11)

[T]hey had neglected God and had cast

Part I: Folly (Damnation)

him off, and therefore he justly rejected them and *gave them to the curse* .... Those who neglect to call upon God do in effect tell him they are weary of him and have a mind to change their Master. (Isaiah 43:28)

Those that threw themselves out of God's service, threw themselves out of his protection. (Judges 4:1-2)

Those that cast off the dominion of their religion forfeit all the benefit and comfort of it. (2 Chronicles 36:16-17)

God, sometimes, in a way of righteous judgment, ceases to correct those who have long been incorrigible, and whom therefore he designs to destroy. The reprobate silver shall be cast, not into the furnace, but to the dunghill.... He that is *filthy, let him be filthy still.* (Isaiah 1:7)

Let the *lying spirit prevail* to entice those to their ruin that will not be persuaded to their duty and happiness. (2 Chronicles 18:20-21)

God suffers the lying spirit to do strange things, that the faith of some may be tried and manifested ... that the infidelity of others may be confirmed, and that he who is filthy may be filthy still.... (Exodus 7:11)

God will justly deny those understanding to keep out of the way of danger that will not use their understanding to keep out of the way of sin. He that will be foolish, let him be foolish still. (Obadiah 7)

Of all judgments spiritual judgments are the sorest, and to be most dreaded, though they make the least noise. (Romans 11:8)

It is a righteous thing with God to give those up to their own heart's lusts that indulge them ... for why should his Spirit always strive? His grace is his own, and he is debtor to no man, and yet, as he never gave his grace to any that could say they deserved it, so he never took it away from any but such as had first forfeited it. *They would have none of me, so I gave them up;* let them take their course. (Psalm 81:11-12)

God will be no loser in his glory at last by the disobedience of men .... (2 Chronicles 36:21)

[E]very wilful sin is a quarrel with God, it is *striving with our Maker* (Isa. 45:9), the most desperate contention. (Romans 2:8-9)

Wilful sinners are haters of God; for the carnal mind is enmity against him. (Deuteronomy 7:10)

Wilful sinners are self-destroyers. Obstinate impenitence is the grossest self-murder. Those that are *destroyed of the destroyer* have their blood upon their own head; they have *destroyed themselves*.... This will aggravate the condemnation of sinners, not only that they did that which tended to their own ruin, but that they opposed the offers God made them and the methods he took with them to prevent it: *I*

## 2: Willful Disobedience

*would have gathered them,* and they *would not.* (Hosea 13:9)

Why do men oppose religion but because they are impatient of its restraints and obligations? They would break asunder the bands of conscience they are under and the cords of God's commandments by which they are called to tie themselves out from all sin and to themselves up to all duty; they will not receive them, but cast them away as far from them as they can. (Psalm 2:3)

[A]ll obstinate sinners, who will not be reclaimed … are given over to disobedience. Disobedience is the very malignity of sin. (Ephesians 5:6)

Obstinate sinners stand upon their guard against convictions; and those that are resolvedly impenitent, look with disdain upon the penitent. (Matthew 27:4)

Wilfull impenitence is the grossest self-murder; and that is *a horrible thing,* which we should abhor the thought of. (Jeremiah 18:13)

[Impenitent sinners are] the most stupid senseless people in the world, that would not be made wise by all the methods that Infinite Wisdom took to bring them to themselves and their right mind, and so prevent the ruin that was coming upon them…. They would not act in the affairs of their souls with the same common prudence with which they acted in other things. Sinners would become saints if they would but show themselves men, and religion would soon rule them if right reason might. (Jeremiah 8:4-6)

Our souls must shortly be gathered, to return to God that gave them and will call for them again. (Psalm 26:9)

Let but reason rule us, and religion will. (Deuteronomy 11:17)

Many that have long lived in sin are, through grace, saved by a timely repentance from *dying in sin;* but for those who go out of this world of probation into that of retribution under the guilt of sin unpardoned, and the power of sin unbroken, there remaineth no relief: salvation itself cannot save them…. (John 8:21)

It is not owing to God, that sinners perish, but to themselves. (Matthew 22:8)

All the wickedness of the wicked world is owing to the wilfulness of the wicked will. The reason why people are not religious is because they will not be so. (Psalm 81:11)

The reason why sinners perish is because they *do not harken to the sound of the trumpet;* and the reason why they do not is because they will not; and they have no reason to give why they will not but because they will not, that is, they are herein most unreasonable. One may more easily deal with ten men's reasons than one man's will. (Jeremiah 6:17)

There needs no more to show the absurdity of sin than to produce the reasons that are given in defence of it, for they carry with them their own confutation. (Isaiah 41:21)

Many whose consciences condemn them are very industrious to justify themselves before men, and put a good face on it.... (Matthew 26:25)

Those that promise themselves secrecy in sin deceive themselves.... [S]ometimes it proves a mercy to sinners to have their sin brought to light, that they may *do no more presumptuously*. Better our sin should *shame* us than *damn* us, and be set in order before us for our conviction than for our condemnation. (John 8:3)

The day is coming when impenitent sinners will have their mouths for ever stopped and be struck speechless. What confusion will they be filled with when God shall set their sins in order before their eyes! They would not see their sins to their humiliation, but cast them behind their backs, covered them, and endeavoured to forget them, nor would they suffer their own consciences to put them in mind of them; but the day is coming when God will make them see their sins to their everlasting shame and terror; he will set them in order, original sin, actual sins, sins against the law, sins against the gospel, against the first table, against the second table, sins of childhood and youth, of riper age, and old age. He will set them in order, as the witnesses are set in order, and called in order, against the criminal, and asked what they have to say against him. (Psalm 50:21)

Shame came into the world with sin, and is still the certain product of it—either the shame of repentance, or, if not that, eternal shame and contempt. Who would wilfully do that which sooner or later he is sure to be ashamed of? (Romans 6:21)

It is a shame to do amiss, but a greater shame to deny it; for thereby we add iniquity to our iniquity. Fear of a rebuke often betrays us into this snare. (Genesis 18:15)

Impenitent sinners are not willing to own any thing to be the word of God that makes against them, that tends either to part them from, or disquiet them, in their sins. (Jeremiah 5:12)

Galled consciences kick at the least touch; and those who are resolved not to be ruled by reason commonly resolve not to hear it if they can help it. (Acts 22:22)

Those who cannot bear the light of truth do all they can to *eclipse* it, and hinder the discovery of it. (John 9:19)

Christianity was not only destitute of the advantage of the countenance and support of kings and rulers (it had neither their power nor their purses), but it was opposed and fought against by them, and they combined to run it down and yet it made its way. (Acts 4:26)

The reason why men deny the scriptures to be the word of God is because they are resolved not to conform to

## 2: Willful Disobedience

scripture-rules, and so an obstinate infidelity is made the sorry subterfuge of a wilful disobedience. (Jeremiah 43:2)

Those that are resolved not to walk in God's ways desire not to know them, because their knowledge will be a continual reproach to their disobedience, John 3:19. (Job 21:14)

The reason why some people blame the pains and expense of zealous Christians, in religion, is because they are not willing themselves to come up to it, but resolve to rest in a *cheap* and *easy* religion. (Luke 7:46)

Those know not what religion is whose chief care it is to make it cheap and easy to themselves, and who are best pleased with that which costs them least pains or money. (2 Samuel 24:24)

Persons may taste religion, and seem to like it, if they could have it upon easier terms than denying themselves, and taking up their cross, and following Christ. (Hebrews 6:4)

*Therefore* it is that people run into mistakes, because they *read their Bibles by the halves*, and are as partial in the prophets as they are *in the law*. They are only for the *smooth things*, Isa. 30:10. (Luke 18:34)

It is the secret wish of many wicked men that the church of God might not have a being in the world, that there might be no such thing as religion among mankind. Having banished the sense of it out of their own hearts, they would gladly see the whole earth as well rid of it, all its laws and ordinances abolished, all its restraints and obligations shaken off, and all that preach, profess, or practise it cut off. (Psalm 83:4)

[Those who are not God's children, are the devil's] for God and Satan divide the world of mankind; the devil is *therefore* said to *work in the children of disobedience*, Eph. 2:2. All wicked people are the devil's children, *children of Belial* (2 Cor. 6:15), the serpent's seed (Gen. 3:15), children of the wicked one, Matt. 13:38. They partake of his nature, bear his image, obey his commands, and follow his example. (John 8:44)

Impenitent sinners God will be angry with for ever; for what is hell but the wrath of God drawn out unto endless generations? (Psalm 85:5)

Impenitent sinners will not escape the damnation of hell by saying that they can never believe there is such a thing, but they will feel what they will not fear. (Jeremiah 14:16)

Many will show respect to good ministers that will not take their advice, Ezek. 33:31. (Acts 27:11)

God keeps account, whether we do or no, how often he has called to us to turn to him and we have refused. (Jeremiah 3:7-8)

God keeps an account, whether we do or no, of the sermons we hear; and those that have long enjoyed the means of grace in purity, plenty, and power, that have been frequently, faithfully, and familiarly, told the mind of God, will have a great deal to answer for another day if they persist in a course of iniquity. (Hosea 12:10)

Many are made worse by the gifts of Christ's bounty, and are confirmed in their impenitency by that which should have led them to repentance. The *coals of fire heaped upon their heads,* instead of melting them, harden them. (John 13:27)

When God sends to us by his ministers he observes what entertainment we give to the message he sends us; he hearkens and hears what we say to them, and what enquiries we make upon them, and is much displeased if we pass them by without taking any notice of them. (Ezekiel 12:9)

Wise and good men may be guilty of an oversight, which, as soon as they are aware of, they will correct. (1 Chronicles 15:2)

The words of the covenant shall not fall to the ground. If we do not by our obedience qualify ourselves for the blessings of it, we shall by our disobedience bring ourselves under the curses of it. (Jeremiah 11:8)

Set aside the instructions of the Christian doctrine, and we know little of the difference between good and evil. He is going to destruction, and knows not his danger, for he is either sleeping or dancing at the pit's brink. (John 12:35)

Those that concur not with the word of God do thereby evince that there is *no light,* no morning light (so the word is) *in them;* they have no right sense of things; they do not understand themselves, nor the difference between good and evil, truth and falsehood. (Isaiah 8:20)

Those are to be reckoned rebellious that shut their eyes against the divine light and stop their ears to the divine law. The ignorance of those that are wilfully ignorant, that have faculties and means and will not use them, is so far from being their excuse that it adds rebellion to their sin. (Ezekiel 12:2)

Those that wilfully persist in sin consider not the power of God's anger.... [They] ... confound and overthrow the distinctions between moral good and evil, *who call evil good and moral evil,* (*v.* 20), who not only live in the omission of that which is good, but condemn it, argue against it, and, because they will not practise it themselves, run it down in others, and fasten invidious epithets upon it—not only do that which is evil, but justify it, and applaud it, and recommend it to others as safe and good.... Virtue and piety are good, for they are light and sweet, they are pleasant and right; but sin and wickedness are evil; they are darkness, all the fruit of ignorance and mistake, and will be bitterness in the latter end. (Isaiah 5:20)

As his mercies are new every morning towards his people, so his anger is new every morning against the wicked,

## 2: Willful Disobedience

upon the fresh occasions given for it by their renewed transgressions. (Psalm 7:11)

Those that live in disobedience to God commonly grow worse and worse, and the heart is more and more hardened by *the deceitfulness of sin*. (Jeremiah 44:16-17)

An erroneous mind and vicious life often go together and help forward one another. (2 Thessalonians 2:11-12)

Many have so debauched their own consciences, and have got to such a pitch of daring wickedness, that they stick at nothing; and this they trust to carry them through those difficulties which embarrass men who make conscience of what they say and do. (Isaiah 47:10)

Shameful sins shall have shameful punishments. (Hosea 12:14)

What bands are strong enough to hold those who can so easily break through the most sacred ties of common justice, and violate the maxims which even nature itself teaches? (John 12:10)

The contempt and violation of the laws of domestic duties are a sad symptom of a universal corruption of manners. Those are never likely to come to good that are undutiful to their parents, and study to be provoking to them and cross them. (Micah 7:6)

The ungrateful rebellions of God's children against him are a vexation to his Holy Spirit.... Thereupon he justly withdraws his protection, and not only so, but makes war upon them, as a prince justly does upon the rebels. He who had been so much their friend was *turned to be their enemy and fought against them,* by one judgment after another.... (Isaiah 63:10)

Those that continue impenitent in sin, when they are preserved from one judgment, are but reserved for another. (Isaiah 16:9)

Those that go on in sin while they are endeavouring to ward off mischiefs with one hand are at the same time pulling them upon their own heads with the other. (Jeremiah 4:18)

Those are the children of pride that are the *children of disobedience,* Job 41:34; Eph. 5:6. Proud men think themselves too good to stoop even to God himself, and would not be under control, Jer. 43:2. (Exodus 5:2)

[T]hose who thus take a pride in venturing upon the borders of sin, and the brink of it, are in danger of falling into the depths of it. (Isaiah 65:7)

Those have reason to fear perishing in their sins that cannot bear to be frightened out of them. (Isaiah 30:11-12)

The less provocation we have from men to do a wrong thing the more provocation we give to God by doing it. (Isaiah 33:1)

Those that commit a wilful sin know

not how far the mischievous consequences of it may reach, nor what mischief may be done by it. (Jonah 1:10)

There are many things which people would not do if they knew the wisdom of God in the great work of redemption. They act as they do because they are blind or heedless. They know not the truth, or will not attend to it. (1 Corinthians 2:8)

Those that are deaf to the reproofs of wisdom are manifestly marked for ruin. (1 Samuel 2:25)

[T]hose that will not cease to sin, God will make to cease. (Isaiah 14:4)

Those that go on in a course of sin are treasuring up unto themselves wrath.... Every wilfull sin adds to the score, and will inflame the reckoning; it brings a *branch to their wrath*.... (Romans 2:5)

Those that are willingly ignorant of the wrath of God revealed from heaven against sin and sinners shall be made to know it. (Isaiah 9:8)

God lives for ever, to see how his laws are observed, and is in readiness to revenge all disobedience. (Jeremiah 35:14)

## -3-

# Scorners

God, to whom vengeance belongs, will render shame for shame. Those that put contempt and reproach upon God's people will, sooner or later, have it *burned upon themselves*, perhaps in this world (either their follies or their calamities, their miscarriages or their mischances, shall be their reproach), at furthest in that day when all the impenitent shall *rise to shame and everlasting contempt*.

Matthew Henry
on Ezekiel 36:7

God, to whom vengeance belongs, will render shame for shame. Those that put contempt and reproach upon God's people will, sooner or later, have it *burned upon themselves*, perhaps in this world (either their follies or their calamities, their miscarriages or their mischances, shall be their reproach), at furthest in that day when all the impenitent shall *rise to shame and everlasting contempt*. (Ezekiel 36:7)

There is a day coming when those that now hate and despise the people of God would gladly receive kindness from them. (Luke 16:24)

Those that will not so much as ask and seek now will knock shortly, and cry, *Lord, Lord*. Slighters of Christ will then be humble suitors to him. (Genesis 27:34)

Omissions make way for commissions, and by these the heart is so hardened that at length they come to be *scorners*, that is, they openly defy all that is sacred, scoff at religion, and make a jest of sin. Thus is the way of iniquity downhill; the bad grow worse, sinners themselves become tempters to others and advocates for Baal. (Psalm 1:1)

The devil, as he is a liar, so he is a scoffer, from the beginning: and the scoffers of the last days are his children. (Genesis 3:1)

Thus the *scoffers of the latter days* think the promise of Christ's coming is broken, because he does not come in their time, though it is certain he will come at the set time. (1 Samuel 13:11)

We are not to think it strange if sacred truths of the greatest certainty and importance are made the scorn of profane wits. (Acts 17:32)

Perhaps those are cried up as the wits of the age that ridicule religion and sacred things; but really they are the greatest fools, and will shortly be made to appear so before all the world. (Psalm 74:18)

Great wits have not always the most wisdom .... Many ruin themselves by consulting their humour more than their interest. (1 Kings 12:8-14)

It is not strange if those who make a jest of the most sacred oaths can make a jest likewise of the most sacred oracles; for where will a profane mind stop? But shall their unbelief invalidate the counsel of God? Are they safe because they are secure? By no means .... (Ezekiel 21:23-24)

Those that can do wickedly and then think to turn it off with a jest, though they may deceive themselves and others, will find at last that God is not mocked. (Genesis 29:26)

It is good to enquire into the reason of our laughter, that it may not be the laughter of the fool, Eccl. 7:6. (Genesis 18:13)

Profane scoffers are not to be humoured, nor pearls cast before swine. (Psalm 137:4)

The curses of the law, though they may be bantered by profane wits, cannot be baffled. (Ezekiel 33:33)

Scorners are fools. Those that ridicule things sacred and serious do but make themselves ridiculous. (Proverbs 19:29)

Nothing is more grievous to those who have a true concern for the glory of God, nor is more lamented, than the violation of God's laws, and the contempt they see put upon sacred things. (Lamentations 1:10)

The dishonour done to God's name, and the profanation of his holy word, are the greatest grief imaginable to a gracious soul. (Jeremiah 23:9)

A scorner is one that not only makes a jest of God and religion, but bids defiance to the methods employed for his conviction and reformation.... (Proverbs 15:12)

There is little hope of those that will not so much as *hear rebuke* with any patience, but scorn to submit to government and scoff at those that deal faithfully with them. How can those mend a fault who will not be told of it, but count those their enemies who do them that kindness? (Proverbs 13:1)

It is common for those whose hearts are *fully set in them to do evil* to rage at those who give them good counsel. Those who hate to be reformed hate those that would reform them, and count them their enemies because they tell them the truth. (Numbers 14:10)

People's being unwilling to hear of their faults is no good reason why they should not be faithfully told of them. (Acts 5:30)

As it is the praise of great saints that they pray for those that are enemies to them, so it is the shame of many great sinners that they are enemies to those who pray for them.... (Amos 7:10)

Though we are to pray for our enemies as such, yet we are to pray against God's enemies as such, against their enmity to him and all their attempts upon his kingdom. (Psalm 68:1)

[*Reprove not*] scorners and *wicked men* who would mock the messengers of the Lord ... *cast not these pearls before swine*, Matt. 7:6. ... In justice to them, for those have forfeited the favour of further means who scorn the means they have had. Those that are thus *filthy, let them be filthy still*.... (Proverbs 9:8)

[Scorners are] not fit to be discoursed with concerning Christ's authority; for men of such a disposition could not be convinced of the truth, nay, they could not but be provoked by it, and therefore, *he that is thus ignorant, let him be ignorant still*. (Matthew 21:27)

There is a time to keep silence, as well as a time to speak, and there are those to whom to offer any thing religious or rational is to cast pearls before swine. What can be said to a madman? (2 Kings 18:36)

The father corrects not the rebellious son any more when he determines to disinherit him. (Hosea 4:17)

Those are justly forbidden God's house that profane his house. (Ezekiel 20:39)

"Woe unto them that call evil good, and good evil; that put darkness for light, and light for darkness ..." who not only live in the omission of that which is good, but condemn it, argue against it, and, because they will not practise it themselves, run it down in others, and fasten invidious epithets upon it.... (Isa.5:20)

We must answer, another day, not only for our enmity in opposing truth, but for our cowardice in defending it. (Jeremiah 9:3)

Immorality and dishonesty are commonly attended with a contempt of religion and the worship of God. (Ezekiel 22:8)

Those that are strangers to the covenant are often enemies to it. (Daniel 11:30)

Tertullian pleads [that] those [who] opposed Christianity ... were generally the worst of men. ... It is the honour of religion that those who hate it are generally the *lewd fellows of the baser sort*, that are lost to all sense of justice and virtue. (Acts 17:5)

Those that are base, and design ill themselves, are apt to be jealous and to suspect ill of others without cause. (1 Chronicles 19:3)

Many that are themselves guilty of the greatest crimes are forward to censure others for the most innocent and inoffensive actions. (Luke 6:2)

Innocence itself cannot secure a man's reputation. Not every one that keeps a good conscience can keep a good name. ... It is no new thing for the best of men to be falsely accused of the worst of crimes by those who themselves are the worst of criminals. (Genesis 39:13-18)

It is no new thing for the greatest kindnesses to be misinterpreted and basely represented as the greatest injuries. The worst colours are sometimes put upon the best actions. (Exodus 16:2-3)

It is an unspeakable comfort to a good man, when he lies under the censure of his brethren, that there is a God in heaven who knows his integrity and will clear it up sooner or later. ... This one witness instead of a thousand. (Job 16:19)

Those most defile themselves, who are most forward to censure the defilements of others. (Matthew 15:11)

Such should the eyes of our mind be, reflecting nearer on ourselves than on other people, looking much within, to judge ourselves, but little without, to censure our brethren. (1 Kings 6:4)

## 3: Scorners

It is common for people to be angry at those sins in others which they allow of and indulge in themselves. Those that are proud and covetous themselves do not care to see others so. (Matthew 20:24)

Those who resemble others in their sins may expect to resemble them in their plagues, especially those who seem zealous against such sins in others as they allow themselves in; the house of Jehu was reckoned with for the blood of the house of Ahab, Hos. 1:4. (1 Kings 16:3-4)

[A]nd so, in judging others, they condemn themselves, Rom. 2:1; 14:22. (Genesis 38:24)

It is gross hypocrisy to *condemn* that in those who *reprove* us which yet we *allow* in those that *flatter* us. (Luke 11:19)

It is a common thing, but a very bad thing, to cover malice against men's persons with a show of zeal against their vices. (Genesis 38:24)

It is the way of malicious people, especially the malicious persecutors of Christ and Christianity, to condemn the same thing in those they hate, which they approve of and applaud in those they have a kindness for: the judgments of envy are made, not by things, but persons; not by reason, but prejudice. (Matthew 12:24)

The enemies of piety would never suffer themselves to be bound by the laws of equity. (Jeremiah 20:2)

The pious devotion of God's people sometimes provokes and exasperates their enemies more than any thing else. (Joshua 9:1-2)

The faithfulness of God's servants to him has often been the wonder of their enemies and persecutors, who *think it strange* that they *run not with them to the same excess of riot.* (Daniel 3:14)

Those that dote upon worldly things themselves think every body else should do so too, and true or false, right or wrong, speak and act for their secular interest only. (1 Kings 22:13)

Those that themselves will be held by no bonds of reason or religion are ready to think that others should as easily break those bonds. (1 Samuel 19:17)

It is common for those who will not be wrought upon by the word to pick quarrels with it; it is either too plain or too obscure, too fine or too homely, too common or too singular; something or other is amiss in it. (Ezekiel 20:49)

The reason why some people seek wisdom and do not find it, is because they do not seek it from a right principle and in a right manner. They are scorners, and it is scorn that they ask instruction, that they may ridicule what is told them and may cavil at it. Many put questions to Christ, tempting him, and that they might have whereof to accuse him, but they were never the wiser. (Proverbs 14:6)

The benefit we have had by the word of God greatly aggravates our sin and folly if we put any slight upon the word of God. (Hosea 12:13)

The character of one that is marked for ruin: he that *"despises the word"* of God, and has no regard to it, no veneration for it, nor will be ruled by it, certainly he *shall be destroyed*, for he slights that which is the only means of curing a destructive disease and makes himself obnoxious to that divine wrath which will certainly be his destruction. Those that prefer the rules of carnal policy before divine precepts, and the allurements of the world and the flesh before God's promises and comforts, despise his word, giving the preference to those things that stand in competition with it; and it is to their own just destruction: they would not take warning. (Proverbs 13:13)

And justly will those die of their disease that will not take God for their physician. We are certainly enemies to ourselves if we will not be subjects to him. (Isaiah 30:16)

Ministers that reject knowledge, that are grossly ignorant and scandalous, ought not to be owned as ministers; but that which they *seem to have* should be *taken away*, Luke 8:18. (Hosea 4:6)

Those are wicked indeed that lay the blame of their wickedness upon God. (Isaiah 63:17)

Greater impiety can scarcely be imagined than to vent a devilish passion in the language of the sacred writ, to kindle strife with coal's snatched from God's altar, and to call for fire from heaven with a tongue set on fire of hell. (Psalm 109:6-7)

Ruin is not far off from those that lie under the guilt of wrong done to God's people. (Jeremiah 51:34-35)

Neither the patience of the saints under their sufferings, nor the counsel of God concerning their sufferings, will be any excuse for those that have any hand in their sufferings, or that persecute them. (Luke 22:22)

God's suffering people will lose nothing by their sufferings, and their enemies will gain nothing by their advantages against them. (2 Thessalonians 1:6)

The designs of enemies for the ruin of the church often prove ruining to themselves; and thereby they prepare themselves for destruction and put themselves in the way of it; they are *snared in the work of their own hands*. (Micah 4:12-13)

When men are projecting the church's ruin God is preparing for its salvation. (Exodus 2:2)

The God of heaven easily can, and certainly will, break down all the opposing power of his and his church's enemies. Gates of brass and bars of iron are, before him, but as straw and rotten wood. ... Thus shall Satan's kingdom fall, nor shall any prosper

## 3: Scorners

that harden themselves against God. (Joshua 6:20)

The persecutors of God's people had best look to themselves, lest they fall into the pit which they dig. (Acts 5:35)

Ruin comes gradually, but at last comes effectually, upon a provoking people. (Ezekiel 21:14)

The malignant world shall in a little time give an account to the great God of all their evil speeches against his people, Jude 14, 15. (1 Peter 4:5)

Those that are *glad at calamities,* especially the calamities of God's church, *shall not* long *go unpunished.* ... All the fury and all the falsehood of the church's enemies are perfectly known to God, whatever the pretenses are with which they think to cover them.... (Jeremiah 48:26-30)

The enemies of the church are apt to take its shocks for its ruins, and to triumph in them accordingly; but they will find themselves deceived; *for the gates of hell shall not prevail against the church.* (Lamentations 2:16)

Those that have a perpetual enmity to God and his people, as the carnal mind has, can expect no other than to be made a perpetual desolation. Implacable malice will justly be punished with irreparable ruin. (Ezekiel 35:9)

The most unspotted innocency, and the most unparalleled excellency, will not always be a fence *against the reproach of tongues.* ... The best of our actions may become the worst of our accusations, as David's fasting.... (Matthew 11:18)

It is no new thing for the most pious devotions of the best men to be ridiculed and abused by profane scoffers; nor are we to think it strange if what is well said in praying and preaching be misconstrued, and turned to our reproach; Christ's words were so, though he spoke as never man spoke. (Matthew 27:47)

See how restless Satan's agents are in their opposition to the gospel of Christ and the salvation of the souls of men. This is an instance of the enmity that is in the serpent's seed against the seed of the woman. (Acts 17:13)

So implacable, so incurable, is the enmity of the serpent against that of the woman, so deceitful and desperately wicked is the heart of man without the grace of God.... (1 Samuel 19:10)

Thus Satan and his instruments make war upon those that make peace with God. (Joshua 10:4)

What Christ did by his wisdom, we must labour to do by our well-doing— *put to silence the ignorance of foolish men....* (Mark 11:33)

It is no new thing for that which is both well-*done,* and well-*designed,* to be misrepresented, and turned to the reproach of the wisest and best of men. ... Those are too tender of their own *good name,* who, to preserve it with

## Part I: Folly (Damnation)

some nice people, will decline a *good work*. (Mark 2:16)

Those greatly provoke God who misrepresent religion, cast reproach upon it, and raise prejudices in men's minds against it, or give occasion to those to do so who seek occasion. (Numbers 14:37)

[T]he best services [to God] are no fences against malice and slander. ... Those that are resolved to contradict the great ends of the ministry are industrious to bring a bad name upon it. (Jeremiah 43:3)

Yet it is *impotent* malice, for we cannot hurt the heavens. Nay, it is foolish malice; what is shot *against the heavens* will return upon the head of him that shoots it.... (Luke 15:18)

Of the church in general, and particular believers; hell shoots its arrows against the saints, but Heaven protects and strengthens them, and will crown them. (Genesis 49:23-24)

Those very persons whom men load with slanders God loads with benefits and honours. (Psalm 31:19)

Men that fret and rage at God's counsels are impiously aiming to defeat them; but they imagine a vain thing, Ps. 2:1-3. God's counsels will stand. (Genesis 37:20)

[I]t is no new thing for the church's best friends to be represented as in the interest of her worst enemies. Thus have the blackest characters been put upon the fairest purest minds, and, in such a malicious world as this is, innocency, nay excellency itself, is no fence against the basest calumny. (Jeremiah 37:13-14)

It is no new thing for the best of benefactors to be branded and run down as the worst of malefactors. (John 18:38)

It is no new thing for a man's modesty to be turned against him, and improved to his prejudice; but it is better that men should take advantage of our low thoughts of ourselves, to *trample upon us*, than the devil take advantage of our high thoughts of ourselves, to *tempt us* to pride and draw us into his condemnation. (John 1:25)

The people of God have always had a great deal of ill-will borne them by this wicked world; and their calamities have been their neighbours' entertainments. See to what unnatural instances of malice the enmity that is in the seed of the serpent against the seed of the woman will carry them. (Ezekiel 25:6)

It is as much the meat and drink of a wicked man to do mischief as it is of a good man to do good. He is like *a young lion lurking in secret places*, disguising his cruel designs. (Psalm 17:9-12)

The dog that bites is not always the dog that barks. (Proverbs 10:10)

[M]alice harboured will last long, and find an occasion to break out with violence a great while after the provoca-

## 3: Scorners

tions given. Angry men have good memories. (Genesis 32:6-7)

Whom Christ blesseth the world curseth. The favourites and heirs of heaven have never been the darlings of this world, since the old enmity was put between the seed of the woman and of the serpent. Why did Cain hate Abel, but *because his works were righteous?* Esau hated Jacob because of the blessing; Joseph's brethren hated him because his father loved him; Saul hated David because *the Lord was with him;* Ahab hated Micaiah because of his prophecies; such are the causeless causes of the world's hatred. (John 15:19)

Cain hated Abel because *his own works were evil and his brother's righteous. The wicked devours the man that is more righteous than he,* for that very reason, because he shames him; they have an ill will to the image of God, and *therefore* devour good men, because they bear that image. (Habakkuk 2:13)

The one that continues in unbelief will be provoked, and will hate and persecute the one that by his faith and obedience witnesses against, and condemns, his unbelief and disobedience. A spirit of bigotry and persecution will break through the strongest bonds of relation and natural affection.... (Luke 12:53)

It is common for those who have rendered themselves unworthy of God's favour by their presumptuous sins to have indignation against those who are dignified and distinguished by it. (Genesis 4:5)

It is common for those who walk in false ways themselves to rejoice at the false steps which they sometimes see others make. (Genesis 9:22)

[T]ake heed of doing any thing which may give occasion to others to speak evil, either of the Christian religion in general, or of your Christian liberty in particular. (Romans 14:16)

See how the greatest instance of heaven's power and grace is branded with the blackest note of hell's enmity. (Matthew 9:3)

It is very common for those that will not be convinced by reason to be provoked and exasperated by it, and to push on with fury what they cannot support with equity. (Daniel 2:12)

Those are fittest to be employed against Christ and Christianity that are governed least by reason and most by passion. (Acts 21:27)

If there is no life to come, what harm can other men's hopes of it do them? But in depraved souls all faculties are vitiated. (Acts 4:1-2)

Such a rooted enmity there is in the hearts of wicked men to goodness for its own sake that they hate it, even when they themselves have the benefit of it; they hate prayer even in those that pray for them, and hate peace even in those that would be at peace with them. (Psalm 38:20)

Those that are unmindful of their other benefactors, it is to be feared, will forget the supreme benefactor, 1 John 4:20. (Exodus 1:8)

Call a man ungrateful and you can call him no worse. ... Thus disingenuously do sinners deal with the great intercessor, crucifying him afresh, and speaking against him on earth, while his blood is speaking for them in heaven. (Jeremiah 18:20)

What a pity it is that this earth, which is so full of God's goodness, should be so empty of his praises, and that of the multitudes that live upon his bounty there are so few that live to his glory! (Psalm 33:5)

It is sad to think how empty the earth is of the glory of God, how little service and honour he has from a world to which he is such a bountiful benefactor. (Psalm 72:18-19)

Ignorance is at the bottom of ingratitude. (Hosea 11:3)

It is no new thing for those who have been very civil and obliging to their neighbours to find them very unkind and unneighbourly and for those who do no injuries to suffer many. (Joel 3:4)

We must not think it strange if in this world we have hatred shown us for our love, and slights for our respects. (Genesis 40:23)

It is much more honourable to clothe a company of decrepit widows with needful clothing for night and day, who will pray for their benefactors when they do not see them, than to clothe a company of lazy footmen with rich liveries, who perhaps behind their backs will curse those that clothe them.... (Acts 9:39)

Charity misplaced is a great hindrance to true charity; there should be prudence in the choice of the objects of charity, that it may not be thrown away upon those who are not properly so, that there may be the more for those who are real objects of charity. (1 Timothy 5:16)

To give rough answers to those who give us soft answers is one way of rendering evil for good; and those are wicked indeed, and it is to be feared incurable, with whom that which usually turns away wrath does but make bad worse. (Isaiah 36:11-12)

To render good for good is human, evil for evil is brutish, good for evil is Christian, but evil for good is devilish; it is so very absurd and wicked a thing that we cannot think but God will avenge it. (Jeremiah 18:20)

It is the devil that stirs up his instruments, wicked men, to persecute the people of God; tyrants and persecutors are the devil's tools, though they gratify their own sinful malignity, and know not that they are actuated by a diabolical malice. (Revelation 2:10)

## 3: Scorners

Of all sinners persecutors are set up as the fairest marks of divine wrath; against them, more than any other, God has ordained his arrows. They set God at defiance, but cannot set themselves out of the reach of his judgments. (Psalm 7:12-13)

No wicked men are such *absurd* and *unreasonable* men as *persecutors* are, who study to *do evil* to men for *doing good*. (Luke 6:7)

The reason why men are not good is because they will not be so; they will not consider, will not comply; and therefore, *if thou scornest, thou alone shalt bear it*. (Zechariah 8:11)

Those who scorn to submit to the discipline of religion, scorn to take God's yoke upon them, scorn to be beholden to his grace, who scoff at godliness and godly people, and take a pleasure in bantering and exposing them, God will scorn them, and lay them open to scorn before all the world. He despises their impotent malice, *sits in heaven and laughs at them* (Ps 2:4). (Proverbs 3:34)

Sometimes God makes the enemies of his church a vexation one to another, while he that sits in heaven laughs at them, and the efforts of their impotent malice. (Numbers 23:11)

God delights to baffle his enemies when they most strengthen themselves; he gives them all the advantages they could wish for, and yet conquers them. *Associate yourselves, and you shall be broken in pieces,* Isa. 3:9, 10. (Matthew 22:41-46)

There are none so blind as those who will not see, who shut their eyes against the clearest conviction of guilt and wrath, who ascribe that to chance, or common fate, which is manifestly a divine rebuke, who regard not the threatening symptoms of their own ruin, but cry Peace to themselves, when the righteous God is waging war with them. ... [B]*ut they shall see,* shall be made to see, whether they will or no, that God is angry with them. Atheists, scorners, and the secure, will shortly feel what now they will not believe, that *it is a fearful thing to fall into the hands of the living God*. (Isaiah 26:11)

# -4-

# Corruption

Satan teaches men first to doubt and then to deny; he makes them sceptics first, and so by degrees makes them atheists.

Matthew Henry
on Genesis 3:4

Satan teaches men first to doubt and then to deny; he makes them sceptics first, and so by degrees makes them atheists. (Genesis 3:4)

The design of the devil is to keep men in ignorance; and, when he cannot keep the light of the gospel out of the world, he makes it his great business to keep it out of the hearts of men. (2 Corinthians 4:4)

Many of the reproaches cast upon the word of God and the people of God, take rise from gross mistakes. Divine truths are often corrupted by ignorance of the language and style of the scripture. Those that hear by the halves, pervert what they hear. (Matthew 27:47)

The divine law cannot be reproached unless it be first misrepresented. ... [I]t is the subtlety of Satan to blemish the reputation of the divine law as uncertain or unreasonable, and so to draw people to sin.... (Genesis 3:1-5)

The misunderstanding of scripture is a great prejudice to the entertainment of truth. (Mark 9:11)

The devil is for nothing that is humbling, but every thing that is assuming; and gains his point, if he can but bring men off from their dependence upon God, and possess them with an opinion of their self-sufficiency. (Matthew 4:3)

Ever since Adam ate forbidden fruit, we have all been fond of forbidden paths; the diseased appetite is carried out most strongly towards that which is hurtful and prohibited. (Romans 7:8)

When there is thought to be no more harm in forbidden fruit than in other fruit sin lies at the door, and Satan soon carries the day.... [I]f it had nothing in it more inviting than the rest, yet it was the more coveted because it was prohibited. ... [W]e find that in us, (that is, in our flesh, in our corrupt nature) there dwells a strange spirit of contradiction. (Genesis 3:6)

There is nothing about which the natural man is more blind than about original corruption, concerning which the understanding is altogether in the dark till the Spirit by the law reveal it, and make it known. (Romans 7:7)

When man sinned, the ground was cursed for man's sake, and with it all the creatures (especially of this lower world, where our acquaintance lies) became subject to that curse, became mutable and mortal. *Under the bondage of corruption.* (Romans 8:21)

The understanding, through the corruption of nature by the fall, and through the confirmation of this disorder by customary sin, is utterly unapt to receive the rays of divine light; it is prejudiced against them. The truths of God are foolishness to such a mind. (1 Corinthians 2:14)

It is to be sadly lamented by every one of us that we brought into the world with us a corrupt nature, wretchedly

## 4: Corruption

degenerated from its primitive purity and rectitude; we have from our birth the snares of sin in our bodies, the seeds of sin in our souls, and a stain of sin upon both. This is what we call *original sin,* because it is as ancient as our original, and because it is the original of all our actual transgressions. (Psalm 51:5)

*As for* our *nativity, in the day that we were born* we were shapen in iniquity and conceived in sin, our understandings darkened, our minds alienated from the life of God, polluted with sin, which rendered us loathsome in the eyes of God. *Marvel not* then that we are told, *You must be born again.* (Ezekiel 16:4-5)

The disciples of the Saviour are, as well as others, born after the flesh. They come into the world endued with a corrupt carnal disposition, which is enmity to God. This disposition must be mortified and abolished. A new nature must be communicated. Old lusts and corruptions must be eradicated, and the true disciple become a new creature. The regeneration or renovation of souls is a testimony to the Saviour. (1 John 5:6-9)

The things of this world, which are seen, draw strongly from the pursuit of the things of the other world, which are not seen. The magnetic virtue of this earth prevails with most people above the attractives of heaven itself. (Numbers 10:30)

Many never think of religion but just when it falls in their way and they cannot avoid it, like chance customers. (Judges 18:5)

In nothing is the corrupt memory of man more treacherous than in this, that it is apt to forget God; because out of sight, he is out of mind; and here begins all the wickedness that is in the world: they *have perverted their way,* for they have *forgotten the Lord their God.* (Judges 3:6-7)

The mind of man is a busy thing; if it be not employed in doing good, it will be doing evil. (2 Thessalonians 3:11)

Man was made the same day that the beasts were, because his body was made of the same earth with theirs; and, while he is in the body, he inhabits the same earth with them. God forbid that by indulging the body and the desires of it we should make ourselves like the beasts that perish. (Genesis 1:26)

As the death of the body is the corruption and putrefaction of it, so sin is the corruption or depravation of the soul. (Colossians 2:13)

That which ruins sinners is affecting to live as they lust. They call it liberty to live at large; whereas for a man to be a slave to his lusts is the worst of slaveries. (Jeremiah 18:12)

Those who live a carnal sensual life, who instead of employing themselves to the honour of God and the good of others, spend all their thoughts, and care, and time, about the flesh, must expect no other fruit of such a course than corruption—a mean and short-lived satisfaction at present, and ruin and misery at the end of it. (Galatians 6:8)

Our original corruptions are the sickness and disease of the soul, an habitual indisposition; our actual transgressions are the wounds of the soul, which put conscience to pain, if it be not seared and senseless. (Isaiah 53:4)

Man, by reason of his actual transgressions, is obnoxious to God's justice and cannot in himself be justified before him: he can neither plead *Not guilty*, nor plead any merit of his own to balance or extenuate his guilt. The scripture has concluded all under sin. (Job 25:4)

Through the corruption of men's nature, those things that should be detestable to them are desirable and delectable; but those are far gone in a distemper to whom that which is the food and fuel of it is most agreeable. (Isaiah 44:9-11)

When we make God's gifts the food and fuel for our lusts, and his providence the patron of our wicked projects, especially when we encourage ourselves to continue in sin because grace has abounded, then we make God to serve with our sins. (Isaiah 43:24)

God is angry with the wicked even in the merriest and most prosperous of their days, even in the days of their devotion; for, if they be suffered to prosper, it is in wrath; if they pray, their very prayers are an abomination. The wrath of God abides upon them (John 3:36) and continual additions are made to it. (Psalm 7:11)

We must not think that one smiling providence either justifies an unrighteous cause or secures its success. (1 Samuel 23:7)

There is a strange proneness in those that are tempted to say that they are tempted of God, as if our abusing God's gifts would excuse our violation of God's laws. God gives us riches, honours, and relations, that we may serve him cheerfully in the enjoyment of them; but, if we take occasion from them to sin against him, instead of blaming Providence for putting us into such a condition, we must blame ourselves for perverting the gracious designs of Providence therein. (Genesis 3:12)

The transgression we are guilty of is the sin of our soul, for the soul acts it (without the soul's act it is not a sin) and the soul suffers by it; it is the disorder, disease, and defilement of the soul, and threatens to be the death of it: *What shall I give for my transgressions?* (Micah 6:6)

Every sin against God is a sin against ourselves, and so it will be found sooner or later. (Jeremiah 11:17)

Where there is one abomination it will be found that there are many more. Sins do not go alone. (Ezekiel 8:6)

## 4: Corruption

The way of sin is downhill; a man cannot stop himself when he will. The beginning of it is as the breaking forth of water, to which it is hard to say, "Hitherto thou shalt come and no further." Therefore it is our wisdom to suppress the first emotions of sin, and to leave it off before it be meddled with. (Genesis 3:6)

[T]hose that make a slight excuse to serve in daring to commit one sin will have their hearts so hardened by it that they will venture upon the next without such an excuse; for the way of sin is downhill. (Joshua 7:21)

Those that take one bold step in a sinful way give Satan advantage against them to tempt them to take another, and provoke God to leave them to themselves, to go from bad to worse. It is therefore our wisdom to take heed of the beginnings of sin. (Acts 12:3)

If men did but consider as they ought, what would be the end of sin, they would be afraid of the beginnings of it. (Numbers 32:14-15)

Where sin has been general, and all flesh have corrupted their way, what can be expected but a general desolation? (Isaiah 16:6-9)

When the hearts of the sons of men are fully set in them to do evil, the fairest warnings both of the sin they are about to commit and of the consequences of it make no impression upon them. (Luke 20:19)

Thus it is the folly of sinners to please themselves with that which will certainly be their grief, and pride themselves in that which will certainly be their shame. (Jeremiah 2:26)

See what mischievous work sin makes. If the things that have been our comforts prove our crosses, we must thank ourselves: it is sin that turns our waters into blood. (Exodus 8:20)

Those who will get to heaven must fight their way thither. There must be a conflict with corruption and temptations, and the opposition of the powers of darkness. (1 Timothy 6:12)

Their case is very miserable who have brought themselves to such a pass that their corruptions triumph over their convictions; they know they should reform, but own they cannot, and therefore resolve they will not. (Jeremiah 2:25)

Many a man sins with regret, that never has any true regret for his sin; is sorry to sin, yet is utterly a stranger to godly sorrow; sins with reluctancy, and yet goes on to sin. (Matthew 14:9)

It is very common for those that have been hardened with presumption when they were warned against sin to sink into despair when they are called to repent, and to conclude there is no hope of life for them. (Ezekiel 33:10)

Those are wicked indeed that sin to the utmost of their power, that never refuse to comply with a temptation because they should not, but because they cannot. (Jeremiah 3:2)

Strong inclinations to sin within are often justly punished with strong temptations to sin without. (John 12:6)

But there are some sins in their own nature so exceedingly sinful, and to which there is so little temptation from the world and the flesh, that it is plain Satan lays the egg of them in a heart disposed to be the nest to hatch them in. (John 13:2)

It is by the breaking out of the corruption that is in our hearts; the mind and conscience are defiled, guilt is contracted, and we become odious in the sight of God by that which *comes out* of us; our wicked thoughts and affections, words and actions, these defile us, and these only. (Mark 7:15)

Most of our danger from outward troubles arises from the occasion they give for inward trouble. (Matthew 14:26)

Those that have themselves done ill are commonly willing to draw in others to do the same. As was the devil, so was Eve, no sooner a sinner than a tempter. (Genesis 3:6)

Sinners love company in sin; the angels that fell were tempters almost as soon as they were sinners. (Proverbs 1:10)

Those that are willing to justify themselves are commonly very forward to condemn others, and to lay the blame upon any rather than take it to themselves. Sin is a brat that nobody cares to have laid at his doors. It is the sorry subterfuge of an impenitent heart, that will not confess its guilt, to lay the blame on those that were tempters, or partners, or only followers in it. (1 Samuel 15:15)

It is natural to us to endeavour thus to transfer our guilt; we have it in our kind, Adam and Eve did so; sin is a brat that nobody is willing to own. (Exodus 32:22)

Those who draw men to wickedness, and encourage them in it, are the devourers and murderers of their souls. (Ezekiel 22:25)

It is no breach of the law of meekness to show our displeasure at the wickedness of the wicked. Those are *angry and sin not* that are angry at sin only, not as against themselves, but as against God. (Exodus 32:19)

[T]ake heed of having fellowship with sinners, and of being in league with them, lest we share in their guilt. Many a careful tradesman has been broken by a careless partner. And it concerns us to watch over one another for the preventing of sin, because others' sins may redound to our damage. (Joshua 7:1)

Partners in sin are justly made partners in the punishment. Those that serve other's lusts must expect to share in their plagues. (Genesis 12:17-20)

When partners in sin come to be shar-

## 4: Corruption

ers in woe, as tares bound in bundles for the fire, they will be a terror to one another. (Luke 16:27-28)

That which is rotten will sooner corrupt that which is sound than be cured or made sound by it. (Psalm 106:34-35)

[T]here is more reason to fear that the bad will corrupt the good than to hope that the good will reform the bad, as there is in laying two pears together, the one rotten and the other sound. (Judges 3:6)

[S]uch is the corruption of nature that the bad are much more likely to debauch the good, than the good to reform the bad. The way of sin is downhill…. (Exodus 34:15-16)

It is not strange if people that are vicious and debauched covet to have ministers that are altogether such as themselves, for they are willing to believe God is so too, Ps. 50:21. (Micah 2:11)

It is not strange if those who do not live up to their religion, but in their conversations *do wickedly against the covenant*, are easily *corrupted by flatteries* to quit their religion. Those that make shipwreck of a good conscience will soon *make shipwreck of the faith*. (Daniel 11:32)

The filthiness of the spirit and the filthiness of the flesh often go together. Corrupt doctrines and a corrupt worship often lead to a corrupt conversation. (Revelation 2:14)

Coldness of love to Christ, and a secret contempt of serious piety, when they appear in professors of religion, are sad presages of a final apostasy. (John 12:4-5)

If those who have made a profession of religion, and have had a pious education, apostatize from it, they are commonly more profane and vicious than those who never made any profession; they have *seven other spirits more wicked*. (Ezekiel 5:6)

Those that suffer vain worldly thoughts to lodge within them when they are at their devotions, turn the *house of prayer* into a *house of merchandise*; but they that make long prayers for pretence to devour widows' houses, turn it into a *den of thieves*. (Mark 11:17)

Those who have themselves apostatized from the truths of God are often the most subtle and barbarous persecutors of those who still adhere to them. (Hosea 5:2)

It is no new thing for the show and form of godliness to be made a cloak to the greatest enormities. But dissembled piety, however it passeth now, will be reckoned for as double iniquity, *in the day when God shall judge the secrets of men*. (Matthew 23:14)

Those have a great deal to answer for who grieve the spirits, and weaken the hands, of good people, and who gratify the lusts of sinners, and animate them in their opposition to God and religion. (Ezekiel 13:22)

Those who hinder the conversion of souls withstand God; and those take too much upon them who contrive how to exclude from their communion those whom God has taken into communion with himself. (Acts 11:17)

The case is bad indeed, and in a manner deplorable and past relief, if the conscience which should rectify the errors of the other faculties is itself a mother of falsehood and a ring-leader in the delusion. What will become of a man if that in him which should be *the candle of the Lord* give a false light...? (Jeremiah 17:9)

[W]isdom will preserve us, (1.) From men of corrupt principles, atheistical profane men, who make it their business to debauch young men's judgments, and instill into their minds prejudices against religion and arguments for vice.... (Proverbs 2:10-11)

It is bad to do mischief upon a sudden thought, but much worse to devise it, to do it with design and deliberation; when the craft and subtlety of the old serpent appear with his poison and venom, it is wickedness in perfection. (Micah 2:2)

Those that contrive wickedness and command it are as truly guilty of it as those that execute it. (2 Samuel 12:9)

Anger and wrath are bad, but malice is worse, because it is more rooted and deliberate; it is anger heightened and settled. (Colossians 3:8)

*Thou shalt not hate thy brother in thy heart;* for malice is murder begun. (Leviticus 19:17)

Malice is ingenious in its devices, as well as industrious in its prosecutions. (Jeremiah 11:19)

The more there is of craft and contrivance in any wickedness the more there is of the devil in it. (Psalm 52:2)

Observe how inveterate is the malice that wicked men have towards the righteous, how far it will go, and what a variety of cruelties it will invent and exercise upon those against whom they have no cause of quarrel, except in the matters of their God. (Hebrews 11:35-36)

See how restless and unwearied the church's enemies are in their malicious attempts to ruin it; they leave no stone unturned, no project untried, to compass it. O that we were as full of contrivance and resolution in prosecuting good designs for the glory of God! (Numbers 23:13)

So full is the world of wicked people that, which way soever God's judgments go forth, they will find work, will find matter to work upon. That fire will never go out on this earth for want of fuel. (Ezekiel 21:15-16)

Wicked men will never want wicked instruments to be employed in carrying on their wicked counsels. (Matthew 22:16)

## 4: Corruption

Pause a little here and wonder, (1.) That men should be thus cruel and inhuman, and so utterly divested of all compassion; and in it see how corrupt and degenerate the nature of man has become. (2.) That the God of infinite mercy should suffer it, nay, and should make it to be the execution of his justice, which shows that, though he is gracious, yet he is the God to whom vengeance belongs. (3.) That little infants, who have never been guilty of any actual sin, should be thus abused, which shows that there is an original guilt by which life is forfeited as soon as it is had. (Isaiah 13:18)

What pleasure could an unsanctified soul take in the vision of a holy God? As *he* cannot endure to look upon their iniquity, so *they* cannot endure to look upon his purity.... (Matthew 5:8)

We may glory before men, who are short-sighted, and cannot search our hearts,—who are corrupt, as we are, and well enough pleased with sin; but there is no glorying before God, who cannot endure to look upon iniquity. (Romans 3:23)

Those deal treacherously with God indeed who not only turn from following him themselves but train up their children in wicked ways. (Hosea 5:7)

Though those children are happy that have that in them which justly recommends them to their parents' particular love, yet it is the prudence of parents not to make a difference between one child and another, unless there be a great and manifest cause given for it by the children's dutifulness or undutifulness; paternal government must be impartial, and managed with a steady hand. ... [W]hen parents make a difference, children soon take notice of it, and it often occasions feuds and quarrels in families. (Genesis 37:4)

The case of those children is very sad, whose parents are *their counsellors to do wickedly*, as Ahaziah's (2 Chron. 22:3); who instruct them and encourage them in sin, and set them bad examples; for the corrupt nature will sooner be quickened by bad instructions than restrained and mortified by good ones. (Matthew 14:8)

Children will be more apt to imitate the vices than the virtues of their parents, and to tread in the steps of their sin than in the steps of their repentance. Parents should therefore be careful not to set their children any bad example.... (Ezekiel 35:5)

See what enemies wicked men are to their own children and families; those that damn their own souls, care not how many they take to hell with them. (Matthew 27:25)

Those are not always in the right that have antiquity and the fathers on their side; for there are errors and corruptions of long standing: and it is so far from being an excuse for walking in a bad way that our fathers walked in it that it is really an aggravation, for it is

Part I: Folly (Damnation)

justifying the sin of those that have gone before us. (Ezekiel 2:3)

The wickedness of the master of a family often brings ruin upon a family; and he that should be the house-keeper proves the house-breaker. (Leviticus 20:4-5)

Let parents take heed of sin, especially the sin of cruelty and oppression, for their poor children's sake, who may be smarting for it by the just hand of God when they themselves are in their graves. Guilt and a curse are a bad entail upon a family. (2 Samuel 21:5-6)

It is not at all inconsistent with the honour and duty which children owe their parents humbly and modestly to advise them, and, as occasion is, to reason with them. (Genesis 43:3-4)

We must never dishonour God in honour to our earthly parents. (2 Kings 18:4)

Those that outdo their predecessors in sin may justly expect to fall under greater and sorer judgments than any of their predecessors knew. (Joel 1:2)

We must not follow the examples of our dear fathers unless they were God's dear children, nor any further than they were dutiful and obedient to him. (Zechariah 1:4)

It is a great aggravation of the wickedness of any family or people that their ancestors were famed for virtue and probity; and commonly those that thus degenerate prove the most wicked of all men. *Corruptio optimi est pessima—that which was originally the best becomes when corrupted the worst....* (Isaiah 1:21-23)

Parents cannot give grace to their children, nor does it run in the blood. Many that are sincerely pious themselves live to see those that come from them notoriously impious and profane; *for the race is not to the swift.* (1 Samuel 2:12)

Families which generally may be most pious and orderly may yet have one or other in them impious and wicked. (Philemon 2)

It is common for a sinking decaying family to boast of the glory and dignity of its ancestors, and to borrow honour from that name to which they repay disgrace; ... It is the common fault and folly of those that have pious parentage and education to trust to their privilege and boast of it, as if it would atone for the want of real holiness. (John 8:33)

[T]hose that are past shame (we say) are past hope. Those that have an adulterer's heart, if they indulge that, will come at length to have a whore's forehead, void of all shame and modesty. (Jeremiah 3:3)

The righteous are the precious be they ever so lowly and poor; the wicked are the vile be they ever so rich and great. In our congregations these are mixed, wheat and chaff in the same floor. (Jeremiah 15:19)

# -5-

# Pride, Vanity, Misplaced Faith in Man

Great men are but instruments which the great God makes use of to serve his own purposes. ... [But] the pride of men sets God against them and ripens them apace for ruin.

Matthew Henry
on Jeremiah 50:21, 32

Great men are but instruments which the great God makes use of to serve his own purposes. ... [But] the pride of men sets God against them and ripens them apace for ruin. (Jeremiah 50:21, 32)

No man's greatness, or honour, or interest, or valour, or victory, can set him out of the reach of the sorest calamities of human life; there is many a sickly crazy body under rich and gay clothing. (2 Kings 5:1)

Pride and self-conceitedness are sins that most easily beset great men, who have great things in the world. They are apt to take the glory to themselves which is due to God only. ... [But] God resists the proud, and delights to abase them and put contempt upon them. Nebuchadnezzar would be more than a man, and therefore God justly makes him less than a man, and puts him upon a level with the beasts who set up for a rival with his Maker. (Daniel 4:30)

There is not a greater enemy to the power of religion, and the fear of God in the heart, than conceitedness of our own wisdom. (Proverbs 3:7)

Let not the highest be proud, nor the strongest secure, for they know not how low they may be brought before they die. (Judges 1:7)

Who can tell what the day may prove which yet begins with a bright morning? (Job 1:1-3)

Let no man glory then in his own wisdom, nor depend upon that, nor upon the wisdom of those about him; for he that gives understanding can when he please take it away. And from those it is most likely to be taken away that boast of their policy. (Isaiah 19:3)

Those who are comparatively *innocents* seldom know how to be compassionate towards those who are manifestly *penitents*. ... O what need have good men to take heed of pride, a corruption that arises out of the ashes of other corruptions! Those that have long served God, and been kept from gross sins, have a great deal to be humbly thankful for, but nothing proudly to boast of. ... Let the rich call the poor *brethren*, and let the innocents call the penitents so. (Luke 15:29-30)

How far will pride carry Christians in opposition to one another! Even so far as to set Christ and his own apostles at variance, and make them rivals and competitors. (1 Corinthians 1:12-13)

It is presumption to say of any creature, "It is, and there is not its like, there is none besides it" (for creatures stand very nearly upon a level with one another); but it is insufferable arrogance for any to say so of themselves, and an evidence of their self-ignorance. (Isaiah 47:8)

It is folly for us to think that there will be any great irreparable loss of us when we are gone, or that we can be ill spared, since God has the residue of the Spirit, and can raise up others, more fit than we are, to do his work. (Job 12:2)

## 5: Pride, Vanity, Misplaced Faith in Man

God is infinitely above us, and happy without us, and whatever good we do it is all from him; so that we are indebted to him, not he to us. (Psalm 16:2-3)

[N]ot by the permission of Providence and the blessing of God ... [d]ownright atheism and profaneness, as well as pride and vanity, are at the bottom of men's attributing their prosperity and success thus to themselves and their own conduct, and raising their own character upon it. (Isaiah 10:13)

[H]e who glories must not glory in himself, but in the Lord. There is no room for any man's boasting of his own abilities and power; or as though he had done any thing that might deserve such immense favours from God. (Ephesians 2:9)

All those whom God rejects are rejected for their own wickedness: but none of those whom he accepts are accepted for their own righteousness. (Deuteronomy 9:4-5)

We have no reason to be proud of our attainments, enjoyments, or performances; all that we have, or are, or do, that is good, is owing to the free and rich grace of God. Boasting is forever excluded. (1 Corinthians 4:7)

Pride is a great prejudice to our improvement. He is stopped from growing wiser or better who thinks himself at the height.... (1 Corinthians 4:8)

Even in good thoughts there is a fickleness and inconstancy which may well be called *vanity*. It concerns us to keep a strict guard upon our thoughts, because God takes particular notice of them. Thoughts are words to God, and vain thoughts are provocations. (Psalm 94:11)

Proud men scorn to be taught, especially by their inferiors, whereas we should never think ourselves too old, nor too wise, nor too good, to learn. ... [T]hose are to be valued by whom we may improve in learning. (John 9:34)

Commonly those are most proud who know least; for with all their knowledge they do not know themselves. (1 Timothy 6:4)

Many have their eyes open that have not their hearts open, are enlightened, but not sanctified; and that knowledge which puffs men up with pride will but serve to light them to hell, whither many go with their eyes open. (Numbers 24:1-2)

[H]e who founds all his knowledge upon principles of science, and the mere light of reason, can never be a judge of the truth or falsehood of what is received by revelation. ... It is the great privilege of Christians that they have the mind of Christ revealed to them by his Spirit. (1 Corinthians 2:16)

Men arrive gradually at the height of impiety and wickedness. *Nemo repente fit turpissimus—No man reaches the height of vice at once.* But, where pride has got the ascendant in a man, he is on the high road to all abominations. (Ezekiel 16:50)

When impiety grows very impudent we may see its ruin near. ... When God's time shall come to bring proud oppressors to their end none shall be able to help them, nor perhaps inclined to help them.... (Daniel 11:45)

Pride is at the bottom of men's obstinacy and disobedience; they think it below them to bow their necks to God's yoke, and a piece of state to set up their own will in opposition to the will of God himself. (Nehemiah 9:16)

Those that are lifted up with great pride are commonly reserved for some great disgrace in life or death. (Jeremiah 22:19)

God takes notice of the degrees of men's pride, the pride of some and the great pride of others; and he will mar it, he will stain it. Pride will have a fall, for God resists the proud. (Jeremiah 13:11)

How proper a method it is to beat down pride to let persons know the true value of what they pride themselves in! It is but too common a thing for men to value themselves most on what is least worth; and it is of great use to bring them to a sober mind by letting them know how much they are mistaken. (1 Corinthians 12:28)

[T]hose who *exalt themselves shall be abased*. (Proverbs 29:23)

(1.) Those that think well of themselves are apt to fancy that others think well of them too; but, when they come to make trial of them, they will find themselves mistaken, and thus their pride deceives them and by it slays them. (2.) God can easily lay low those that have magnified and exalted themselves, and will find out a way to do it, for he *resists the proud;* and we often see those small and greatly despised who once looked very big and were greatly caressed and admired. (Obadiah 1:3)

See what real enemies those are to themselves that think too well of themselves, and what mischiefs those run upon that are impatient of contempt. That will break a proud man's heart that will not break a humble man's sleep. (2 Samuel 17:23)

Those who know their strength are too apt to cause terror, to pride themselves in frightening those they are an overmatch for. ... Note, the strongest cities in this world, the best-fortified and best-furnished, are subject to decay, and may in a little time be brought to nothing. ... It is just with God to make those a terror to their neighbours, by the suddenness and strangeness of their punishment, who make themselves a terror to their neighbours by the abuse of their power. (Ezekiel 26:17-21)

Let us not therefore fear the pride and power of evil men, nor be discouraged by their impotent menaces, for the moth shall eat them up as a garment, but *God's righteousness shall be for ever*, Isa. 51:7, 8. (Psalm 92:7-8)

## 5: Pride, Vanity, Misplaced Faith in Man

"Let not him that begins a war, and is girding on his sword, his armour, his harness, boast of victory, or think himself sure of it, *as if he had put it off*, and had come home a conqueror." (1 Kings 20:11)

God knows all men better than they know themselves, knows their length, their strength, what is in them, and what they will do if they come into such and such circumstances. (1 Samuel 23:11)

Where there is pride in the heart, and no wisdom in the head to suppress it, it commonly shows itself in the words. ... The proud man with his tongue lays about him and deals blows at pleasure, but it will in the end be a rod to himself; the proud man shall come under an ignominious correction by the words of his own mouth, not cut as a soldier, but caned as a servant ... beaten with his own rod. (Proverbs 14:3)

God made but one male and one female, that all the nations of men might know themselves to be made of one blood, descendants from one common stock, and might thereby be induced to love one another. (Genesis 1:27)

The fall of those who have affected to make a noise with their pomp and power will make so much the greater noise. (Jeremiah 49:21)

It is common for men to be most elevated with the hope of success when they are upon the brink of ruin, which makes their ruin so much the sorer.

(Exodus 15:9)

It is common for those that are most elated in their prosperity to be most dejected and disheartened in their adversity. (Ezekiel 30:24)

It is common for those who were honoured in their wealth to be despised in their poverty. (Job 17:6)

Those that are least courageous are commonly most cruel. (Amos 1:11)

Those that are most haughty, insolent, and imperious, when they are in power and prosperity, are commonly the most abject and poor-spirited when the wheel turns upon them. Cowards, they say, are most cruel, and then consciousness of their cruelty makes them the more cowardly. (Esther 7:7-8)

Those that slight God in their prosperity will find themselves under a necessity of seeking him when they are in trouble. (Judges 4:3)

Those that admire with complacency the pomp of this world will admire with consternation the ruin of that pomp, which to those that know the vanity of all things here below is no surprise at all. (Ezekiel 32:9-10)

Great pomp is but great fancy. It neither adds any real excellency, nor gains any real respect, but feeds a vain humour, which wise men would rather mortify than gratify. (Acts 25:23)

The falls of others, both into sin and

ruin, are intended as admonitions to us not to be secure or *high-minded,* nor to think we stand out of danger. (Ezekiel 31:2)

It is good for us to shame ourselves out of our presumptuous confidence in ourselves. Shall a bruised reed set up for a pillar, or a sickly child undertake to be a champion? ... The most secure are commonly the least safe; and those most shamefully betray their own weakness that confidently presume upon their own strength, 1 Cor. 10:12. (John 13:37-38)

[I]t is a common instance of the calamitous state of human life that when we seek to avoid one mischief we fall into a worse, and that the end of one trouble is often the beginning of another; so that we are least safe when we are most secure. (Isaiah 24:18)

We know not the uneasiness of many that live in great pomp, and, one would think, in pleasure, too. We look into their houses, and are tempted to envy them; but, could we look into their hearts, we should pity them rather. (Daniel 2:1)

The place appointed for Adam's residence was a garden; not an ivory house nor a palace over-laid with gold, but a garden, furnished and adorned by nature, not by art. What little reason have men to be proud of stately and magnificent buildings, when it was the happiness of man in innocency that he needed none! As clothes came in with sin, so did houses. (Genesis 2:8)

Those therefore that are enlarging their houses, and making them more sumptuous, have need to look well to the frame of their own spirits in the doing of it, and carefully to watch against all the workings of vain-glory. (Jeremiah 22:13-15)

Those that follow after lying vanities weary themselves with the pursuit. (Ezekiel 24:12)

Those make a bad bargain for themselves that part with their wisdom for the gratifying of their gaiety, and, to please a vain humour, lose a real excellency. (Ezekiel 28:17)

It is a pity that music, which may be so serviceable to the good temper of the mind, should ever be abused by any to the support of vanity and luxury, and made an occasion of drawing the heart away from God and serious things: if this be to any the effect of it, it drives away the good Spirit, not the evil spirit. (1 Samuel 16:23)

Self is the great idol that all the world worships, in contempt of God and his sovereignty. (Ezekiel 29:3)

Abundance of young people are ruined by pride and particularly pride in their beauty. *Rara est concordia formae atque pudicitiae—Beauty and chastity are seldom associated.* (Ezekiel 16:15)

Handsome are those that handsome do. Many a polluted deformed soul dwells in a fair and comely body.... (2 Samuel 14:25)

## 5: Pride, Vanity, Misplaced Faith in Man

We must not be proud of our bodies, because the matter is from the earth, yet not dishonour our bodies, because the mould and shape are from the divine wisdom. ... What a pity it is that these bodies should be instruments of unrighteousness which are capable of being temples of the Holy Ghost! (Job 10:10-11)

The pride and vanity of young people betray them into many snares. (Genesis 34:2)

A believing foresight of the defacing of all worldly glory will help to take us off from admiring it and overvaluing it. The most beautiful body will be shortly worm's meat, and the most beautiful building a ruinous heap. (Matthew 24:2)

Death will strip us; naked we came into the world, and naked we must go out. We shall see little reason to be proud of our clothes, our ornaments, or marks of honour, if we consider how soon death will strip us of our glory, divest us of all our offices and honours, and take the crown off from our head. (Numbers 20:28)

While a saint can ask proud Death, *Where is thy sting?* Death will ask the proud sinner, *Where is thy wealth, thy pomp?* and the more he was fattened with prosperity the more sweetly will death feed on him. (Psalm 49:14)

Let none be proud of the beauty of their grounds any more than of their bodies, for God can soon change the face of both. (Joel 2:3)

It is the folly of the children of this world to value themselves on the pomp and pleasure they live in, to call themselves beauties for the sake of them, and, if in these they excel others, to think themselves perfect. But God takes notice of the vain conceits men have of themselves in their prosperity when the mind is lifted up with the condition, and often, for the humbling of the spirit, finds a way to bring down the estate. Let none reckon themselves beautified any further than they are sanctified, nor say that they are of perfect beauty till they come to heaven. (Ezekiel 27:3)

It is the common folly of those that are sinking in their estates to covet to make a fair show. Many have unhumbled hearts under humbling providences, and look most haughty when God is bringing them down. This is striving with our Maker. (Jeremiah 22:14)

It is not only our wisdom, but our duty, to live according to our estates, and not to spend above what we have. As it is unjust on the one hand to hoard what should be laid out, so it is much more unjust to lay out more than we have; for what is not our own must needs be another's, who is thereby robbed and defrauded. (Deuteronomy 12:15)

*Vanity of vanities, all is vanity.* ... The truth itself here asserted is, that *all is vanity*, all besides God and considered as abstract from him, the *all* of this world, all worldly employments and enjoyments. ... It is *all vanity*. ...Man ... is vanity (Ps. 39:5, 6), and, if there were not another life after this, were made in vain ... and those things, considered in reference to man (whatever they are in themselves), are *vanity*. They are impertinent to the soul, foreign, and add nothing to it; they do not answer the end, nor yield any true satisfaction; they are uncertain in their continuance, are fading, and perishing, and passing away, and will certainly deceive and disappoint those that put a confidence in them.... (Ecclesiastes 1:2-3)

The honours, pleasures, and profits of the world are the vanities, the aspect and prospect of which draw multitudes away from the paths of religion and godliness. (Psalm 119:37)

The world we live in is a world of disappointment, a vale of tears, and a dying world; and the children of men in it are but of a few days, and full of trouble. (Isaiah 24:6)

We are out in our aim, if we look for a heaven here upon earth. (Matthew 17:4)

The frowns of the world would not disquiet us as they do if we did not foolishly flatter ourselves with the hopes of its smiles and court and covet them too much. (Jeremiah 45:4-5)

Those who make any creature their expectation and glory, and so put it in the place of God, will sooner or later, be ashamed of it, and their disappointment in it will but increase their fear. (Isaiah 20:4-6)

Nothing is more grievous than the disappointment of a raised expectation. ...

[H]ope quite dashed kills the heart, and the more high the expectation was raised the more cutting is the frustration of it. It is therefore our wisdom not to promise ourselves any great matters from the creature, nor feed ourselves with any vain hopes from this world, lest we lay matter for our own vexation.... (Proverbs 13:12)

It is not wisdom to raise our expectations high in this world, for the most valuable of our glories and joys here are vanishing, even those of near communion with God are so, not a continual feast, but a running banquet. (Matthew 17:8)

The creature that we make our hope commonly proves our hurt. (Isaiah 7:17)

[A]nd the less confidence is to be put in men's words let us with the more assurance trust in God's word. (Psalm 12:6)

Among men it is too often found that those who are most able to break their word are least careful to keep it.... (Psalm 89:6-8)

Let none of God's children distrust their Father, nor take any sinful course for the supply of their own necessities; some way or other, God will provide for them in the way of duty and honest diligence, *and verily they shall be fed.* (Deuteronomy 8:3)

Those that are holy must nevertheless not trust in themselves, nor in their

## 5: Pride, Vanity, Misplaced Faith in Man

own righteousness, but only in God and his grace. (Psalm 86:1)

Men are false to one another; there is no faith in man, but a universal dishonesty. Truth, that sacred bond of society, has departed, and there is nothing but treachery in men's dealings. (Isaiah 24:16)

Men are barbarous, but God is gracious; men are false, but God is faithful. (Psalm 86:14-15)

Thus true is that of Solomon, *Confidence in an unfaithful man in time of trouble is like a broken tooth or a foot out of joint*. Let us therefore cease from man. (Acts 27:29-30)

Those that had been unfaithful to their God were so to one another, and it was a part of their punishment as well as their sin, for even those that love to cheat, yet hate to be cheated. (Jeremiah 9:8)

Those hearts go a whoring from God that take a complacency in the pomp of the world and put a confidence in its wealth, and in an *arm of flesh,* Jer. 17:5. (Ezekiel 23:43-44)

Those that can live better by sense than by faith, that stay themselves upon an arm of flesh rather than upon the almighty arm, forsake a fountain of living waters for broken cisterns. (1 Samuel 10:19)

Those that make flesh their arm, arm it against them. (Obadiah 7)

Many are beaten with that arm of flesh which they trusted to rather than to the arm of the Lord. (Isaiah 8:18)

[As] ... it can do nothing but by divine permission ... we must not trust to an arm of flesh when it is engaged for us, so we must not be afraid of an arm of flesh when it is stretched out against us. (Psalm 56:4)

If we value men, if we over-value them, for their worldly wealth and power, it is just with God to make them thereby a scourge to us. ... [R]*ich men oppress us*.... (Isaiah 8:7-8)

Those that trust in man perhaps draw nigh to God with their mouth and honour him with their lips ... but really *their heart departs from him*; they distrust him. ... Cleaving to the cistern is leaving the fountain, and is resented accordingly. ... We need not be solicitous about the breaking of a cistern as long as we have the fountain. ... God is to all that are his a *fountain of living waters.* (Jeremiah 17:5-6, 18:13)

It is better to have one fountain than a thousand cisterns, one all-sufficient God than a thousand insufficient ones. (Deuteronomy 6:4-5)

It is good to foresee the failing of all our creature-confidences, then when we are most in temptation to depend upon them, that we may *cease from man.* (Ezekiel 29:2)

Though others fail in their duty to us, yet we must not therefore neglect ours to them. (Exodus 18:13)

The insufficiency of creatures should drive us to the all-sufficiency of the Creator. (Daniel 2:28)

When great men *appear in their glory* they are apt to look with disdain upon the poor that apply to them; but the great God will not do so. (Psalm 102:17)

"… Be not only so just to your God, but so wise for yourselves, as not to throw away your adorations upon those who are not able to help you, and thereby provoke him who is able to destroy you." Well, this is all that God insists upon. (Jeremiah 7:3)

Wisdom is a gift of God, which he grants to some and withholds from others, grants at some times and withholds at other times. Those that are void of compassion are so far void of understanding. Where there is not the tenderness of a man one may question whether there be the understanding of a man. … *Therefore shalt thou not exalt them.* Those are certainly kept back from honour whose hearts are hidden from understanding. (Job 17:4)

It is a dishonour to the children of men, who are endued with the powers of reason, to worship that as their god which is the creature of their own fancy and the work of their own hands, to bow down to the stock of a tree. It is much more a dishonour to the children of God, who are blessed with the privilege of divine revelation, to forsake such a God as they know theirs to be for a thing of nought, their own mercies for lying vanities. They likewise debase themselves by truckling to their heathen neighbours, and depending upon them, when they had a God to go to who is all-sufficient and in covenant with them. (Isaiah 57:9)

# -6-

# Judges, Politicians, National Sins

God never perverts judgment upon personal regards and considerations, nor countenances a wicked man in a wicked thing for the sake of his beauty, or stature, his country, parentage, relations, wealth, or honour in the world.

Matthew Henry
on Acts 10:34

God never perverts judgment upon personal regards and considerations, nor countenances a wicked man in a wicked thing for the sake of his beauty, or stature, his country, parentage, relations, wealth, or honour in the world. (Acts 10:34)

God's laws were never designed to be like cobwebs, which catch the little flies, but suffer the great ones to break through. (2 Samuel 14:21)

The judges [who] would not do right, would not protect or vindicate oppressed innocency. ..."*Do you indeed speak righteousness, or judge uprightly?*" No; you are far from it. ... [Y]ou do not discharge the trust reposed in you as magistrates, by which you are bound to be *a terror to evil-doers and a praise to those that do well.* ... Remember you are sons of men; mortal and dying, and that you stand upon the same level before God with the meanest of those you trample upon, and must yourselves be called to an account and judged. (Psalm 58:1-2)

"Is it not your business to administer justice impartially, and not to *know faces*" (as the Hebrew phrase for partiality and respect of persons is), "but to *know judgment,* and the merits of every cause?" (Micah 3:1)

Judges, when they receive the complaints of the accuser, must always reserve in their minds room for the defence of the accused, for they have two ears, to remind them to hear both sides. ... Facts, and not faces, must be known in judgment; and the *scale* of justice must be used before the *sword* of justice. (John 7:51)

*In multitude of counsellors there is safety;* and judges should consult both with themselves and others before they pass sentence. (Acts 25:12)

God is greatly offended with corruptions, not only in his own worship, but in the administration of justice between man and man, and the dishonesty of a people shall be the ground of his controversy with them as well as their idolatry and impiety; for God's laws are intended for man's benefit and the good of the community, as well as for God's honour, and the profanation of courts of justice shall be avenged as surely as the profanation of temples. (Hosea 10:4)

Those shame themselves that bring a reproach on their profession. And justly will that beauty, that excellency, at length be made the object of the loathing of others which men have made the matter of their own pride. (Ezekiel 16:31)

[B]ad magistrates ... neglect their duty and abuse their power, forgetting that God standeth among them. ... [T]hey *judge unjustly,* contrary to the rules of equity and the dictates of their consciences, giving judgment against those who have right on their side, out of malice and ill-will, or for those who have an unrighteous cause, out of favour and partial affection. To do unjustly is bad, but to judge unjustly is

## 6: Judges, Politicians, National Sins

much worse, because it is doing wrong under the colour of right. (Psalm 82:1-5)

When malice and envy sit upon the bench, reason and justice may even be silent at the bar, for whatever they can say will undoubtedly be over-ruled. (John 5:18)

Those who will wrong their consciences for any thing will come at length to do it for next to nothing; those who begin to sell justice for silver will in time be so sordid as to sell it *for a pair of shoes,* for a pair of old shoes. (Amos 2:6)

[T]he judge that will not do right without a bribe will no doubt do wrong for a bribe. (Acts 24:25-27)

Such a prevalency of irreligion and inhumanity is bad in any, but very bad in a *judge,* who has power in his hand, in the use of which he ought to be guided by the principles of religion and justice, and, if he be not, instead of doing good with his power he will be in danger of doing hurt. *Wickedness in the place of judgment* was one of the sorest evils Solomon saw under the sun, Eccl. 3:16. (Luke 18:2)

It is sad that the power which magistrates have from God, and should use for him, should ever be employed against him. But *marvel not at the matter,* Eccl. 5:8. (Psalm 119:161)

Miserable is the people's case when the judge's enquiry upon a cause is not, "What is to be done in it?" but, "What is to be got by it?" (Micah 4:11)

[J]udges on the bench, like Pilate (John 19:11) ... have no power but what is given them from above. (Ezekiel 30:25)

[W]hat an offence it is to God, 1. When those that are entrusted with the administration of public justice, judges, juries, witnesses, prosecutors, counsel, do either acquit the guilty or condemn those that are not guilty, or in the least contribute to either; this defeats the end of government, which is to protect the good and punish the bad. (Proverbs 17:15)

Wise governors should be careful to keep up the credit of their government and the authority of the laws, by punishing presumptuous offenders; but then in such cases there should be good evidence of the fact. (Hebrews 10:28)

He that does wrong must expect one way or other to receive *according to the wrong he has done,* Col. 3:25. God sometimes brings men's violent dealings upon their own heads (Ps. 7:16); and magistrates are in this the ministers of the justice, that they are *avengers* (Rom. 13:4), and they shall not bear the sword in vain. (Exodus 21:22)

Those that have power may do a great deal for the protection of an honest man and an honest cause, and when they so use their power they are ministers of God for good. (Judges 6:31)

Those who have power ought to use it for the protection and comfort of those whom they have power over; for to that end they are entrusted with power.

Even the bramble, if he be anointed king, invites the trees to come and *trust in his shadow*. Judg. 9:15. (Ezekiel 31:6)

In demanding and recovering even a just debt we must take heed lest we act either unjustly or uncharitably. (Amos 5:11)

The plentiful enjoyment of God's ordinances in their power and purity is the most valuable instance of a nation's prosperity and the greatest blessing that can be desired. (Joel 2:12-17)

It is the real honour of great men to be quiet men, and it is the wisdom of princes to put such into places of trust. (Jeremiah 51:59-61)

It is well with a kingdom when its great men know how to value its good men, when its governors look upon religion and religious people to be their strength, and consider it their interest to support them, and learn to call godly praying people, and skillful faithful ministers, *the chariots and horsemen of Israel*, as Joash called Elisha, and not the troublers of the land, as Ahab called Elijah. (Zechariah 12:5-7)

Good men are the blessings of their country, and it is their unspeakable honour and happiness to be made so. (Genesis 12:2)

It is the misery of this world that so many who are fit for public stations are buried in obscurity, and so many who are unfit for them are preferred to them. (Daniel 1:3-4)

[T]hose are most fit for government who are least ambitious of it. (Numbers 11:26)

Those are commonly most fit for places of honour and trust that are least fond of them. (Psalm 101:6)

Those are fittest to rule that have learnt to obey. (Joshua 1:1-2)

[T]he case is bad, when the leaders of the people *cause them to err*. ... Though the condition of those whose guides are blind is very sad, yet that of the blind guides themselves is yet more woeful. Christ denounces a woe to those blind guides that have the blood of so many souls to answer for. (Matthew 23:16)

Satan is in a special manner busy with great men and men of power, to keep them from being religious; because he knows that their example, whether good or bad, will have an influence upon many. And those who are in any way instrumental to prejudice people against the truths and ways of Christ are doing the devil's work. (Acts 13:8)

[I]f *the wicked* get power in their hands, wickedness will abound, religion and religious people will be persecuted, and so the ends of government will be perverted. (Proverbs 29:2)

Satan, the great accuser of the brethren, has his agents in all places, and particularly in the courts of those princes that encourage them and give ear to them, who make it their business to represent the people of God as

## 6: Judges, Politicians, National Sins

enemies to Caesar and hurtful to kings and provinces, that, being thus dressed up in bear-skins, they may "be baited." (1 Samuel 24:9)

It is a very hard and rare thing for men to have an absolute arbitrary power, and not to make an ill use of it. (Daniel 5:19)

Those rulers that are of a persecuting spirit shall never want ill instruments about them, that will blow the coals, and make them worse. (John 9:13)

If we did but duly *consider the ways* of wicked men, we should all dread being associates with them and followers of them. (Ezekiel 18:14)

[To an unrighteousness nation] the rod of government shall be turned into the serpent of tyranny and oppression. (Isaiah 19:4)

Tyranny is the inlet to anarchy; and, when the rod of government is turned into the serpent of oppression, it is just with God to say, "There shall be no strong rod to be a sceptre to rule; but let men be as *are the fishes of the sea,* where the greater devour the less." (Ezekiel 19:14)

Nothing gives greater advantage to a mastiff-like tyranny, that is fierce and furious, than a spaniel-like submission, that is fawning and flattering. (Hosea 5:11-13)

It is sad with a people when the powers that should be for edification are for destruction, and they are ruined by those by whom they should be ruled.... (Isaiah 19:4)

It is a barbarous thing to *add affliction to the afflicted.* (Ezekiel 34:21)

A nation is certainly marked for ruin when God hides the things that belong to its peace from the eyes of those entrusted with its counsels. (Obadiah 8)

One party shall be for a thing for no other reason than because the other is against it; that is a perverse spirit, which, if it mingles with the public counsels, tends directly to the ruin of the public interests. ... Their politics shall be all blasted, and turned into foolishness. (Isaiah 19:14)

A secret enmity to Christ and his gospel is often gilded over with a pretended affection to Caesar and his power. (Ezra 4:14-15)

It is no new thing for that to be represented, and with great assurance too, as the sense of the nation, which is far from being so; and that which few approve of is sometimes confidently said to be that which all agree to. (Daniel 6:6-7)

It is common for that which is the sense only of the malicious to be falsely represented by them as the sense of the many. (Nehemiah 6:5-7)

A few madmen may out-shout many wise men, and then fancy themselves to speak the sense (when it is but the nonsense) of a nation, or of all mankind; but it is not so easy a thing to change the sense of the people as it is to misrepresent it, and to change their cry. (John 19:15)

A few factious, discontented, ill-natured people, may do a great deal of mischief in the best societies, if great care be not taken to discountenance them. (Numbers 11:4)

Those that bring sin into a country or family bring a plague into it and will have to answer for all the mischief that follows. (2 Kings 17:17-20)

Those that help to bring sin into a country do but thereby prepare for the throwing of themselves out of it. Those must expect to be first in the punishment who have been ringleaders in sin. (Micah 1:13)

Ring-leaders in sin may expect to fall under particular marks of the wrath of God, who will severely reckon for the blood of souls, which is thus spilt. (Numbers 14:36)

Princes and scholars must not exercise themselves in matters too great, too high, for men; and those in a low station, and of ordinary capacities, must not pretend to that which is out their reach, and which they were not cut out for. Those will fall under due shame that affect undue honours. (Psalm 131:1)

It is common for self-seeking men thus to grasp at more than they can manage, and so the business of their places is neglected, while the pomp and profit of them wholly engage the mind. (Isaiah 22:15-16)

*He* may be said to boast of a false gift, 1. Who pretends to have received or given that which he never had, which he never gave, makes a noise of his great accomplishments and his good services, but it is all false; he is not what he pretends to be. Or, 2. Who promises what he will give and what he will do, but performs nothing, who raises people's expectations of the mighty things he will do for his country ... but either he has not wherewithal to do what he says or he never designs it. Such a one is like the morning-cloud, that passes away, and disappoints those who looked for rain from it to water the parched ground (Jude 12), *clouds without water.* (Proverbs 25:14)

High places are slippery places; and those are justly deprived of their honour that are proud of it and puffed up with it, and deprived of their power that do hurt with it. (Isaiah 22:19)

The high ones, that are on high, that are puffed up with their height and grandeur, that think themselves so high that they are out of the reach of any danger, God will visit upon them all their pride and cruelty, with which they have oppressed and injured their neighbours and subjects, and it shall return upon their own heads. (Isaiah 24:21)

The higher bad men sit above the resentments of the earth the nearer they

## 6: Judges, Politicians, National Sins

ought to think themselves to the vengeance of Heaven. (Job 39:28)

Those who abuse their power will justly be stripped of it; and God, as King of nations, will find out a way to maintain the injured rights and liberties, not only of his own, but of other nations. (Ezekiel 29:14-15)

We need not fear great men against us while we have the great God for us. (1 Chronicles 20:6-7)

Let not those that are advanced in the world set their inferiors at too great a distance, because they know not how soon they may be set upon a level with them. *The rich man's wealth is his strong city* in his own conceit; but it does not always prove so. (Isaiah 24:1-2)

The most mighty and magnificent kingdoms and states, sooner or later, have their day to come down. They have their period; and, when they are in their zenith, they will begin to decline. ... It is ill with a people when those that sit at the stern, instead of putting them into the harbour, run them aground. (Ezekiel 27:26-27)

Sometimes the valour of a nation strangely sinks, and it becomes cowardly and effeminate, so that what was the head of the nations in an age or two becomes the tail. (Daniel 7:4)

What is got by oppression cannot long be enjoyed with satisfaction. (Amos 4:2)

There are some in whom ambition and affectation of dominion seem to be bred in the bone; such there have been and will be, notwithstanding the wrath of God often revealed from heaven against them. Nothing on this side hell will humble and break the proud spirits of some men, in this like Lucifer.... (Genesis 10:8-9)

It is common for the greatest abusers of their power to be the most rigorous asserters of it, and to take a pride and pleasure in any thing that looks like the exercise of it. (Matthew 21:23)

The fear of man brings a snare, and many are driven to sin by the dread of death.... (Genesis 12:12)

Tyrants have their fears. Those who are, and affect to be, *the terror of the mighty*, are many times the greatest terror of all to themselves; and when they are most ambitious to be feared by the people, are most afraid of them. (Matthew 14:5)

Those who design ill themselves are commonly most apt to suspect that others design ill. (Judges 9:2)

As rulers by the ordinance of God are made a terror and restraint to wicked people, so people are sometimes by the providence of God made a terror and restraint to wicked rulers. (Acts 4:21)

Thus many are restrained from evil practices by the fear of man who would not be restrained from them by the fear of God. (Acts 22:29)

Those could not but fear the people, who studied only how to make the people fear them. (Matthew 21:26)

The righteousness of God is to be acknowledged when those who have terrified and enslaved others are themselves terrified and enslaved, when those who by the abuse of their power to destruction which was given them for edification make themselves as wild beasts, as *roaring lions and ranging bears*.... (Ezekiel 19:1-9)

The death or disuniting of the mighty often proves the death and destruction of the many; and it is in vain to depend upon mighty men for our protection if we have not an almighty God for us, much less if we have an almighty God against us. (Obadiah 9)

There is a woe to those who are in public trusts, but consult only their own private interest, and are more inquisitive about the benefice than about the office, what money is to be got than what good to be done. (Ezekiel 34:2)

Those in public trusts, if they raise great estates, must take heed that it be not at the expense of a good conscience, which is much more valuable. (Genesis 47:24-26)

Great care ought to be taken in the distribution of public charity, [1.] That it be given to such as have need; such as are not able to procure a competent maintenance of themselves, through age, infancy, sickness, or bodily disability, or incapacity of mind.... (Acts 4:35)

The public revenues must be applied to the public service, and not to gratify the avarice of private persons. (Luke 3:13)

Those that hate to be reformed hate to be reproved, and do all they can to silence faithful ministers. Amos was forbidden to prophecy.... (Micah 2:6)

Those have a great deal to answer for that cannot bear faithful preaching, and those much more that suppress it. (Amos 2:12)

It bodes ill to a people when prayer is restrained among them. (Isaiah 64:7)

When princes begin to persecute God's people and ministers, let them expect no other than vexation on all sides. The way for any country to be quiet is to let God's church be quiet in it. If Saul fight against David, the Philistines shall fight against his country. (1 Samuel 23:1)

There is not a greater service done to the devil's kingdom than the silencing of faithful ministers; and putting those under a bushel that are the lights of the world. (Acts 4:18)

The restraining of public assemblies for religious worship, the scattering of them by their enemies, or the forsaking of them by their friends, so that either there are no assemblies or not solemn ones, is a very sorrowful thing to all good people. (Zephaniah 3:18)

It has often been the hard fate of Christ's holy religion, unjustly to fall under the suspicions of the civil pow-

# 6: Judges, Politicians, National Sins

ers, as if it were hurtful to kings and provinces, whereas it tends mightily to the benefit of both. (Matthew 27:11)

Religion teaches good manners, and obliges us to give honour to those to whom honour is due. It is an instance of great degeneracy and disorder in a land when *the child behaves himself proudly against the ancient, and the base against the honourable*.... (Leviticus 19:32)

Those are enemies not only to God, but to the world, they are enemies to their country, that silence good ministers, and obstruct the means of knowledge and grace; for it is certainly for the public common good of states and kingdoms that religion should be encouraged. (Micah 2:7-8)

Nothing contributes more to the making of a nation considerable abroad, valuable to its friends and formidable to its enemies, than religion reigning in it; for who can be against those that have God for them? And he is certainly for those that are sincerely for him, Prov. 14:34. (Deuteronomy 11:25)

Those that faithfully perform the service of God do one of the best services that can be done to the public; God's ministers, while they keep within the sphere of their office and conscientiously discharge the duty of it, must be looked upon as some of the most useful servants of their country. (Numbers 8:24)

It is the greatest relief of the cares of magistrates and ministers, when those under their charge make them uneasy, that they may have recourse to God by prayer. (Exodus 15:25)

Public charities should be encouraged, for they bring upon a nation public blessings; and though there may be some mismanagement of them, yet that is not a good reason why we should not bring in our *quota* to them. (Mark 12:41)

They were *a hypocritical nation*, that made a profession of religion ... but were not truly religious, not truly reformed, not so good as they pretended to be. ... Being a profane hypocritical nation, they are the people of God's wrath. ... Nothing is more offensive to God than dissimulation in religion. See what a change sin made: those that had been God's chosen and hallowed people, above all people, had now become the *people of his wrath*. (Isaiah 10:5-6)

A people may be filling up the measure of their iniquity apace, and yet may keep up a course of external performances in religion. (Joel 1:13)

[I]f this nation, which God is thus loading with benefits, *do evil in his sight* and *obey not his voice*,—if it lose its virtue, and become debauched and profane,—if religion grow into contempt, and vice to get to be fashionable, and so be kept in countenance and reputation, and there be a general decay of serious godliness among them,—then God will turn his hand against them, will pluck up what he was planting, and pull down what he was building ... the good work that was in the doing shall stand still and be let fall. (Jeremiah 18:9-10)

The debauching of a nation will certainly be the debasing of it. (2 Kings 13:6)

National impiety and immorality bring national desolation. (Isaiah 1:4)

Though God grieves long, and bears long, when pressed with the weight of general and prevailing wickedness, yet he will at length ease himself of public offenders by public judgments. (Hebrews 3:17-19)

It is a sign religion is going to decay when good ministers are neglected and at a loss for a livelihood. (Judges 17:7-8)

Universal neglect of religion is a more dangerous symptom to any people than particular instances here and there of daring irreligion. (Matthew 24:38)

National sins bring national disorders and the disturbance of the public repose: *For the transgression of a land,* and a general defection from God and religion to idolatry, profaneness, or immorality ... by which the people are crumbled into parties and factions, biting and devouring one another, or many successively, in a little time, one cutting off another. ... As the people suffer for the sins of the prince ... so the government sometimes suffers for the sins of the people. ... We cannot imagine what a great deal of service one wise man may do to a nation in a critical juncture. (Proverbs 28:2)

Let us not be frightened with an apprehension of the continual decay of virtue, as if, when times and men are bad, they must needs, of course, grow worse and worse; that does not follow, for, after many bad kings, God raised up one that was like David himself. (2 Kings 18:1-3)

If God has mercy in store for a people, he will either prevent the rise or hasten the ruin of hypocritical rulers. (Job 34:29-30)

It may be some encouragement to zealous reformers, that frequently the purging out of corruptions, and the correcting of abuses, prove an easier piece of work than was apprehended. Prudent attempts sometimes prove successful beyond expectation, and there are not those lions *found* in the way, that were feared to be. (Mark 11:15-16)

One man may be of public service to a whole country. (Ezekiel 33:1-4)

Good magistrates are in pain if their subjects are in tears. (1 Samuel 11:5)

The pardon of a national sin, as such, consists in the turning away of the national punishment.... (Numbers 14:19)

National justice prevents national judgments. (Psalm 106:30)

Those that will not tremble and mourn as they ought for national sins shall be made to tremble and mourn for nation-

## 6: Judges, Politicians, National Sins

al judgments; those that look without concern upon the sins of the oppressors, which should make them tremble, and upon the miseries of the oppressed, which should make them mourn, God will find out a way to make them tremble at the fury of those that oppress them and mourn for their own losses and sufferings by it. (Amos 8:8)

God's judgments often look a great way back, which obliges us to do so when we are under his rebukes. It is not for us to object against the people's smarting for the sin of their king (perhaps they were aiding and abetting), nor against this generation's suffering for the sin of the last. God often *visiteth the sins of the fathers upon the children, and his judgments are a great deep*. He gives not account of any of his matters. (2 Samuel 21:1)

When the sins of a people reach up to heaven, the wrath of God will reach down to the earth. (Revelation 18:5)

Wickedness, as it is the shame of human nature, so it is the ruin of human society. (Genesis 6:11-12)

When iniquity is universal we have reason to expect that calamity should be so too. (Jeremiah 48:21-24)

When the disease of sin has become epidemical, it is fatal to any place, Isa. 1:5-7. (Genesis 19:4)

It is one bad effect of the abounding of iniquity, and its becoming fashionable, that it often gives occasion to suspect the innocent. When a disease is epidemical every one is suspected to be tainted with it. (1 Samuel 1:12-13)

The way of the most is neither the best, the wisest, nor the safest way to follow: better to follow the eight in the ark than the eight millions drowned by the flood and damned to hell. (1 Peter 3:20)

*Nations that forget God shall be turned into hell*, and no reproach at all to God's infinite goodness. (Joshua 10:42)

When all are involved in guilt nothing less can be expected than that all should be involved in ruin. (Hosea 4:5)

God's judgments come upon a people by steps, that they may meet him repenting. (Ezekiel 30:20-26)

Under public judgments there ought to be public humiliations; for by them the *Lord God calls to weeping and mourning*. With all the marks of sorrow and shame sin must be confessed and bewailed, the righteous God must be acknowledged, and his favour implored. (Joel 1:14-15)

If God speak concerning it [a nation] to build and to plant, and it do wickedly, he will recall his favours and leave it to ruin. But if he speak concerning it to pluck up and destroy, and it repent, he will revoke the sentence and deliver it. (Ezekiel 33:10-12)

It is the great concern of those who have revolted from God to return to him. And those who have gone from him by consent, and in a body, drawing one another to sin, should by consent, and in a body, return to him, which will be for his glory and their mutual edification. ... The consideration of the judgments of God upon us and our land, especially when they are tearing judgments, should awaken us to return to God by repentance, and prayer, and reformation. (Hosea 6:1)

National sin or disobedience is the great and only thing that retards and obstructs national deliverance. (Psalm 81:15)

Nothing but reformation will prevent the ruin of a sinful people. (Amos 4:12)

Reformation is not sincere if it be not universal. (Genesis 35:4)

When we seek to God for national mercies we ought to humble ourselves before him for national sins. (Daniel 9:5-6)

National holiness would secure national happiness. (Psalm 80:7)

When God returns in mercy to a people that return to him in duty, all their grievances will be soon redressed and their honour retrieved. (Ezekiel 36:15)

Personal and particular reformation must be insisted on as necessary to national deliverance: *every one* must *turn from his* own *evil way*. The street will not be clean unless every one sweep before his own door. (Jeremiah 25:5-6)

# -7-

# Pharisees (Hypocritical Teachers)

… Christ was quarrelled with. … They that quarrelled with him were the Pharisees; a proud generation of men, conceited of themselves, and censorious of others; of the same temper with those in the prophet's time…

Matthew Henry
on Matthew 9:11

... Christ was quarrelled with. ... They that quarrelled with him were the Pharisees; a proud generation of men, conceited of themselves, and censorious of others; of the same temper with those in the prophet's time, who said, *Stand by thyself, come not near me; I am holier than thou*: they were very strict in avoiding *sinners*, but not in avoiding *sin*.... (Matthew 9:11)

The scribes and Pharisees were the great men of the Jewish church, men whose gain was godliness, great enemies to the gospel of Christ, but colouring their opposition with a pretence of zeal for the law of Moses, when really nothing was intended but the support of their own tyranny over the consciences of men. (Matthew 15:1-2)

Many that make a great profession of religion, have much knowledge, and abound in the exercise of devotion, are yet ruined by the love of the world; nor does any thing harden the heart more against the word of Christ. (Luke 16:14)

[S]ome of the greatest scholars and the greatest statesmen have been the greatest strangers to gospel mysteries. *The world by wisdom knew not God*, 1 Cor. 1:21. (Matthew 11:25)

[M]any excel in worldly wisdom who are utterly destitute of heavenly grace, because those who set up for oracles themselves are apt to despise the oracles of God. *God has chosen the foolish things of the world;* and the greatest statesmen are seldom the greatest saints. (2 Samuel 17:23)

Frequently the greatest pretenders to knowledge are most ignorant in the things of God. (John 10:6)

A man may seem to be learned who has not learned Christ, and appear virtuous when he has not a principle of grace in his heart. (2 Corinthians 10:7)

It is possible for men to be very studious in the letter of the scripture, and yet to be strangers to the power and influence of it. (John 5:39)

It is a profanation of God's solemn ordinances when those that are grossly and openly profane and vicious impudently and impenitently so intrude upon the services and privileges of them. *Give not that which is holy unto dogs.* (Ezekiel 23:39)

It will be more tolerable with those that perish for lack of vision than with those that *rebel against the light*. ... And as those are most blind who *will not see*, so their blindness is most dangerous who fancy they do see. (John 10:41)

Hypocrisy in religion is of all things most abominable to the God of heaven. ... [The elder] Jews in Christ's time ... pretended a great zeal for the law and the temple, but made themselves and all their services abominable to God by filling their hands with the blood of Christ and his apostles, and so filling up the measure of their iniquities. (Isaiah 1:10-15)

Thus objections are made against the gospel from the advancement and im-

## 7: Pharisees (Hypocritical Teachers)

provement of gospel light, as if childhood and manhood were contrary to each other, and the superstructure were against the foundation. (John 3:26)

Those who are your enemies are the seed and successors of them who of old mocked the messengers of the Lord.... (Matthew 5:12)

It is no new thing for bad men to be found employed in the external performances of religion. (Ezekiel 14:1-4)

Many seem enemies to sin in others, while they indulge it in themselves. Saul will drive the devil out of his kingdom, and yet harbour him in his heart, by envy and malice. (1 Samuel 28:3-4)

Those are of all sinners most inexcusable that allow themselves in the sins they condemn in others, or in worse. This doth especially touch wicked ministers, who will be sure to have their portion appointed them with hypocrites ... for what greater hypocrisy can there be, than to press that upon others, to be believed and done, which they themselves disbelieve and disobey; pulling down in their practice what they build up in their preaching; ... living so ill that it is a pity they should ever come in; like bells, that call others to church, but hang out of it themselves.... (Matthew 23:1-8)

Hypocrisy is the high road to apostasy. Those that do not set their hearts aright will not be stedfast with God, but play fast and loose. (Psalm 78:8)

Nothing ripens a people more for ruin, nor fills the measure faster, than the sins of their priests and prophets. (Lamentations 4:13-14)

"... They are notorious for their obstinacy; they sacrifice to the Lord as their God, but they will not be ruled by him as their God; they will not receive either the instruction of his word or the correction of his rod; they will not be reclaimed or reformed by either. *Truth has perished* among them; they cannot receive it; they will not submit to it nor be governed by it. They will not speak truth; there is no believing a word they say, for it is *cut off from their mouth,* and lying comes in the room of it. They are false both to God and man." (Jeremiah 7:28)

They know not that way of duty which God had prescribed them, though it be written both in their hearts and in their books. ... They would not attend to the dictates of the written word. (Jeremiah 8:7-9)

It is a pity that those who are so far convinced of the divine origin of gospel preaching as to protect it from the malice of others do not submit to the power and influence of it themselves. (Jeremiah 26:16)

Those that pretend to an inspiration of the Spirit, in imposing upon the church their own fancies, either in opinion or practice—that say they are moved from above when they are carried on by their pride, covetousness, or affectation of dominion, belie the Holy Ghost. (Acts 5:3)

All that minister about holy things must have an eye to God's command as their rule and warrant; for it is only in the observance of this that they can expect to be owned and accepted of God. (Leviticus 8:5)

Those must be very wicked and ungodly men who set themselves to seduce and deceive others into false doctrines and errors. (Ephesians 4:14)

Deceivers of souls are murderers of souls. Those that steal away the scripture by keeping it in an unknown tongue, that steal away the sacraments by maiming them and altering the property of them, that steal away Christ's ordinances to put their own inventions in the room of them, they *kill and destroy*.... (John 10:10)

Great corruptions and abuses come into the church by the practices of those whose *gain is godliness*, that is, who make worldly gain the end of their godliness, and counterfeit godliness their way to worldly gain (1 Tim. 6:5); *from such withdraw thyself*. (Matthew 21:12)

Note, 1. In order to our judging aright of the different persuasions in religion which there are among Christians, it concerns us to enquire whether they come of him that calleth us, whether or no they are founded upon the authority of Christ and his apostles. 2. If, upon enquiry, they appear to have no such foundation, how forward soever others may be to impose them upon us, we should by no means submit to them, but reject them. (Galatians 5:8)

Those that take upon them to control and contradict God's appointment take too much upon them. It is enough for us to submit; it is too much to prescribe. (Numbers 16:3)

Illegal impositions will be laid to the charge of those who support and maintain them, and keep them up, as well as those who first invented and enjoined them. ... Those who are most zealous of their own impositions, are commonly most careless of God's commands.... (Matthew 15:3-6)

There is a day coming when vengeance will be taken on those that have introduced errors and corruptions into the church, and the devil that deceived man will be *cast into the lake of fire*. (Numbers 31:3)

False doctrines are like winds, that toss the water to and fro, and they are apt to unsettle the minds of men, who are sometimes as unstable as water. (2 Thessalonians 2:1-3)

There is a strange proneness in us to make our opinion and practice a rule and a law to every body else, to judge of all about us by our standard, and to conclude that because we do well all do wrong that do not just as we do. (Acts 15:1)

## 7: Pharisees (Hypocritical Teachers)

Those who are strict in restraining their own liberty yet ought not to impose those restraints upon the liberties of others, nor to judge of them accordingly. We must not make ourselves the standard to measure others by. A good man will deny himself that liberty which he will not deny another, contrary to the practice of the Pharisees…. (Genesis 14:23-24)

[I]t is common for men of corrupt minds, by their zeal in rituals, and the external services of religion, to think to atone for the looseness of their morals. But they are cursed who *add to*, as well as they who *take from, the words of this book*, Rev. 22:16, 19; Prov. 30:6. (Matthew 12:1-7)

The power of the church, and of church rulers, is not a legislative, but only a judicial power. The high priest might not make any new laws for God's house, nor ordain any other rites of worship than what God had ordained; but he must judge God's house, that is, he must see to it that God's laws and ordinances were punctually observed, must protect and encourage those that did observe them, and enquire into and punish the violation of them. (Zechariah 3:7)

Those are no friends to Christ and his disciples, who make that to be unlawful which God has not made to be so. (Matthew 12:2)

Men often run into gross mistakes by understanding that literally which the scripture speaks figuratively. (John 2:19-23)

How apt we are to misunderstand scripture—to understand that literally which is spoken figuratively, and to expound scripture by our schemes, whereas we ought to form our schemes by the scriptures. (Acts 1:6)

[Pharisees] were very severe in imposing upon others those things which they were not themselves willing to submit to the burthen of…. (Matthew 23:4)

Corruptions in worship make way for corruptions in morals. The *mother of harlots* is the *mother of* all other *abominations,* Rev. 17:5. (Hosea 9:17)

[Pharisees are] men made up of error and enmity, mistakes and malice. Sore eyes cannot bear clear light; and nothing is more provoking to these proud imposers than the undeceiving of those whom they have first blindfolded, and then enslaved. (Matthew 15:10-12)

Good and useful offices and powers are not *therefore* to be condemned and abolished, because they fall sometimes into the hands of bad men, who abuse them. We must not *therefore* pull down Moses's seat, because scribes and Pharisees have gotten possession of it. … We must not think the worst of good truths for their being preached by bad ministers; nor of good laws for their being executed by bad magistrates. (Matthew 23:1-3)

We must take heed of being prejudiced against the ways and people of God by the follies and peevishness of some

## Part I: Folly (Damnation)

particular persons that profess religion. (Exodus 2:11-15)

Those who have the choice of the keepers of the holy things, if, to serve some secular selfish purpose, they choose such as are unfit and unfaithful, will justly have laid it at their door, that they have betrayed the holy things by lodging them in bad hands. (Ezekiel 44:7-9)

If that place which should have been a centre of devotion be made a centre of wickedness, it is not strange if God make it a rendezvous of destroyers. (Jeremiah 21:4)

It is sad with a people when those who should be as shepherds to them are as young lions to them. (Zechariah 11:3)

They barbarously devour those whom they should protect, and, as unfaithful shepherds, fleece the flock they should feed; nay, instead of feeding it, they feed upon it.... (Micah 3:1-3)

The righteous God will certainly reckon for injuries done to the widows and fatherless, who, being helpless and friendless, cannot otherwise expect to be righted. (Micah 2:9)

Hypocrites, while they fancy themselves heirs of heaven, are, in the judgment of Christ, the children of hell. The rise of their hypocrisy is from hell, for the devil is the father of all lies; and the tendency of their hypocrisy is toward hell ... which was the principle ... of Pharisaism. (Matthew 23:28-33)

Disciples are in most danger from hypocrites; against those that are openly vicious they stand upon their guard, but against Pharisees, who are great pretenders to devotion, and Sadducees, who pretend to a free and impartial search after truth, they commonly lie unguarded: and therefore the caution is doubted, *Take heed, and beware*. (Matthew 16:6)

Two traitors within the garrison may do more hurt to it than two thousand besiegers without. (2 Timothy 3:1-9)

What greater indignity can be done to the God of truth than to lay the brats of the father of lies at his door? (Jeremiah 23:32)

The external performances of religion, if they do not harden men against sin, harden them in it, and embolden carnal hearts to venture upon it, in hopes that when they come to count and discount with God he will be found as much in debt to them for their peace-offerings and their vows as they to him for their sins. But it is sad that a show of piety should become the shelter of iniquity (which really doubles the shame of it, and makes it more exceedingly sinful) and that men should baffle their consciences with those very things that should startle them. The Pharisees made long prayers, that they might the more plausibly carry on their covetous and mischievous provisions. (Proverbs 7:14-15)

[N]othing is more opposite to true Christianity than Pharisaism is, nor any

## 7: Pharisees (Hypocritical Teachers)

thing more disrelishing to a soul truly devout than their hypocritical devotions. (John 10:8)

There will always be a difference between those who worship the true God; some will compass him about with lies, others will be faithful with the saints; some, like the Pharisee, will lean to their own righteousness; others, like the publican, will confess their sin, and cast themselves upon the mercy of God in Christ. (Hebrews 11:4)

Those that have no inward principle of love to God's ordinances may yet be found much in the external observance of them. Cain brought his sacrifice as well as Abel; and the Pharisee went up to the temple to pray as well as the publican. (Ezekiel 34:31)

Many can freely give God their beasts, their lips, their knees, who would not give him their hearts; the Pharisees gave alms. (Proverbs 21:27)

It is a gracious ambition to covet to be really more holy than others, but it is a proud ambition to covet to appear so. It is good to excel in real piety, but not to exceed in outward shows; for overdoing is justly suspected of design, Prov. 27:14. (Matthew 23:5)

It is true prayer is not a thing we have reason to be ashamed of, but we must avoid all appearances of ostentation. Let what passes between God and our souls be kept to ourselves. (1 Samuel 1:13)

Men may go far in the external performances of religion, and keep long to them, merely by the power of their education and the influence of their friends, who yet have no hearty affection for divine things nor any inward relish of them. Foreign inducements may push men on to that which is good who are not actuated by a living principle of grace in their hearts. ... In the outward expressions of devotion it is possible that those who have only the form of godliness may out-strip those who have the power of it. (2 Chronicles 24:1-5)

*Ye cannot serve God and Mammon.* ... To some their belly is their *mammon* ... to others their ease, their sleep, their sports and pastimes, are their *mammon* ... to others worldly riches ... to others honours and preferments; the praise and applause of men was the Pharisees' *mammon*.... (Matthew 6:24)

Great shows of piety and devotion may be found even among those who, though they keep up these *forms of godliness,* are strangers and enemies to *the power* of it. But what will such hypocritical services avail? (Jeremiah 36:9)

[Pharisees] made but a jesting matter of the methods God takes to do them good. ... This is the ruin of multitudes, they can never persuade themselves to be *serious* in the concerns of their souls. ... O the amazing stupidity and vanity of the blind and ungodly world! (Luke 7:31)

[The Pharisees] pretended a deal of kindness for the memory of prophets that were dead and gone, while they hated and persecuted those that were present with them. (Matthew 23:31)

Many good men have had more honour done to their memories than ever they had to their persons, witness those that were persecuted while they lived, but when they were dead had their sepulchers garnished. (Numbers 21:29)

It is common for men to hate and persecute the power of that religion in others which yet they pride themselves in the form of. (Acts 26:6-7)

Mean and prejudiced spirits are apt to judge of men by their education, and to enquire more into their rise than their reasons. *"Whence has this man these mighty works? Did he come honestly by them? Has he not been studying the black art?"* Thus they turned that against him [Christ] which was really for him; for if they had not been wilfully blind, they must have concluded him to be divinely assisted and commissioned, who without the help of education gave such proofs of extraordinary wisdom and power. (Matthew 13:54-56)

Persecuting God's prophets, suppressing and silencing them, is a sin that provokes God as much as anything, for it not only spits in the face of his authority over us, but spurns at the bowels of his mercy to us; for his sending prophets to us is a sure and valuable token of his goodwill. (Micah 2:6)

The prophecies of the Old Testament were so fully accomplished in Christ that those who rejected Christ did in effect deny those prophecies, and set them aside. (John 5:46-47)

The Old Testament set forth in shadows what was to come; the New Testament is the accomplishment of the Old. (Hebrews 9:11)

For as the New Testament explains the Old, so the Old Testament confirms the New, and Jesus Christ is the Alpha and Omega of both. (Psalm 110:1-4)

The canon of scripture is now perfected, *the Spirit of prophecy has ceased,* the mystery of God is finished, he has put his last hand to it. The gospel church may be made more large, more prosperous more purified from contracted pollution, but it shall never be altered for another dispensation; those who perish under the gospel perish without remedy. (Hebrews 12:25)

Blindness and deafness in spiritual things are worse in those that profess themselves to be God's servants and messengers than in others. It is in them the greater sin and shame, the greater dishonour to God, and to themselves a greater damnation. (Isaiah 42:18-19)

The sins of those who have made a profession of religion and relation to God are more provoking to him than the sins of others. (Hosea 9:1)

Those will have a great deal to answer for in the judgment-day who take upon

## 7: Pharisees (Hypocritical Teachers)

them the care of souls and yet take no care of them. (Ezekiel 34:10)

Sinners, and especially degenerate professors, are in God's account as dross, vile, and contemptible, and of no account, as the *evil figs* which *could not be eaten, they were so evil.* They are useless and fit for nothing; of no consistency with themselves and no service to man. (Ezekiel 22:18)

Ringleaders in sin are the worst of sinners, especially if those that by their office should have been guides to the friends of Christ are guides to his enemies. (Acts 1:15)

Ringleaders in sin may expect to be first met with by the judgments of God; and the sins of those who are in the most eminent and public stations call for the most exemplary punishments. (Ezekiel 9:6)

Leaders in sin are the worst of sinners; and the proselytes which the scribes and Pharisees make often prove seven times more the children of hell than themselves. (Acts 9:1-2)

Nothing in men is more odious and offensive to God than a proud conceit of themselves and contempt of others; for commonly those are most unholy of all that think themselves holier than any. (Isaiah 65:5)

Many can easily prognosticate the dismal consequences of other people's sins, that see not what will be the end of their own. (Matthew 21:40-41)

Those that pretend to honour God by a profession of religion, and yet live wicked lives, put an affront upon him, as if he were the patron of sin. (Isaiah 66:1-4)

The practice of profaneness appears most odious in those that make a profession of religion. (Ezekiel 16:2)

It is very possible, and too common, for those that declare God's statutes to others to live in disobedience to them themselves, and for those that take God's covenant in their mouths yet in their hearts to continue their covenant with sin and death; but they are guilty of an usurpation, they take to themselves an honour which they have no title to, and there is a day coming when they will be thrust out as intruders. ... (1.) They are charged with a daring contempt of the word of God ... (2.) A close confederacy with the worst of sinners ... 3) A constant persisting in the worst of tongue-sins: [lying and slandering]. (Psalm 50:16-20)

Usurpers must expect to resign. Let no man therefore set his heart on that to which he is not entitled. (2 Samuel 3:14-16)

*The* [false] *priest and the prophet ... have healed the hurt of the daughter of my people slightly,* or *according to the cure of some slight hurt*, skinning over the wound and never searching it to the bottom, applying lenitives only, when there is need of corrosives, soothing people in their sins, and giving them opiates to make them easy for the present, while the disease was preying upon the vitals. (Jeremiah 6:13-14)

If ministers, who are reprovers by office, connive at sin and indulge sinners, either show them not their wickedness or show them not the fatal consequences of it, for fear of displeasing them and getting their ill-will, they hereby make themselves partakers of their guilt and are rebellious like them. (Ezekiel 2:8)

Love to this present world is often the cause of apostasy from the truths and ways of Jesus Christ. (2 Timothy 4:10)

An apostate church is a harlot. (Ezekiel 16:35)

When the holy seed degenerate, they are commonly worse than the worst of the profane. (2 Kings 21:3)

Apostates are usually the worst of men, the most vain and profligate, the most bold and daring; their consciences are seared, and their sins of all others the most aggravated. God often sets marks of his displeasure upon them in *this* world, and in the other world they will *receive the greater damnation*. Let us therefore hear, and fear, and hold fast our integrity. (Luke 11:26)

Professors of religion, if they do not live up to their profession, but contradict it, if they degenerate and depart from it, are the most unprofitable creatures in the world, like the *salt* that has *lost its savour* and is thenceforth *good for nothing*, Mark 9:50. (Ezekiel 15:1-8)

Apostasy will be punished with everlasting burnings, the fire that shall never be quenched. This is the sad end to which apostasy leads, and therefore Christians should go on and grow in grace, lest, if they do not go forward, they should go backward, till they bring matters to this woeful extremity of sin and misery. (Hebrews 6:6-8)

Those that are sincere in religion may trust in God that they shall not slide, that is, that they shall not apostasize from their religion. (Psalm 26:1)

Those that follow God fully in times of general apostasy God will own and honour by singular preservations in times of general calamity. (Numbers 14:24)

Those that preserve their purity in times of general corruption may trust God with their safety in times of general desolation. (Psalm 91:1-8)

In times of general apostasy, there is usually a remnant that keep their integrity—some, though but a few; all do not go one way. ... [I]t is God that reserves to himself that remnant. If he had left them to themselves, they had gone down the stream with the rest. It is his free and almighty grace that makes the difference between them and others. (Romans 11:4)

In times of the greatest degeneracy and apostasy God has always had, and will have, a remnant faithful to him, some that keep their integrity and do not go down the stream. (1 Kings 19:18)

## 7: Pharisees (Hypocritical Teachers)

In the worst of times God has his remnant, and in every age will reserve to himself a holy seed and preserve that to his heavenly kingdom. (Psalm 12:7)

God's part in the world is too often the smallest part. His chosen are comparatively a little flock. (Numbers 3:39)

The wickedness of ministers, though it destroy themselves, yet it shall not destroy the ministry. How bad soever the officers are, the office shall continue always to the end of the world. If some betray their trust, yet others shall be raised up that will be true to it. God's work shall never fall to the ground for want of hands to carry it on. (1 Samuel 2:35)

When the corruptions of the visible church are such, and so provoking, that we have reason to fear its total extirpation, yet then we may be confident of this, to our comfort, that God will secure his own honour, by making good his purpose, that while the world stands he will have a church in it. (Ezekiel 20:24)

## -8-

# Hypocrisy

In matters of religion hypocrisy is counterfeit piety.

Matthew Henry
on 1 Peter 2:1

In matters of religion hypocrisy is counterfeit piety. (1 Peter 2:1)

A false and hypocritical profession of religion commonly withers in this world, and it is the effect of Christ's curse; the fig tree that had no fruit, soon lost its leaves. Hypocrites may look plausible for a time, but, having no principle, *no root in themselves*, their profession will soon come to nothing; the gifts wither, common graces decay, the credit of the profession declines and sinks, and the falseness and folly of the pretender are manifested to all men. (Matthew 21:19)

The acts of devotion which are done in hypocrisy are commonly reflected upon with pride and vain glory. Thus the Pharisee went up to the temple to boast of his religion, Luke 18:11, 12. (Numbers 23:4)

A believing, humble, thankful glorying in God, is the root and summary of all religion. ... But a proud vainglorious boasting in God, and in the outward profession of his name, is the root and summary of all hypocrisy. Spiritual pride is of all kinds of pride the most dangerous. (Romans 2:17)

It is no new thing for the plausible professions and protestations of hypocrites to be contradicted and disproved by the most plain and undeniable evidence. Many boast of their obedience to the command of God; but what mean then their indulgence of the flesh, their love of the world, their passion and uncharitableness, and their neglect of holy duties, which witness against them? (1 Samuel 15:13-14)

When hypocrites screen themselves behind the wall of an external profession, and with it think to conceal their wickedness from the eye of the world and carry on their designs the more successfully, it is hard for them to manage it with so much art that there is some hole or other left in the wall, something that betrays them, to those who look diligently, not to be what they pretend to be. The ass's ears in the fable appeared from under the lion's skin. (Ezekiel 8:7-10)

Those who think by their disguises to hide themselves from God will be wretchedly confounded when they find themselves disappointed in the day of discovery. Sinners now appear in the garb of saints, and are taken to be such; but how they will blush and tremble when they find themselves stripped of their false colours, and are called by their own name: "Go out, thou treacherous false-hearted hypocrite. *I never knew thee. Why feignest thou thyself to be another?*" Tidings of a portion with hypocrites will be heavy tidings. God will judge men according to what they are, not according to what they seem. (1 Kings 14:5-6)

To appear before God is as much the desire of the upright as it is the dread of the hypocrite. (Psalm 42:1-2)

It is possible for a man to continue under the power of sin, and yet to put on a form of godliness. ... The disguises of

## 8: Hypocrisy

hypocrites many times are soon seen through; the nature of the wolf shows itself notwithstanding the cover of the sheep's clothing. (Acts 8:23)

Note, It is possible for a hypocrite to go through the world, not only undiscovered, but unsuspected; like bad money so ingeniously counterfeited that nobody questions it. (Matthew 26:14-16)

The professions and pretences of hypocrites will be produced in evidence against them, and they will be self-condemned. (Mark 12:14-15)

Let this be a warning to us against hypocrisy, that disguises will shortly be stripped off, and every man will appear in his own colours; and an encouragement to us in our sincerity, that God is a witness to it. (Matthew 22:11)

[W]hatever lust reigns in the heart it will break out; diseased lungs make an offensive breath: men's language discovers what country they are of, so likewise *what manner of spirit they are of*.... (Matthew 12:33-35)

It is the hope of hypocrites, and not of the sons of God, that makes an allowance for the gratification of impure desires and lusts. (1 John 3:3)

There is a mixture of bad with good in the best societies, a Judas among the apostles; it will be so till we come to the blessed society into which shall enter nothing unclean or disguised. (John 13:18)

There is a great deal of secret wickedness in the hearts of men, which is long hid under the cloak of a plausible profession, but breaks out at last. As the good seed, so the tares, lie a great while under the clods, and at first springing up, it is hard to distinguish them; but when a trying time comes, when fruit is to be brought forth, when good is to be done that has difficulty and hazard attending it, then you will return and discern between the sincere and the hypocrite: then you may say, This is wheat, and that is tares. (Matthew 13:26)

The pretending mother [1 Kings 3:25] was for dividing the child.... (Matthew 6:24)

How many there are who call Christ, Master and Lord, that are far from him! But they *serve their own belly*—their carnal, sensual, secular interests. It is some base lust or other that they are pleasing; pride, ambition, covetousness, luxury, lasciviousness, these are the designs which they are really carrying on. (Romans 16:18)

A man may be free from gross sin, and yet come short of grace and glory. His hands may be clean from external pollutions, and yet he may perish eternally in his heart-wickedness. What shall we think then of those who do not attain to this; whose fraud and injustice, drunkenness and uncleanness, witness against them, that all these they have broken from their youth up, though they have named the name of Christ? (Matthew 19:20)

A hypocritical attendance on God and his ordinances is so far from being pleasing to him that it is provoking. (Ezekiel 20:3)

Gospel advantages and advancements abused will sink sinners so much lower into hell. ... [T]he higher the precipice is, the more fatal is the fall from it.... (Matthew 11:23)

The greater profession men make of religion, and the more they are employed in the study and service of it, the greater opportunity they have of doing mischief, if their hearts be not right with God. If Judas had not been an apostle, he could not have been a traitor; if men had not known the way of righteousness, they could not have abused it. (Matthew 26:15)

When those that have called themselves disciples afterwards prove traitors, their apostasy at last is a certain evidence of their hypocrisy all along. (John 13:10-11)

Those that apostatize from religion sufficiently indicate that, before, they were hypocrites in religion: those who have imbibed the spirit of gospel truth have a good preservative against destructive error. (1 John 2:19)

There are many who in works deny God, and disown him, yet, to serve a turn, will profess that they *know him*, that they know more of him than some of their neighbours do. But what stead will it stand a man in to be able to say, *My God, I know thee*, when he cannot say, "My God, I love thee," and "My God, I serve thee, and cleave to thee only?" (Hosea 8:2)

The reason why hypocrites do not persevere in religion is because they have no pleasure in it. Those that do not delight in the Almighty will not always call upon him. The more comfort we find in our religion the more closely we shall cleave to it. (Job 27:10)

All our religious professions avail nothing further than they are made in truth and righteousness. If we be not sincere in them, we do but *take the name of the Lord our God in vain*. (Isaiah 48:1)

There is no mean between God's acceptance and his abhorrence. If our persons and performances are sincere and upright, they are accepted; if not, they are an abomination.... (Leviticus 7:18)

[T]here are many whose religion is lip-labour only. They say that which expresses an approach to God and an adoration of him, but it is only from the teeth outward. ... They do not apply their minds to the service. When they pretend to be speaking to God they are thinking of a thousand impertinences: *They have removed their hearts far from me*.... (Isaiah 29:13)

Many that profess faith in Christ have not a due consideration for him; he is not so much thought of as he deserves to be, and desires to be, by those that expect salvation from him. (Hebrews 3:1)

# 8: Hypocrisy

Many are full of good words, who are empty and barren in good works.... (Acts 9:36)

A man may be a good casuist and yet a bad Christian—accurate in the notion, but loose and careless in the application. ... A man may be well skilled in the controversies of religion, and yet a stranger to the power of godliness. (Romans 2:18)

It is an easy thing for bad men to speak very good words, and with their mouth to make a show of piety. There is no judging of men by their words. God knows the heart. (Numbers 22:18)

See the nature of hypocrisy: it lies in the heart, which is for the world and the flesh when the outside seems to be for God and religion. Many that are saints in show and saints in word are hypocrites in heart. (Job 36:13)

Piety from the teeth outward is no difficult thing. (Jeremiah 12:2)

Many have their pangs of piety who, when the pangs are over, show that they have no true piety. (Jeremiah 22:23)

Many are melted under the word that harden again before they are cast into a new mould. (Judges 2:4)

They that take up a profession *in a pang*, will throw it off again *in a fret*.... (Matthew 8:19-20)

The fruits that are the first ripe keep the worst. (1 Samuel 8:1)

Those that take upon them a profession of religion only in complaisance to their relations, to oblige their friends, or for the sake of company, will be converts of small value and of short continuance. (Ruth 1:12-15)

Many have their consciences startled by the law that have them not purified; fair promises are extorted from them, but no good principles fixed and rooted in them. (Deuteronomy 5:27)

This is the true description of one who hears the word of God and does it not. How many are there who, when they sit under the word, are affected with their own sinfulness, misery, and danger, acknowledge the evil of sin, and their need of Christ; but, when their hearing is over, all is forgotten, convictions are lost, good affections vanish, and pass away like the waters of a land-flood: he *straightway forgets*. (James 1:24)

Many are almost persuaded to be religious who are not quite persuaded; they are under strong convictions of their duty, and of the excellency of the ways of God, but yet are overruled by some external inducements, and do not pursue their convictions. (Acts 26:28)

God calls many by the ministry of the word, and they say, as Samuel did, "Here am I;" but not looking at God, nor discerning his voice in the call, the impressions of it are soon lost; they lie down again, and their convictions come to nothing. (1 Samuel 3:4)

[T]hose that have *begun in the spirit and end in the flesh* may reckon all their past services and sufferings *in vain*. ... [U]nless we persevere we *lose what we have gained*, 2 John 8. (Ezekiel 18:24)

It is better never to begin than not to proceed; and therefore before we begin we must consider what it is to proceed. (Luke 14:28)

God's promises pertain to those, and those only, that dwell under the church's shadow, that attend on God's ordinances and adhere to his people, not those that flee to that shadow only for shelter in a hot gleam, but those that *dwell under it*. Ps. 27:4 (Hosea 14:7)

There are sinners in Zion, hypocrites ... but their hearts are not right in the sight of God; they keep up secret haunts of sin under the cloak of a visible profession, which convicts them of hypocrisy. [Hypocrites] ... will have a great deal to answer for above other sinners. (Isaiah 33:14)

This is the worst thing in sin, that it makes us loathsome to God; and the nearer any are to God in profession the more loathsome are they if they rebel against him, like a dunghill at our door. (Psalm 106:40)

The sin of Ananias and Sapphira his wife .... Now their sin was, 1. That they were ambitious of being thought eminent disciples, and of the first rank, when really they were not true disciples; they would pass for some of the most fruitful trees in Christ's vineyard, when really the root of the matter was not found in them. ... It is possible that hypocrites may deny themselves in one thing, but then it is to serve themselves in another; they may forego their secular advantage in one instance, with a prospect of finding their account in something else. (Acts 5:1-4)

Thus hypocrites, when they hear good things promised to good Christians, would put in for a share, though they have no part nor lot in the matter. (Genesis 40:16-19)

In the visible church, it is no strange thing to find plants that our heavenly Father has not planted. (Matthew 15:13)

Many come to the wedding feast without a wedding garment. If the gospel be the wedding feast, then the wedding garment is a frame of heart, and a course of life agreeable to the gospel and our profession of it.... (Matthew 22:11-14)

Many times those who are nearest to the means, are furthest from the end. (Matthew 2:1-4)

Ananias and Sapphira pretended they could come up to the terms, that they might have the credit of being disciples, when they really could not. ... It is often of fatal consequence for people to go to a greater length in profession than their inward principle will admit of. (Acts 5:1-11)

Many are brought to gross lying by reigning pride, and affectation of the

## 8: Hypocrisy

applause of men, particularly in works of charity to the poor. (Acts 5:4)

Those that bind up their happiness in the favour of men make themselves an easy prey to the temptations of Satan. (John 19:12-13)

Those who bind up their happiness in the praise and applause of men, expose themselves to a perpetual uneasiness upon every favourable word said of any other. (Matthew 12:23-24)

Those are like the devil who cannot endure that any body should be praised but themselves, but grudge the just share of reputation others have, as Saul (1 Sam. 18:5, etc.) and the Pharisees, Matt. 21:15. (Job 1:9)

An undue regard to the approbation and applause of men is one great ground of the unhappy strifes and contentions that exist among Christians. (Galatians 5:26)

Hypocrites have their eye to the world's hand; thence *they have their reward* (Matt. 6:2); but true Christians have their eye to God as their rewarder. (Psalm 123:1-4)

They who *desired* nothing more than the *praise* of men, dreaded nothing more than the rage and displeasure of men, (Mark 14:2)

Those who are dead to men's praise can safely bear their contempt. (John 8:49-50)

Those that make most noise in any business are frequently but a noise. Great talkers are often little doers. (Jeremiah 46:17)

Note, 1. It is easy to find those that will pretend to be kind and liberal. Many a man will call himself a man of mercy, will boast what good he has done and what good he designs to do. ... Most men will talk a great deal of their charity, generosity, hospitality, and piety, will sound a trumpet to themselves, as the Pharisees, and what little goodness they have will proclaim it and make a mighty matter of it. 2. But it is hard to find those that are really kind and liberal, that have done and will do more than either they speak of or care to hear spoken of, that will be true friends in a strait; such a one as one may trust to is like a black swan. (Proverbs 20:6)

Hence learn, A man may lawfully acknowledge, and sometimes is bound to assert, the gifts and graces of God to him. To pretend to what we have not is hypocrisy; but to deny what we have is ingratitude. (1 Peter 1:1-2)

Many that are destitute of *the power of godliness* are yet very fond of *the form* of it; and it is just with God to punish them for their hypocrisy by depriving them of that too. ... The church-privileges that men are proud of are profaned by their sins, and it is just with God to profane them by his judgments. (Ezekiel 24:21)

Everlasting misery and sorrow will certainly be the portion of those who

## Part I: Folly (Damnation)

live among sanctified ones, but themselves die unsanctified. (Matthew 14:49-50)

It is possible for those to be confident they are in the right who yet are evidently in the wrong; and for those to think they are doing their duty who are wilfully persisting in the greatest sin. ... Under colour and pretext of religion, the most barbarous and inhuman villainies have been not only justified, but sanctified and magnified. ... There is not a more violent principle in the world than conscience misinformed. (Acts 26:9)

Some confess Christ to be the *holy One of God*, that under the cloak of that profession they may carry on malicious mischievous designs; but their confession is doubly an abomination to the Lord Jesus, as it sues in his name for a license to sin, and shall therefore be put to silence and shame. (Mark 1:23-28)

It is bad in any to rob God of his honour, but worst in ministers, whose office and business it is to bear up his name and to give him the glory due to it. ... As sin is a reproach to any people, so especially to priests; there is not a more despicable animal upon the face of the earth than a profane, wicked, scandalous minister. (Malachi 2:9)

Wicked priests are generally the worst of men. The better any thing is, the worse it is when it is corrupted. Lay persecutors have been generally found more compassionate than ecclesiastics. (Mark 15:3-4)

Great pretenders to sanctity are commonly the worst enemies to those who are really sanctified. Priests have been the most bitter persecutors. (Amos 7:10-11)

Bloody designs have often been covered, and carried on, with a pretence of religion; thus they have been accomplished most plausibly and most securely: but this dissembled piety is, doubtless, double iniquity. Religion is never more injured, nor are God's sacraments more profaned, than when they are thus used for a cloak of maliciousness. (Genesis 34:15)

There are those, even among Christ's followers, that are worse than anyone can imagine them to be, and lack nothing but opportunity to show it. (Matthew 26:15)

Satan's sworn servants would be thought to be his enemies, and they never more effectually do his work, than when they pretend to be fighting against him. (Matthew 10:25)

The hottest place in hell will be the portion of hypocrites and persecutors. (Matthew 21:41)

It is not only the murderer with his sword, but the *hypocrite with his mouth*, that *destroys his neighbour*, decoying him into sin, or into mischief, by the specious pretences of kindness and goodwill. (Proverbs 11:9)

Those are our worst enemies that draw us to sin, for that is the greatest mis-

# 8: Hypocrisy

chief any man can do us. ... We are more endangered by the charms of a smiling world than by the terrors of a frowning world. (Numbers 25:1-3)

When God's professing people quarrel among themselves, snarl at, and devour one another, it is just with God to bring the common enemy upon them, that shall make peace by making a universal devastation. (Habakkuk 1:6)

If professors of religion ruin themselves, their ruin will be the most reproachful of any; and they in a special manner will rise at the last day to everlasting shame and contempt. (Micah 6:16)

[T]o acknowledge that a doctrine is from God, and yet not to receive and entertain it, is the greatest absurdity and iniquity that a man can be charged with. (Matthew 21:25)

For the holy God hates sin in those that are nearest to him, nay, in them he hates it most. A sinful state is, and will be, a woeful state. (Zephaniah 3:1)

Those that have so far thrown themselves out of God's favour that he will not hear their prayers cannot expect benefit by the prayers of others for them. (Jeremiah 11:14)

True believers are as wheat, substantial, useful, and valuable; hypocrites are as chaff, light, and empty, useless and worthless, and carried about with every wind; these are now mixed, good and bad, under the same external profession; and in the same visible communion. ... There is a day coming when the floor shall be purged, and the wheat and chaff shall be separated. ... Hell is the *unquenchable fire*, which will burn up the chaff, which will certainly be the portion and punishment, and everlasting destruction, of hypocrites and unbelievers. (Matthew 3:12)

Those who are not fruitful to the glory of God's grace will be fuel to the fire of his wrath; and thus, if they give not honour to him, he will *get himself honour upon them*, honour that will shine brightly in that flaming fire by which impenitent sinners will be forever consumed. (Ezekiel 15:6)

As God tries believers by their strongest graces, so hypocrites by their strongest corruptions. (Matthew 19:21-22)

Where grace does not work, corruption will. ... Wild grapes are hypocritical performances in religion, that look like grapes, but are sour or bitter, and are so far from being pleasing to God, that they are provoking.... (Isaiah 5:2)

Those to whom God has given a good pasture, if they are wanton in it, will justly be turned out of it; and those who will not be kept within the hedge of God's precept forfeit the benefit of the hedge of God's protection, and will be forced in vain to flee through the breaches they have themselves fearfully made in that hedge. (Amos 4:2-3)

It is a sin against God to be unkind to our friends and to lift up the heel

Part I: Folly (Damnation)

against those that have helped to raise us. (Ezekiel 17:15-16)

It is rare to find even those that have shared with us in our joys willing to share with us in our griefs too. The cankerworms will continue upon the field while there is any thing to be had, but they are gone when all is gone. (Nahum 3:15)

Men may have their fancies pleased by the word, and yet not have their consciences touched nor their hearts changed, the itching ear gratified and yet not the corrupt nature sanctified. ... There are many who take pleasure in hearing the word, but make no conscience of doing it; and so they build upon the sand, and deceive themselves. (Ezekiel 34:31-32)

Many that attend on the word come rather to see and be seen, than to learn and be taught, to have something to talk of, than to be made wise to salvation. ... They who attend on the word will be called to an account, what their intentions and what their improvements were. (Matthew 11:7-9)

*In vain do those worship me* whose *hearts are far from me* while they *draw near with their mouth;* but whose fault is that? Not God's, who is the rewarder of those who seek him diligently, but theirs who seek him carelessly. (Malachi 3:14)

Those do not pray to God at all that do not pray *in the spirit.* (Hosea 7:14)

Spiritual joy is seated in the soul; the joy of the hypocrite is but from the teeth outward. (Proverbs 14:13)

*The joy of the hypocrite is but for a moment.* There is no serenity without a lasting sincerity. (Psalm 97:8-12)

The God with whom we have to do perfectly knows how our hearts are toward him. He knows both the guile of the hypocrite and the sincerity of the upright. (Jeremiah 12:3)

[For] ... the wicked who go on still in their trespasses. Let not them think to have any benefit among God's people. Though in show and profession they herd themselves among them, let them not expect to come in sharers; no ... those among them that ... [are] *wicked* and ... [hate] to be reformed *there is no peace,* no peace with God or their own consciences, no real good, whatever is pretended to. (Isaiah 48:22)

Carnal hearts, in their prayers to God, covet temporal mercies only, and dread and deprecate no other but temporal judgments, for they have no sense of any other. (Hosea 7:14)

[I]t is an abominable thing for those who profess the holiness of the Lord to profane it, particularly by yoking themselves unequally with unbelievers. (Malachi 2:11)

The hypocrite is like the waterman, that looks one way and rows another; the true Christian like the traveller, that has his journey's end in his eye. The hypocrite soars like the kite, with

# 8: Hypocrisy

his eye upon the prey below, which he is ready to come down to when he has a fair opportunity; the true Christian soars like the lark, higher and higher, forgetting the things that are beneath. (Matthew 6:22-23)

There are those who are called *Christians* who will in the great day be condemned by the better tempers and better lives of sober heathens. (Ezekiel 5:7-8)

God can strike a terror upon those that are most secure; fearfulness shall, when he pleases, surprise the most presumptuous hypocrites. (Ezekiel 30:9)

See what foolish fruitless pains sinners take in their sinful ways; they seek deep, they sink deep, to hide their counsel from the Lord who sits in heaven and laughs at them. Note, A practical disbelief of God's omniscience is at the bottom both of the carnal worships and of the carnal confidences of hypocrites.... (Isaiah 29:15)

Even God's Israel get to heaven by hell-gates; so many are their transgressions, and so strong their corruptions, that it is a miracle of mercy that they are happy at last; as hypocrites go to hell by heaven-gates. (Ezekiel 20:27-32)

# -9-

# Carnality and Idolatry

Carnal desires get head by indulgence, and therefore should be observed and checked in their first rise: if once they prevail, and bear sway in us, we know not whither they will carry us. This caution stands first, because carnal appetites indulged are the root and source of much sin.

Matthew Henry
on 1 Corinthians 10:6

Carnal desires get head by indulgence, and therefore should be observed and checked in their first rise: if once they prevail, and bear sway in us, we know not whither they will carry us. This caution stands first, because carnal appetites indulged are the root and source of much sin. (1 Corinthians 10:6)

It is as great a piece of self-denial to control our passions as it is to control our appetites. (1 Samuel 1:9)

We ought always to have such a command of every passion as that, however it may break out, it may soon be restrained and called in again when we are convinced that it is either unreasonable or unseasonable. *He that has such a rule as this over his own spirit is better than the mighty.* (Nehemiah 8:11-12)

Two things we must watch against, lest our hearts be overcharged with them:—(1.) The indulging of the appetites of the body, and allowing of ourselves in the gratifications of sense to an excess ... (2.) The inordinate pursuit of the good things of this world. The heart is overcharged with the *cares of this life.* The former is the snare of those that are given to their pleasures: this is the snare of the men of business, that *will be rich.* We have need to guard on both hands. ... Our caution against sin, and our care of our own souls must be *constant.* (Luke 21:34-35)

Every fair haven is not a safe haven; nay, there may be most danger where there is most pleasure. (Acts 27:8)

It is true, eating good meat and wearing good clothes are lawful; but it is true that they often become the food and fuel of pride and luxury, and so turn into sin to us. (Luke 16:19)

Those that make idols of the flesh and the world will in vain have recourse to them in a day of distress. (Jeremiah 11:12)

Passion often overrules conscience, and forces it, when it is appealed to, to give a false judgment.... (Jonah 4:9)

The lusts of men are the springs of all their wickedness.... (1 Peter 4:2)

God often makes people's sin their punishment. A man needs no greater plague than to be left to the impetuous rage of his own lusts. (Romans 10:19-21)

A man cannot be delivered up to a greater slavery than to be given up to his own lusts. (Romans 1:24)

Ungoverned passion often grows more violent when it meets with some rebuke and check. The troubled sea rages most when it dashes against a rock. (Job 6:8-9)

God sometimes makes sin to be its own punishment, and yet is not the author of sin; and there needs no more to make men miserable than to give them up to their own vile appetites and passions. Let them be put into the hand of their own counsels, and they will ruin themselves and make themselves desolate. (Ezekiel 20:26)

## 9: Carnality and Idolatry

What is asked in passion is often given in wrath. ... Those wretchedly forget themselves that feast their bodies and starve their souls. (Psalm 106:13-14)

See here the fatal consequences of an inordinate love of life; many a man hugs himself to death, and loses his life by over-loving it. He that so loves his animal life as to indulge his appetite, and make *provision for the flesh, to fulfill the lusts thereof,* shall thereby shorten his days, shall lose the life he is so fond of, and another infinitely better. (John 12:25)

Inordinate desires commonly produce irregular endeavours. (Genesis 16:2)

God often gives in anger what we sinfully and inordinately desire, gives it with a curse, and with it gives us up to our own heart's lusts. Thus he gave Israel quails. (Hosea 13:11)

Those that throw off their communion with God, and have fellowship with the unfruitful works of darkness, know not what they do now, and will have nothing to say for themselves in the day of account shortly. ... How they must expect to smart by and by for this their folly. ... Thus those who indulge their lusts and corruptions, which they should mortify, forfeit the grace of God, and it is justly withdrawn from them. If we will not resist the devil, we cannot expect that God should tread him under our feet. ... Those deceive themselves who expect advantage by friendship with those that are enemies to God. ... Those that approach sin are justly left to themselves to fall into sin and to perish in it. (Judges 2:2-3)

Those that drive the good Spirit away from them do of course become prey to the evil spirit. If God and his grace do not rule us, sin and Satan will have possession of us. (1 Samuel 16:14)

The service of virtue is perfect liberty; the service of lust is perfect slavery. (2 Chronicles 12:7-8)

A great deal of sin comes in at the eyes. At these windows Satan throws in those fiery darts which pierce and poison the heart. The eye affects the heart with guilt as well as grief. Let us therefore, with holy Job, make a covenant with our eyes, not to look on that which we are in danger of lusting after.... (Genesis 3:6)

Those that would keep their hearts pure must guard their eyes, which are both the outlets and inlets of uncleanness. (Job 31:1)

Those have eyes, and hearts too, full of adultery (as it is 2 Pet. 2:14), that catch at every bait that presents itself to them and are as tinder to every spark. We have need to make a covenant with our eyes, and to turn them from beholding vanity, lest the eye infect the heart. (Genesis 38:15)

The adulterer not only wrongs and ruins his own soul, but, as much as he can, another's soul too. (2 Samuel 11:4)

## Part I: Folly (Damnation)

[T]he devil has no way of securing men in his interests but by diverting them with continual amusements of one kind or another from the calm and sober consideration of the *things that belong to their peace*. (Proverbs 5:3-8)

It is possible a godly man may sin against a commandment, but a wicked man would sin away the commandment, would repeal God's laws and enact his own lusts. This is the sinfulness of sin and the malignity of the carnal mind. (Psalm 119:126)

Carnal hearts are apt to conceive false and wicked opinions concerning God, and with them to harden themselves in their evil ways. (Matthew 25:24)

See what an enmity there is against God in the carnal mind, and wonder at the patience of God, that he bears with such indignities done to him. (Jeremiah 36:23-25)

When men turn their backs upon God's institutions, and despise them, it is no marvel if they wander endlessly after their own inventions. Impiety is the beginning of idolatry and all iniquity. (Ezekiel 8:13-16)

[T]hose that forsake the only right way wander endlessly in a thousand by-paths, and lose themselves in the many inventions which they have sought out. They ... *wearied themselves to find the door* (Gen. 19:11) and could not find it at last. The pleasures of sin will soon surfeit, but never satisfy; a man may quickly tire himself in the pursuit of them, but can never repose himself in the enjoyment of them. (Isaiah 57:10)

And what an absurd thing it is for a man to dote so much upon such a transient pleasure as *the laughter of the fool* is, which may fitly be compared to the burning *of thorns under a pot*, which makes a great noise and a great blaze, for a little while, but is gone presently, scatters its ashes, and contributes scarcely any thing to the production of a boiling heat, for that requires a constant fire! (Ecclesiastes 7:6)

Incurable griefs are owing to incurable lusts. (Jeremiah 30:15)

Those who abandon themselves to that sin [the lusts of uncleanness] give proof that they are abandoned of God: it *is a deep pit*, which those *fall* into that are *abhorred of the Lord*. ... It is seldom that they recover themselves, for it *is a deep pit*; it will be hard getting out of it, it so besots the mind and debauches the conscience, by pleasing the flesh. (Proverbs 22:14)

Those that have broken the fences of modesty will never be held by the bonds of piety, and those that have dishonoured themselves by fleshly lusts will not scruple to dishonour God by idolatrous worships, and for this they are justly given up yet further to vile affections. (Numbers 25:1-3)

Sinful inclinations and desires are deceitful lusts: they promise men happiness, but render them more miserable, and if not subdued and mortified be-

## 9: Carnality and Idolatry

tray them into destruction. (Ephesians 4:22-24)

The pleasures of sense are putrid puddle-water; those of faith are pure and pleasant, *clear as crystal*, Rev. 22:1. (Psalm 36:8)

If we should approve ourselves to be Christ's, such as are united to him and interested in him, we must make it our constant care and business to crucify the flesh with its corrupt affections and lusts. (Galatians 5:16-18)

The love of women has *cast down many wounded* (Prov. 7:26), and *many* (says Bishop Hall) *have had their head broken by their own rib*. (1 Kings 11:1)

Filthy lusts must be suppressed, in order to the supporting of holy love. *Walk in love,* and *shun fornication and all uncleanness.* (Ephesians 5:3-4)

Vile corruptions, the more they are gratified the more they are inflamed. (Isaiah 57:4-5)

Those sins that dishonour the body and defile it are very displeasing to God and are evidences of vile affections. (Genesis 38:9-10)

Nature is content with little, grace with less, but lust with nothing. (Matthew 15:34)

Unbridled lusts make men *like natural brute beasts,* such monstrous odious things they are .... Fulness of bread was fuel to the fire of Sodom's lusts. *Sine Cerere et Bacchio friget Venu*—*Luxurious living feeds the flames of lust.* Fasting would help tame the unruly evil that is so *full of deadly poison,* and bring the body into subjection. (Jeremiah 5:8)

Man has this advantage above the beasts, in the structure of his body, that whereas they are made to look downwards, as their spirits must go, he is made erect to look upwards, because upwards his spirit must shortly go and his thoughts should now rise. (Psalm 19:1)

[Homosexuality is] ... that most unnatural and worse than brutish lust which was expressly forbidden by the law of Moses, and called an *abomination,* Lev. 18:22. Those that are guilty of it are ranked in the New Testament among the worst and vilest of sinners (1 Tim. 1:10), and such as *shall not inherit the kingdom of God,* 1 Cor. 6:9. Now, (1.) This was the sin of Sodom, and is thence called *Sodomy*. The Dead Sea ... [is] the standing monument of God's vengeance upon Sodom, for its filthiness.... (Judges 19:22)

By having fellowship with sin, which is abominable, we make ourselves abominable. That man is truly miserable who is in the sight of God abominable; and none are so but those that make themselves so. (Leviticus 11:43)

Those that allow themselves in unnatural uncleanness are marked for the vengeance of eternal fire. ... Hence daring sinners are said to *declare their sin as Sodom,* Isa. 3:9. Those have hard hearts indeed that sin with a high hand, Jer. 6:15. (Genesis 19:4-7)

The strength of men's lusts is an evidence of the weakness of their hearts; they have no acquaintance with themselves, nor government of themselves. (Ezekiel 16:30)

[L]uxury and sensuality, and the indulgence of the appetite in eating and drinking, [is] a sin that most easily besets us. ... We must alarm ourselves into temperance and moderation.... (Proverbs 23:1-3)

The expectation we have of being without bodily appetites in a future life is a very good argument against being under their power in the present life. (1 Corinthians 6:13)

The delights of sense may ruin the soul, even lawful delights, indulged, and too much delighted in. (Luke 8:14)

Those that are ... [covetous] ... *fall into temptation and a snare*, unavoidably; for, when the devil sees which way their lusts carry them, he will soon bait the hook accordingly. ... It is good for us to consider the mischievousness of worldly fleshly lusts ... [F]or they *drown men in destruction and perdition*. (1 Timothy 6:9)

Satan watches all opportunities, and lays hold of all advantages, to propagate vice and profaneness. The prejudice he does to particular persons is when reason and conscience sleep, when they are off their guard; we have therefore need to *be sober, and vigilant*. (Matthew 13:24-25)

[W]ine is oil to the fire of lust, Prov. 23:33. (Hosea 7:5-7)

[T]here is not a greater drudgery in the world than hard drinking. They are overcome not with the wine, but with the love of it. ... To be ruined by it. They are broken by wine. Their constitution is broken by it, and their health ruined. They are broken in the callings and estates, and their souls are in danger of being eternally undone, and all this for the gratification of a base lust. (Isaiah 28:1-2)

It is a sad thing to die like a fool, as those do that in any way shorten their own days, and much more those that make no provision for another world. (2 Samuel 3:33)

The Lord is for the body, and it is not only folly, but sin against God, to prejudice our health for the pleasing of our appetite. (Leviticus 11:1-8)

Drunkenness is a leading wickedness; they who are slaves to that, are never masters of themselves in any thing else. (Matthew 24:49)

It is a very wicked thing, upon any design whatsoever, to make a person drunk. ... God will put a cup of trembling into the hands of those who put into the hands of others the cup of drunkenness. Robbing a man of his reason is worse than robbing him of his money, and drawing him into sin

## 9: Carnality and Idolatry

worse than drawing him into any trouble whatsoever. (2 Samuel 11:10-11)

Let all Christians oblige themselves to be very moderate in the use of wine and strong drink; for, if the love of these once gets the mastery of a man, he becomes a very easy prey to Satan. (Numbers 6:3-4)

Satan and his agents are very busy to corrupt the minds of young people that look heavenward; and many that we thought would have been Nazarites they have overcome by giving them wine to drink, by drawing them into the love of mirth and pleasure, and drinking company. Multitudes of young men that bade fare for eminent professors of religion have *erred through wine*, and been undone for ever. And how do the factors of hell triumph in the debauching of a Nazarite! (Amos 2:12)

Drunkenness is bad in any, but it is especially scandalous and pernicious in ministers, who of all men ought to have the clearest heads and the cleanest hearts. ... [T]hose that live after the flesh can have no experimental acquaintance with the things of the Spirit ... because such teachers pull down with one hand what they build up with the other. (Leviticus 10:9)

See what an odious thing the sin of drunkenness is, what an affront it is to human society; it is rude and ill-mannered enough to sicken the beholders, for the tables where they eat their meat are filthily stained with the marks of this sin, which the sinners declare as Sodom. Their tables are full of vomit, so that the victor, instead of being proud of his crown, ought rather to be ashamed of it. It bodes ill to any people when so sottish a sin as drunkenness has become national. (Isaiah 28:7-8)

The bench of the drunkards is the seat of the scornful. (Psalm 69:12)

The mischief of drunkenness: *Wine is a mocker; strong drink is raging.* ... [I]t mocks him, makes a fool of him, promises him that satisfaction which it can never give him. It smiles upon him at first, but *at the last it bites*. It ... rages in his conscience. ... *When the wine is in, the wit is out*, and then the man, according as his natural temper is, either mocks like a fool, or rages like a madman. Drunkenness, which pretends to be a sociable thing, renders men unfit for society, for it makes them abusive with their tongues, and outrageous in their passions.... (Proverbs 20:1)

Observe here the great evil of the sin of drunkenness. (1.) It discovers men. What infirmities they have, they betray when they are drunk, and what secrets they are entrusted with are then easily got out of them. Drunken porters keep open gates. (2.) It disgraces men, and exposes them to contempt. As it shows them, so it shames them. (Genesis 9:21)

Death comes easily upon men when they are drunk. Besides the chronic diseases which men frequently bring themselves into by hard drinking, and which cut them off in the midst of their days, men in that condition are more easily overcome by an enemy, as Amnon by Absalom, and are liable to more bad accidents, being unable to help themselves…. (1 Kings 16:9-10)

Justly are men stripped of that which they have served their idols with and have made the food and the fuel of their lusts. … What we make for a sin, God will make for a spoil. (Jeremiah 17:3)

We forfeit the good things of this world if we love them as the best things. (Hosea 9:1-3)

We know not what is good for ourselves; and that often proves afflictive, and sometimes fatal, which we are most fond of and have our hearts most set upon. (Jeremiah 42:22)

What we hold closest we commonly lose soonest, and that proves least safe which is most dear. (Micah 6:14)

Whatever men make a god of they will mourn for the loss of; and an inordinate sorrow for the loss of any worldly good is a sign we made an idol of it. (Hosea 10:5)

Any man will rather make shipwreck of his goods than of his life; but many will rather make *shipwreck of faith and a good conscience* than of their goods. (Acts 27:16-18)

Let the idols that have been *delectable* things, be cast away as *detestable* things;

keep at a distance from that which is a temptation, though ever so pleasing. It is necessary that the part which is gangrened, should be taken off for the preservation of the whole. … We must put ourselves to pain, that we may not bring ourselves to ruin; self must be denied, that it may not be destroyed. (Mark 9:47)

Pride makes a god of self, covetousness makes a god of money, sensuality makes a god of the belly; whatever is esteemed or loved, feared or served, delighted or depended on, more than God, that (whatever it is) we do in effect make a god of. (Exodus 20:3)

Whatever we make a god of but the true God only, it will stand us in no stead on the other side death and the grave, nor for the body, much less for the soul. (Jeremiah 8:2)

A good man will soon have enough of this world; not only of living in it, but of receiving from it. A covetous worldling, if he has ever so much, would still have more; but a heavenly Christian, though he has little, has enough. (Philippians 4:18)

It is the maddest thing in the world to make a god of any creature; and those who are proud against the Lord, the true God, are justly given up to strong delusions, to be mad upon idols that cannot profit. But this madness is wickedness, for which sinners will be certainly and severely reckoned with. (Jeremiah 50:33-38)

# 9: Carnality and Idolatry

How mad are idolaters, who forsake the *rock of salvation* to run themselves upon the *rock of perdition!* (Deuteronomy 32:16-18)

Wilful sinners are haters of God. ... Idolaters are so in a special manner, for they are in league with his rivals. (Deuteronomy 7:9-10)

Idolaters change God's glory into shame (Rom. 1:23) and so they do their own; in dishonouring him, they disgrace and disparage themselves, and are enemies to their own interest. Note, whatever those turn to who forsake God, it will never do them any good; it will flatter and please them, but it *cannot profit them*. (Jeremiah 2:11)

[T]hose that forsake the true God wander endlessly after false ones. (Jeremiah 7:18)

Those who think one God too little will not think a hundred sufficient, but will still be for trying more, as finding all insufficient. (Ezekiel 23:20)

The God of Israel is the one only living and true God, and those that have him for their God need not make their application to any other; nay, to set up any other in competition with him is the greatest affront and injury that can be done him. (Jeremiah 10:10)

... *God only is to be served and worshipped;* and therefore whoever set up any creature as the object of religious worship, though it were a saint or an angel, or the virgin Mary herself, they directly thwart Christ's design, and relapse into heathenism. (Luke 4:8)

[Those who worshipped] ... the *sun, moon, and stars* ... paid those respects to them which they should have paid to God only.... [I]t might be observed how little they got by worshipping the creature, for the creatures they worshipped when they were in distress saw it, but regarded it not, nor gave them any relief, but were rather pleased to see those abused in being vilified by whom they had been abused in being deified. (Jeremiah 8:2)

God put a great honour upon man when, in respect of the powers and faculties of his souls, he made him after the image of God; but man does a great dishonour to God, when he makes him, in respect of bodily parts and members, after the image of man. ... [F]or all the *beauty of a body of a man*, when pretended to be put upon him who is an infinite Spirit, is a deformity and diminution to him. (Isaiah 44:9-13)

Idolatry is spiritual whoredom; it is the breach of a marriage-covenant with God; it is the setting of the affections upon that which is a rival with him, and the indulgence of a base lust, which deceives and defiles the soul, and is a great wrong to God in his honour. (Ezekiel 6:8-10)

Idolatry is spiritual adultery, so vile, and base, and perfidious a thing is it, and so hardly are those reclaimed that are addicted to it. (Judges 3:17-19)

## Part I: Folly (Damnation)

The heart is the place which God has chosen to *put his name there*; if sin have the innermost and uppermost place there, we pollute the temple of the Lord, and therefore he resents nothing more than *setting up idols in the heart*, Ezek. 14:4 (Jeremiah 7:30)

Persons of strong passions, as they are apt to be cast down with a trifle that crosses them, so they are apt to be lifted up with a trifle that pleases them. A small toy will serve sometimes to pacify a cross child, as the gourd did Jonah. … Creature-comforts we ought to enjoy and be thankful for, but we need not be exceedingly glad of them; it is God only that must be our *exceeding joy*, Ps. 43:4. (Jonah 4:6)

We cry out that this and the other creature-comfort are taken away, and we know not how to retrieve them, when indeed the removal of our temporal comforts, which we lament, is in order to the resurrection of our spiritual comforts, which we should rejoice in too. (John 20:2)

Those creature-comfort and confidences that we promise ourselves most from may fail us as soon as those that we promise ourselves least from, for they are all what God makes them, not what we fancy them. (Jeremiah 44:30)

The love of worldly wealth is a spiritual whoredom, and therefore covetous people are called *adulterers and adulteresses* (James 4:4), and covetousness is spiritual idolatry. (Isaiah 23:16)

Some *lavish gold out of the bag* to make an idol of it in the house, while others *hoard up gold in the bag* to make an idol of it in the heart; for *covetousness is idolatry*, as dangerous, though not as scandalous, as the other. (Isaiah 46:6-7)

Those that are for getting wealth at any time, and by any ways and means whatsoever, right or wrong, lay themselves open to a great deal of temptation. Those that will be rich (… *by fair means, by foul means; careless of principle, intent only on money) drown themselves in destruction and perdition.* (2 Kings 6:26)

There are many whose wealth is their snare and ruin. The gaining of the world is the losing of their souls; it makes them proud, secure, covetous, oppressive, voluptuous; and that which, if well used, might have been the servant of their piety, being abused, becomes *the stumbling-block of their iniquity.* (Ezekiel 7:19)

There are those on whom success is ill bestowed; they know not how to serve God, or their generation, or even their own true interests, with their prosperity. *Let favour be shown to the wicked, yet he will not learn righteousness.* (1 Kings 20:34)

The gifts of common providence are bestowed on many to whom are denied the gifts of a special grace, without which the gifts of providence often do more hurt than good. (Ecclesiastes 6:2)

Worldly wealth, though it is to many an objection in religion's way, yet, in

## 9: Carnality and Idolatry

some services to be done for Christ, it is an advantage and an opportunity, and it is well for those who have it, if withal they have a heart to use it for God's glory. (Matthew 27:57-60)

Poverty in the way of duty is to be chosen rather than plenty in the way of sin. Better to live upon alms, or die in a prison, with a good conscience, than roll in wealth and pleasure with a prostituted one. (2 Chronicles 11:13-14)

The prosperity of the soul is the best prosperity.... (John 17:11)

There is a proneness in us to take the glory of our outward prosperity to ourselves, and to say, *My might, and the power of my hands, have gotten me this wealth,* Deut. 8:17. This is idolizing ourselves.... (Habakkuk 1:16)

Prosperity is the unhappy occasion of much iniquity; it makes people conceited of themselves, indulgent of the flesh, forgetful of God, in love with the world, and deaf to the reproofs of the word. (Psalm 119:67)

In covetousness the heart walks after the eyes. ... The eyes and the heart are then for covetousness when the aims and affections are wholly set upon the wealth of this world; and, where they are so, the temptation is strong to murder, oppression, and all manner of violence and villainy. (Jeremiah 22:13)

Money is a bait for the blackest temptation; mercenary tongues will sell the truth for it. (Matthew 28:15)

Those that will not be content with their allotments shall not have the comfort of their achievements. (Habakkuk 2:5)

It is not the *lack* of money, but the *love* of money, that is the root of all evil, and particularly of apostasy from Christ; witness Demas, 2 Tim. 4:10. (Matthew 26:14-16)

A heart divided between God and mammon, though it may trim the matter so as to appear plausible, will, in the day of discovery, be *found faulty.* (Hosea 10:2)

It is the folly of men that they know not when they are well off, and often ruin themselves by endeavouring to better themselves.... (Jeremiah 43:4-7)

1. Those that are eager to get abundance of this world, and solicitous to lay up what they have gotten, little consider what may become of it and in how short a time it may all be taken from them. Great abundance, by tempting the robbers, exposes the owners; and those who depend upon it to protect them often find it does but betray them. 2. In times of distress great riches are often great burdens, and do but increase the owner's care or the enemies' strength. (Isaiah 15:7)

See here the uncertainty of worldly possessions, how often they change their owners, and how soon we may be deprived of them, even when we think ourselves most sure of them; *they make themselves wings.* It is our wisdom therefore to secure the good part which cannot be taken away from us. (Numbers 22:25-26)

Outward losses drive good people to their prayers, but bad people to their curses. (Judges 17:2)

There is a burden of care in getting them, fear in keeping them, temptation in using them, guilt in abusing them, sorrow in losing them, and a burden of account, at last, to be given up concerning them. Great possessions do but make men heavy and unwieldy. (Genesis 13:2)

Those wretchedly deceive themselves who think their present prosperity is a lasting security.... (Jeremiah 22:15)

Want is the just punishment of wantonness. Those who could not be content without dainties and varieties are brought, they or theirs, to want necessaries, and the Lord is righteous in thus visiting them. ... Plenty and power are forfeited when they are abused. (1 Samuel 2:31-32)

Their fault is, (1.) That they are inordinate in their desires to enrich themselves, make it their whole care and business to raise an estate, as if they had nothing to mind, nothing to seek, nothing to do in this world, but that. They never know when they have enough, but the more they have, the more they would have .... They cannot enjoy what they have, nor do good with it, but are constantly contriving and studying to make it more. ...They would live so as to let nobody live but themselves. (Isaiah 5:8)

1. That which is ill-got, though it may increase much, will not last long. A man may perhaps raise a great estate, in a little time, by usury and extortion, fraud and oppression of the poor, but it will not continue; he gathers it for himself, but it shall prove to have been gathered for somebody else that he has no kindness for. His estate shall go to decay, and another man's shall be raised out of the ruins of it. 2. Sometimes God in his providence so orders it that that which one got unjustly, another uses charitably.... (Proverbs 28:8)

And see what folly it is to set our hearts upon possessions of lands, be they ever so fruitful, ever so pleasant; if they lie ever so little neglected and uncultivated, or if they be abused by a wasteful careless heir or tenant, or the country be laid waste by war, they will soon become frightful deserts. But Heaven is a paradise not subject to such changes. (Isaiah 7:25)

# -10-

# Flattery, Lies, Deception

A wise man will ... be more afraid of a flatterer that kisses and kills, than of a slanderer that proclaims war.

Matthew Henry
on Proverbs 26:28

There are two sorts of lies equally detestable: —1. A slandering lie, which avowedly hates those it is spoken of .... The mischief of this is open and obvious; it afflicts, it hates, and owns it, and every body sees it. 2. A flattering lie, which secretly works the ruin of those it is spoken to. In the former the mischief is plain, and men guard against it as well as they can, but in this it is little suspected, and men betray themselves by being credulous of their own praises and the compliments that are passed upon them. A wise man will therefore be more afraid of a flatterer that kisses and kills, than of a slanderer that proclaims war. (Proverbs 26:28)

We may sometimes be in as much or more danger from false and pretended friends as from open and avowed enemies. (2 Thessalonians 3:2)

Thus the most malicious slanderers of *good men* are commonly the most sordid flatterers of *great men*. (Matthew 27:63-64)

[A] double tongue comes from a double heart; flatterers and slanderers are double-tongued. (1 Timothy 3:8)

Compliments and flatteries become not Christians; but the sincere expressions of sacred affection, and the services or labours of love, do. (1 John 3:18)

Whoever are our friends, if, notwithstanding, they are God's enemies, we dare not speak peace to them. (Jeremiah 50:1-2)

It is a pitiable thing, and that which every good man greatly laments, to see people flattered into their own ruin, and promising themselves peace when war is at the door.... (Jeremiah 4:10)

Those deserve to be bantered that love to be flattered; and it is just with God to give up those to their own counsels that give up themselves to their own lusts. Eccl. 11:9. (1 Kings 22:15)

In civil conversation hypocrisy is counterfeit friendship, which is much practised by those who give high compliments, which they do not believe, make promises which they never intend to perform, or pretend friendship when mischief lies in their hearts. (1 Peter 2:1-3)

Fair words, when they are not attended with good intentions, are despicable, but when they are intended as a cloak and cover for wicked intentions they are abominable. (Jeremiah 9:6)

See the danger of enticing words; how many are ruined by the flattery of those who lie in wait to deceive, and by the false disguises and fair appearances of evil principles and wicked practices. (Colossians 2:4)

We have reason to be afraid of those that speak well of us when we do ill.... (Isaiah 9:16)

Flatterers ... are commonly talebearers. If a man fawn upon you, compliment and commend you, suspect him to have some design upon you,

## 10: Flattery, Lies, Deception

and stand upon your guard; he would pick that out of you which will serve him to make a story of to somebody else to your prejudice; therefore *meddle not with him that flatters with his lips.* (Proverbs 20:19)

Those that are in high places will have many hanging upon them as favourites whom they are proud of and trust to; but they are heavy burdens upon them, and perhaps with their weight break the nail, and both fall together, and by deceiving ruin one another — the common fate of great men and their flatterers, who expect more from each other than either performs. (Isaiah 22:19)

When men indulge a proud vainglorious humour, and please themselves with that which feeds it, they know not what vexations they are preparing for themselves; their flatterers may prove their tormentors, and are but *spreading a net for their feet.* (Daniel 6:14)

Thus great men are made an easy prey to flatterers if they lend an ear to them, and encourage them. (Acts 12:22)

Flatterers may please those for a time who, upon second thoughts, will detest and despise them. If ever they come to be convinced of the evil of those sinful courses they were flattered in, and to be ashamed of the pride and vanity which were humoured and gratified by those flatteries, they will hate the fawning flatterers as having had an ill design upon them.... (Proverbs 28:23)

God knows more evil of us than we do of ourselves, which is a good reason why we should not flatter ourselves, but always stand in awe of the judgment of God. (Jeremiah 17:10)

Of all flattery, self-flattery is the worst, and self-applause is seldom any better than self-flattery and self-deceit. At the best, self-commendation is no praise, and it is oftentimes as foolish and vain as it is proud; therefore, instead of praising or commending ourselves, we should strive to approve ourselves to God, and his approbation will be our best commendation. (2 Corinthians 10:18)

David concluded concerning those who lived at large that they lived without God in the world. 2. From their conceit of themselves and a cheat they wilfully put upon their own souls (*v.* 2): *He flattereth himself in his own eyes;* that is, while he goes on in sin, he thinks he does wisely and well for himself, and either does not see or will not own the evil and dangers of his wicked practices; he calls evil good and good evil; his licentiousness he pretends to be but his just liberty, his fraud passes for his prudence and policy, and his persecuting the people of God, he suggests to himself, is a piece of necessary justice. (Psalm 36:1-4)

[I]f it be lawful to kill for prevention, who then can be safe, since malice always suspects the worst? (Jeremiah 40:15)

Part I: Folly (Damnation)

[T]hose who do not as they teach, pull down with one hand what they build up with the other, and give themselves the lie, and tempt men to think that all religion is a delusion.... (Matthew 5:17-20)

"If you destroy the foundations, if you take good people off from their hope in God, if you can persuade them that their religion is a cheat and a jest and can banter them out of that, you ruin them, and break their hearts indeed, and make them of all men the most miserable." (Psalm 11:1-2)

They who can *swallow* a profane oath, will not *strain at a* lie. (Matthew 5:37)

It is bad to tell a lie, but it is much worse to swear to it. (Leviticus 19:12)

Every man hates to have a lie told him; but we should more hate telling a lie because by the former we only receive an affront from men, by the latter we give an affront to God. ... The more we see of the amiable beauty of truth the more we shall see of the detestable deformity of a lie. (Psalm 119:163)

Lying is wickedness, and we should not only refrain from it, but it should be an abomination to us, and as far as what we say as from what God says to us. His word to us is *yea, and amen*; never then let ours be *yea and nay*. (Proverbs 8:7)

*Let lying lips be put to silence, that speak grievous things proudly and contemptuously against the righteous.* (Psalm 31:18)

Those who, by giving invidious characters and telling ill-natured stories of their neighbours, sow discord among brethren, will be accountable for all the mischief that follows upon it; as he that kindles fire will be accountable for all the hurt it does. (Ezekiel 22:9)

We find (Rev. 22:15), that hell is the portion of those that *make a lie*, and of those that *love* it when it is made. *The deceived and the deceiver* are obnoxious to the judgment of God, Job 12:16. (Matthew 15:14)

A course of lying, of deceit and dissimulation, is that which every good man dreads and which we are all concerned to beg of God by his grace to keep us from. (Psalm 119:28-29)

Those that make lies their refuge build upon the sand, and the building will fall when the storm comes, and bury the builder in the ruins of it. Those that make any thing their hiding place but Christ shall find that the waters will overflow it, as every shelter but the ark was over-topped and overthrown by the waters of the deluge. (Isaiah 28:16)

*A lying tongue is but for a moment*, and truth will be the daughter of time. (Joshua 9:16)

Things revealed belong to us, and we ought diligently to enquire into them. (Exodus 3:3)

"... Take all occasions to discourse with those about thee of divine things; not of unrevealed mysteries, or mat-

## 10: Flattery, Lies, Deception

ters of doubtful disputation, but of the plain truths and laws of God, and the things that belong to our peace." (Deuteronomy 6:7)

The being of God may be apprehended, but cannot be comprehended. We cannot by searching find him out, Job. 11:7-9. Finite understandings cannot perfectly know an infinite being. ... [A]nd these things revealed belong to us and to our children, while secret things are not to be pried into, Deut. 29:29. (Romans 1:19-20)

When we cannot, by searching, find the bottom, we must sit down at the brink, and adore the depth, Rom. 11:33. (Psalm 145:3)

*It is not for us to know,* or covet to know, *the times and the seasons,* any further than God has thought fit to make them known, and so far we may and must take notice of them. ... God makes his mind known by degrees.... (Isaiah 16:14)

(2.) We can know nothing of future events but what God is pleased to discover to us; they are within the veil, till God opens the door. But, (3.) So far as God reveals his designs to us we may and ought to receive them, and not pretend to be wise above what is revealed. (Revelation 4:1)

There are many things which our vain curiosity desires to know which there is no necessity at all of our knowing, nor would our knowledge of them do us good. (1 Thessalonians 5:1-2)

In divine things we must not covet to know more than God would have us know; and he has allowed us as much as is good for us. A desire for forbidden knowledge was the ruin of our first parents. (Exodus 20:21)

Those that are most inquisitive concerning the secret things which belong not to them are most easily imposed upon by seducers, 2 Thess. 2:3. (Matthew 24:4)

[L]et those give heed to fortune-tellers, or go to wizards for the discovery of things secret, that use spells for the cure of diseases, are in any league or acquaintance with familiar spirits, or form a confederacy with those that are—let them know that they can have no fellowship with God while thus they have fellowship with devils. It is amazing to think that there should be any pretenders of this kind in such a land and day of light as we live in. (Deuteronomy 18:9-12)

Those are not taught nor sent of the holy God, whose lives evidence that they are led by the unclean spirit. (Matthew 7:15-16)

Errors in the mind tend greatly to weaken our faith, and cause us trouble; and such as are weak in faith and of troubled minds are oftentimes apt to be deceived, and fall a prey to seducers. (2 Thessalonians 2:2-3a)

Because men receive not the love of the truth, but conceive a hatred of it, and by the multitude of their iniquities bid defiance to it, therefore God shall *send them strong delusions, to believe a lie,* so strong that they shall not be undeceived till the day of visitation and recompense comes, which will convince them of the folly and madness of those that seduced them and of their own folly and madness in suffering themselves to be seduced by them. (Hosea 9:7)

That Jesus of Nazareth was the Son of God had been attested by heaven, and earth, and hell. It should seem that some, in the tremendous judgment of God, are given up to strong delusions. (1 John 2:22)

Thus those who easily submit to strong delusions hate to receive the truth in the love of it. (Acts 14:19)

To have a high opinion of our wisdom is but to flatter ourselves, and self-flattery is the very next step to self-deceit. The way to true wisdom is to sink our opinion of our own to a due level, and be willing to be taught of God. He must become a fool who would be truly and thoroughly wise. (1 Corinthians 3:18)

They are *wise in their own eyes;* they think themselves able to disprove and baffle the reproofs and convictions of God's word, and to evade and elude both the searches and the reaches of his judgments; they think they can outwit Infinite Wisdom and countermine Providence itself. ... God resists the proud, those particularly who are conceited of their own wisdom and lean to their own understanding; such must become fools, that they may be truly wise, or else, at their end they shall appear to be fools before all the world. (Isaiah 5:21)

We are very apt to take our measures rather from our own reason than from divine revelation, and thereby often miss our way.... (Genesis 27:1-5)

The wisdom of man is perfect folly, when it pretends to give measures to the divine counsels. (Mark 8:32-33)

There is a great deal of deceitfulness in sin; it appears fair, but is filthy; it appears pleasant, but is pernicious; it promises much, but performs nothing. (Hebrews 7:13)

Such is the deceitfulness of sin, that the very thing by which sinners hope to expiate and atone for their sins will come against them, and make their sins more exceedingly sinful. (Matthew 23:13-14)

When Satan is doing the greatest mischief, he studies most to conceal himself; for his design is in danger of being spoiled if he be seen in it; and therefore, when he comes to sow tares, he *transforms himself into an angel of light,* 2 Cor. 11:13, 14. (Matthew 13:25)

Satan acts most mischievously, when he appears as an angel of light: the colour of the greatest good is often the cover of the greatest evil. (Matthew 24:9-11)

# 10: Flattery, Lies, Deception

Many oppose Christ's holy religion, upon a mistake of the nature of it; they dress it up in false colours, and then fight against it. (Matthew 27:11)

Satan is a subtle enemy, and uses many stratagems to deceive us; and we should not be *ignorant of his devices:* he is also a watchful adversary, ready to take all advantages against us, and we should be very cautious lest we give him any occasion to do so. (2 Corinthians 2:11)

The envious one, who sows tares in God's field, knows how to take an opportunity to do it when the *servants sleep* or are absent, Matt. 13:25. The golden calf was made when Moses was in the mount. (Nehemiah 13:6-7)

Satan himself, though he is the great deceiver, could not deceive us if we did not deceive ourselves; and thus sinners are their own destroyers by being their own deceivers.... (Jeremiah 37:9)

The devil does us more mischief by tempting us to sin against our God than he does by accusing us before our God. He destroys none but by their own hands. (1 Chronicles 21:1)

There is a kind of *peace* in the palace of an unconverted soul, while the devil, as a *strong man armed,* keeps it. The sinner has a good opinion of himself, is very secure and merry, has no doubt concerning the goodness of his state nor any dread of the judgment to come; he flatters himself in his own eyes, and cries peace to himself. (Luke 11:21)

See the nature of sin—it is a *backsliding,* it is going back from the right way, not only into a by-path, but into a contrary path, back from the way that leads to life to that which leads to utter destruction. ... The same subtlety of the tempter that brings men to sin holds them fast in it, and they contribute to their own captivity.... The excuses they make for their sins are deceits.... (Jeremiah 8:4-5)

Those who deceive themselves with groundless hopes of mercy will justly be upbraided with their folly when the event has undeceived them. (Jeremiah 38:19)

It should be more our care to be good really, than to seem good outwardly. (Matthew 12:33)

Many deceive themselves into a good opinion of their state by a partial reformation. They think they are as good as they should be, because, in some one particular instance, they are not so bad as they have been, as if the correcting of one fault would atone for their persisting in all the rest. (Judges 17:13)

*What we wish we readily believe.* Thus those that are to be destroyed are first deceived (Rev. 20:8), and none are so effectually deceived as those that deceive themselves. (2 Kings 3:23)

[W]hat will it avail us to say *We are not so bad as others,* when yet we are not really good ourselves? (Jeremiah 3:11)

When we are lamenting the wickedness of the wicked, it may be, if we duly reflect upon ourselves and give our own hearts leave to deal faithfully with us, we may find something of the same nature, though in a lower degree, that we also have been guilty of. (Ezra 9:5-7)

The way to be truly great is to be truly good and to pray much. (1 Chronicles 4:9-10)

The guilt of others will not acquit us, nor will it avail in the great day to say that others were worse than we, for we are not to be judged by comparison, but we must *bear our own burden*. ... By this it appears that all sins are not equal, but some more heinous than others; some comparatively as gnats, others as camels; some as motes in the eyes, others as beams; some as pence, others as pounds.... (John 19:7-11)

It is possible we may be a great deal better than some others, and yet not be so good as we should be; may go beyond our neighbours, and yet come short of heaven. (Matthew 13:5-8)

It argues a great degree of self-conceit and self-confidence, to think ourselves either safe from the temptations, or free from the corruptions, that are common to men. We should rather say, If it be possible that others may be offended, there is a danger that I may be so. But it is common for those that think too well of themselves, easily to admit suspicions of others. (Matthew 26:33)

Those that do not build upon Christ as their foundation, but rest in a righteousness of their own, will prove in the end thus to have deceived themselves; they can never be easy, safe, nor warm; the bed is too short, the covering is too narrow; like our first parent's fig-leaves, the shame of their nakedness will still appear. (Isaiah 28:20)

Those that act by deceit, with a colour of law and justice, do more mischief perhaps than those wicked men ... that carry all before them by open force and violence.... (Jeremiah 5:26)

How can we think that those will be true to their neighbour that are false to their God? (Jeremiah 3:2)

Those put a cheat upon themselves that think to gain their point by putting cheats upon those they deal with. Those that pursue their designs by trick and fraud, by mean and paltry shifts, may perhaps compass them, but cannot expect comfort in them. Honesty is the best policy. But such refuges as these are those driven to that depart from God, and throw themselves out of his protection. (Isaiah 28:15)

*In all godliness and honesty*. Here we have our duty as Christians summed up in two words: godliness, that is, the right worshipping of God; and honesty, that is, a good conduct towards all men. These two must go together; we are not truly honest if we are not godly, and do not render to God his due; and we are not truly godly if we are not honest, for God hates robbery for burnt-offering. (1 Timothy 2:2)

Those are in a great mistake who think they deal wisely for themselves when they deal deceitfully or unmercifully with their brethren. (Acts 7:19)

A good man cannot, in the reflection, please himself with that which he knows God is displeased with, cannot make use of that, nor take comfort in that, which is obtained by sin. (1 Chronicles 27:23-24)

Industry and honesty are the surest and safest way both of rising and thriving. (Genesis 39:4)

The way to have our days lengthened, and to prosper, is to be just and fair in all our dealings. *Honesty is the best policy.* (Deuteronomy 25:14)

Honesty obliges us to make restitution, not only of that which comes to us by our own fault, but of that which comes to us by the mistakes of others. Though we get it by oversight, if we keep it when the oversight is discovered, it is kept by deceit. (Genesis 43:11-12)

God has his eye upon merchants and traders, when they are weighing their goods and paying their money, whether they do honestly or deceitfully. He observes what balances they have in their hand, and how they hold them; and, though those they deal with may not be aware of that sleight of hand with which they make them balances of deceit, God sees it, and knows it. (Hosea 12:7)

How hateful, particularly, all the arts of deceit are to God, Solomon several times observes, Prov. 11:1, 20:10, 23; and the apostle tells us *that the Lord is the avenger of all such* as overreach and *defraud in any matter,* 1 Thess. 4:6. (Deuteronomy 25:13-14)

[O]ne that judged by the sight of the eye ... might therefore be easily deceived in matters of spiritual concern. Those who make external pomp and splendour a mark of the true church go by the same rule. (Isaiah 10:10-11)

There is a great deal of difference between the state of the children of men on earth and that of the children of God in heaven, a vast unlikeness between *this world* and *that world;* and we wrong ourselves, and wrong the truth of Christ, when we form notions of that world of spirits by our present enjoyments in this world of sense. (Luke 20:35-37)

We deceive ourselves if we think to deceive God by a feigned return to him. I know no religion without sincerity. (Jeremiah 3:7)

The great thing Satan aims at, in tempting good people, is to overthrow their relation to God as a Father, and so to cut off their dependence on him, their duty to him, and their communion with him. ... The devil carries on his designs very much by possessing people with hard thoughts of God, as if he

## Part I: Folly (Damnation)

were unkind, or unfaithful, and had forsaken or forgotten those who had ventured their all with him. (Matthew 4:3-6)

It is natural to proud men to *pre*scribe to God, and then to make that an excuse for not *sub*scribing to him; but a man's *off*ence will never be his *def*ence. (Matthew 12:38)

Unhumbled hearts are ready to charge God with injustice in their afflictions, and pretend they have to seek for the cause of them when it is clearly written in the forehead of them. (Jeremiah 5:19)

[B]ut see what is the effect of sin: by depriving men of their confidence towards God, it deprives them of their courage towards men. (Jeremiah 4:8-9)

Many who lie under guilt and wrath are yet very jocund and merry, and live jovially; but, whether in their laughter their hearts be sad or no, it is certain that the *end of their mirth* will be *heaviness;* for God *will cause all their mirth to cease.* It is as Mr. Burroughs observes here, Sin and mirth can never hold long together; but *if men will not take away sin from their mirth, God will take away mirth from their sin.* (Hosea 2:11)

Before we allow ourselves to be merry, we ought to consider whether we should be merry or no. Should we make mirth, we who are sentenced to the sword, who lie under the wrath and curse of God? (Ezekiel 21:10)

Prosperity in sin is a great bar to conversion from sin. Those that live at ease in their sinful projects, are tempted to think God favours them, and therefore they have nothing to repent of. (Isaiah 57:9-10)

Many justify themselves in their impiety by their prosperity. (Judges 18:27)

*When ... all the workers of iniquity do flourish* in pomp, and power, and all the instances of outward prosperity, are easy and many, and succeed in their enterprises, one would think that all this was a certain evidence of God's favour and an earnest of something as good or better in reserve: but it is quite otherwise; it is *that they shall be destroyed for ever.* The very *prosperity of fools shall slay them,* Prov. 1:32. The sheep that are designed for the slaughter are put into the fattest pasture. (Psalm 92:7)

Many a dangerous temptation comes to us in gay fine colours that are but skin-deep, and seems to come from above; for Satan can seem an angel of light. (Genesis 3:1)

Foul temptations may have very fair pretenses, and be coloured with that which is very plausible. (Genesis 16:3)

When the devil is drawing away disciples and servants after him, he conceals the worst of it, tells them only of the pleasure, but nothing of the peril, of his service; *Ye shall not surely die....* (Mark 8:34-38)

Those that feed themselves with a self-

## 10: Flattery, Lies, Deception

conceit in the day of their prosperity prepare matter for a self-reproach in the day of their calamity. (Ezekiel 21:28-29)

[The] ... proud man is ripened for ruin by the sunshine of prosperity. (Isaiah 37:9-12)

Carnal security is a sin that most easily besets men in the day of their pomp, power, and prosperity, and does, as much as any thing, both ripen men for ruin and aggravate it when it comes. (Obadiah 1:3)

It is the policy of Satan, when by his temptations he has drawn men from God and their duty, to rock them asleep in carnal security, that they may not be sensible of their misery and danger. It concerns us all to *watch therefore.* (Jonah 1:5)

The devil leads men blindfold to hell, but God enlightens men's eyes, sets things before them in a true light, and so leads them to heaven. (Psalm 25:8-9)

God's judgments come with the greatest terror upon those that have been most secure. (Jeremiah 4:13)

We deceive ourselves if we promise ourselves rest any where in this world. Those that are uneasy in one place will be so in another; and, when God's judgments pursue sinners, they will overtake them. (Isaiah 23:12)

# -11-

# Judgment and Retribution

All the children of men are either righteous or wicked, either such as serve God or such as serve him not. This is that division of the children of men which will last forever, and by which their eternal state will be determined; all are either going to heaven or to hell.

Matthew Henry
on Malachi 4:18

All the children of men are either righteous or wicked, either such as serve God or such as serve him not. This is that division of the children of men which will last forever, and by which their eternal state will be determined; all are either going to heaven or to hell. (Malachi 4:18)

There is a judgment to come, in which every man's present character and work, though ever so artfully concealed and disguised, shall be truly and perfectly discovered, and appear in their own colours, and accordingly every man's future state will be, by an irreversible sentence, determined for eternity. (Psalm 1:5)

[O]ur life is a vain life, a dark life, a transient life, and a life that will have its periods either in perfect light or perfect darkness. (1 Chronicles 29:15)

[B]oth dwarfs and giants are all alike to God's judgments; none so great as to over-top them, none so small as to be over-looked by them. (1 Samuel 5:9)

[I]t is *matter of fact* that is true every day, that poor godly people, whom men neglect and trample upon, die away out of their miseries, and go to heavenly bliss and joy, which is made the more pleasant to them by their preceding sorrows; and that rich epicures, who live in luxury, and are unmerciful to the poor, die, and go into a state of insupportable torment, which is the more grievous and terrible to them because of the sensual lives they lived: and that there is no gaining any relief from their torments. (Luke 16:19-23)

1. There is a day of visitation coming, a day of enquiry and discovery, a searching day, which will bring to light, to a true light, every man, and every man's work. 2. The day of visitation will be a day of desolation to all wicked people, when all their comforts and hopes will be lost and gone, and buried in ruin, and themselves left desolate. 3. Impenitent sinners will be utterly at a loss, and will not know what to do in the day of visitation and desolation. ...[T]hey have no refuge. (Isaiah 10:3)

He [Jesus Christ] shall come [again], to the terror of those who have pierced him and have not repented and of all who have wounded and crucified him afresh by their apostasy from him, and to the astonishment of the pagan world. For he comes to take vengeance on those who know not God, as well as on those that obey not the gospel of Christ. (Revelation 1:7)

Christ's sitting at the right hand of God speaks as much terror to his enemies as happiness to his people. (Psalm 110:1)

When sin is in the house, there is reason to fear ruin at the door. (Genesis 35:30)

There is no escaping God's avenging eye, no going out of the reach of his hand; rocks and mountains will be no better shelter at last than fig leaves were at first. (Psalm 21:8)

## 11: Judgment and Retribution

God's curse upon a man will pursue him wherever he goes, and lie heavily upon him whatever he does. There is no avoiding divine judgments.... (Exodus 8:3-4)

It is well that there is a day of judgment, and a future state, before us, in which it shall be eternally well with the righteous, and with them only, and ill with all the wicked, and them only; so the present seeming disorders of Providence shall be set to rights, and there will remain no matter of complaint whatsoever. (Habakkuk 1 Summary)

As sinners never think they have sin enough till it brings them to hell, so saints never think they have grace enough till it brings them to heaven. (Proverbs 14:14)

We ought to lament the punishments of sinners as well as the sufferings of saints in this world.... (Micah 1:8-9)

The sins of sinners are the sorrows of saints. We must mourn for that which we cannot mend. (Psalm 119:136)

(1.) That God has *no pleasure in the death* and ruin of sinners, for he tries all ways and methods with them to prevent their destruction and qualify them for salvation. Both his ordinances and his providences have a tendency this way, to part between them and their sins; and yet, with many it is all lost labour. ...Therefore, (2.) God will be justified in the death of sinners and all the blame will lie upon themselves. He did not reject them till he had used all proper means to reform them.... (Jeremiah 6:30)

This will justify God in the destruction of sinners, and will aggravate their ruin; there is not a damned sinner in hell, but, if he had done well, as he might have done, had been a glorious saint in heaven. (Genesis 4:7)

God will glorify himself in the silencing of many whom he will not glorify himself in the salvation of. Many are convinced, that are not converted, by the word. (Matthew 23:46)

Those are wicked indeed that will not be wrought upon by the favourable methods God takes to subdue and reform them; and it is necessary that God should deal with them in a severe way by his judgments, which shall prevail to humble those that would not otherwise be humbled. (Isaiah 26:8-9)

[I]f the removal of an affliction harden us, and so we lose the benefit of it, we may conclude it goes away with a purpose to return or to make room for a worse. ...Those that are not made better by God's word and providences are commonly made worse by them. (Exodus 8:16-17)

God tries what less judgments will do with a people before he brings greater; but if a light affliction do not do its work with us, to humble and reform us, we must expect to be afflicted more grievously; for when God judges he will overcome. (Isaiah 9:1)

Those that will not know God as their lawgiver shall be made to know him as their judge. (Jeremiah 9:7-11)

Ignorance of the extent and spiritual nature of the divine law, makes people think themselves in a better condition than they really are. (Mark 10:20)

Those that will not consider in time will be made to consider when it is too late. (Jeremiah 23:20)

Those that will not bow before him cannot stand before him. (Isaiah 40:23-24)

Those that will not bow to his golden sceptre will certainly be broken by his iron rod. Thus will God render to every man according to his deeds. (Romans 2:6-9)

We must submit to God's justice with a hope in his mercy. (Judges 10:15)

Even when salvation from God is a comfort to us, yet destruction from God should be a terror to us. (Job 31:23)

[T]hose that will not be monuments of mercy shall be monuments of justice. (Jeremiah 18:6)

The higher any are lifted up in means and mercies, the heavier will their doom be if they abuse them. (Isaiah 22:1-4)

Wild beasts, lions, bears, and wolves, ... tear in pieces all that come their way ... as we read of two bears that in an instant killed forty-two children, 2 Kings 2:24. ... Man was made to have dominion over the creatures, and, though many of them are stronger than he, yet none of them could have hurt him, nay, all of them would have served him, if he had not first shaken off God's dominion, and so lost his own; and now the creatures are in rebellion against him that is in rebellion against his Maker, and, when the Lord of those hosts pleases, they are the executioners of his wrath and the ministers of his justice. (Leviticus 26:22)

When the day of God's abused mercy and patience is over the sword of his justice gives no quarter, spares none. Men have by sin lost the honour of the human nature and made themselves like the beasts that perish; they are therefore justly denied the compassion and respect that are owing to the human nature and killed as beasts, and no more is made of slaying an army of men than of butchering a flock of lambs or goats and feeding on the fat of the kidneys of rams. (Isaiah 34:6)

God has a sword that can reach the soul and affect the mind, and bring men under spiritual plagues. (Jeremiah 50:36)

(1.) Discontent is a sin that is its own punishment and makes men torment themselves; it makes the spirit sap, the body sick, and all the enjoyments sour; it is the heaviness of the heart and the rottenness of the bones. (2.) It is a sin that is its own parent. It arises not from the condition, but from the mind. ...

## 11: Judgment and Retribution

Inordinate desires expose men to continual vexations, and those that are disposed to fret, be they ever so happy, will always find something or other to fret at. (1 Kings 21:4)

Envy is a sin that commonly carries with it both its own discovery, in the paleness of the looks, and its own punishment, in the rottenness of the bones. (Genesis 4:5)

Where envy reigns pity is banished, and humanity itself is forgotten, Prov. 27:4. (Genesis 37:23-24)

*Who can stand before envy? ...* 2. Of the corruption of nature; for that is a bad principle indeed which makes men *grieve at the good of others,* as if it must needs be ill with me because it is well with my neighbour. (Genesis 26:14)

*Fret not thyself, neither be thou envious.* Fretfulness and envy are sins that are their own punishments; they are the uneasiness of the spirit, and the rottenness of the bones. (Psalm 37:1-2)

There is a day coming when he [the Lord] will be afar off, and will not be found, when the day of his patience is over, and his Spirit will strive no more. There may come such a time in this life, when the heart is incurably hardened; it is certain that at death and judgment the door will be *shut....* Mercy is offered, but then judgment without mercy will take place. (Isaiah 55:6)

[A]nd when God goes all good goes, but he goes from none till they first drive him from them. ... God's departures from a people are gradual, but gracious souls are soon aware of the first step he takes toward a remove. (Ezekiel 9:3)

God's patience, which has long been sinned against, will at length be sinned away; and the time will come when those that have been spared often shall be no longer spared. *My spirit shall not always strive.* After frequent reprieves, yet a day of execution will come. (Amos 7:8-9)

The wicked, even murderers, sometimes *live, become old, yea, are mighty in power;* for the day of vengeance is to come in the other world, *the great day of wrath;* and though some are made examples of in this world, to prove that there is a God and a providence, yet many are left unpunished, to prove that there is a judgment to come. (Acts 28:4)

It is worthwhile to enquire into the reasons of the outward prosperity of wicked people. It is not because God has forsaken the earth, because he does not see, or does not hate, or cannot punish their wickedness; but it is because the measure of their iniquities is not full. This is the day of God's patience, and, in some way or other, he makes use of them and their prosperity to serve his own counsels, while it ripens them for ruin; but the chief reason is because he will make it to appear there is another world which is the world of retribution, and not this. (Job 21:7)

When wickedness has become general and universal ruin is not far off; while there is a remnant of praying people in a nation, to empty the measure as it fills, judgments may be kept off a great while; but when all hands are at work to pull down the fences by sin, and none stand in the gap to make up the breach, what can be expected but an inundation of wrath? (Genesis 6:11-12)

Some are spared and reprieved in wrath, that they may be reserved for some greater judgment when they have filled up the measure of their iniquities;… (Isaiah 38:17-18)

When the measure of any man's iniquity is full, and he has sinned to the uttermost, then comes wrath, and that to the uttermost. (1 Thessalonians 2:16)

Some sinners God makes quick work with, while others he bears long with; for which difference, doubtless, there are good reasons; but he is not accountable to us for them. (Acts 5:10)

Preservations from present judgments, if a good use be not made of them, are but reservations for greater judgments. (Hosea 6:11)

Sinners are commonly hardened in their security by the intermissions of judgments and the slow proceedings of them; and those who will not be awakened by the word of God may justly be lulled to sleep by the providence of God. (Jeremiah 37:7-10)

Those that are under the curse of God may yet perhaps thrive and prosper greatly in this world; for we cannot know love or hatred, the blessing or the curse, by what is before us, but by what is within us, Eccl. 9:1. (Genesis 10:15-20)

God often spares wicked people for the sake of the godly; as Zoar for Lot's sake, and as Sodom might have been, if there had been ten righteous persons in it. The good people are hated and persecuted in the world as if they were not worthy to live in it, yet really it is for their sakes that the world stands. (Acts 27:24)

Though God has long seemed to connive at sinners, from which they have inferred that the Lord does not see, does not regard, yet, when the day of his wrath comes, he will look towards them. (Genesis 18:16)

It has been sometimes said that the divine vengeance strikes with iron hands, yet it comes with leaden feet.... (Psalm 74:3)

Where Satan cannot persuade men to look upon the judgment to come as a thing doubtful and uncertain, yet he gains his point by persuading them to look upon it as a thing at a distance, so that it loses its force: if it be sure, yet *it is not near*; whereas, in truth, *the Judge stands before the door*. (Ezekiel 11:3)

Those that make the world their comfort, and their own righteousness their confidence, will certainly meet with a fatal disappointment, which will be

## 11: Judgment and Retribution

bitterness in the end. ... A wicked man's way may be pleasant, but his end and endless abode will be utter darkness. (Isaiah 50:11)

There are many who are under the curse of God and yet bless themselves; but it will soon be found that in blessing themselves they do but deceive themselves. (Deuteronomy 29:19)

Loathsome diseases are often sent as the just punishment of pride, and are sometimes the immediate effect of lewdness, the flesh and the body being consumed by it. (Isaiah 3:17)

Divine Providence has many ways of entailing disgrace upon the wicked practices even of great men, who, though they seek to cover their shame, are *put to a perpetual reproach*. (Matthew 27:8)

Those that make themselves vile by scandalous sins God will make vile by shameful punishments. (Nahum 2:14)

Great laughters commonly end in a sigh. Those that make the world their chief joy cannot rejoice ever more. When God sends his judgments into the earth he designs thereby to make those serious that were wholly addicted to their pleasures. *Let your laughter be turned into mourning*. When the earth is emptied the *noise of those that rejoice in it* ends. Carnal joy is a noisy thing; but the noise of it will soon be at an end, and the end of it is heaviness. (Isaiah 24:3-4)

It is just with God to make those know what hardships mean that indulge themselves too much in their own ease and pleasure. (Hosea 10:9-11)

God not only sees sin in his people, but is much displeased with it; and even those that are delivered from the wrath to come may yet lie under the tokens of God's wrath in this world, and may be denied some particular favour which their hearts are much set upon. God is a gracious, tender, loving Father; but he is angry with his children when they do amiss, and denies them many a thing that they desire and are ready to cry for. (Deuteronomy 3:26)

When sinners turn their back upon God, desert his service, and so cast a reproach upon it, he does, in a way of righteous judgment, not only withdraw his restraining grace and give them up to their own heart's lusts, but order them by his providence into such circumstances as occasion their sin and hasten their ruin. (Ezekiel 3:19-20)

To be hardened in sin and enmity against God by his righteous judgments is a certain token of utter destruction. (Revelation 16:19-21)

Those whom God has marked for destruction, he perplexes and embarrasses in their counsels, and obstructs and retards all the methods they make for their own safety. (Jeremiah 6:21)

The threatenings here will have their full accomplishment in the judgment of the great day and the eternal misery of the impenitent, of which yet there are some earnests in present judgments. [1.] Now sinners are in prosperity and secure; they live at ease, and set sorrow at defiance. But, *First,* Their *calamity will come* (*v.* 26); sickness will come, and those diseases which they shall apprehend to be the very arrests and harbingers of death; other troubles will come, in mind, in estate, which will convince them of their folly in setting God at a distance. *Secondly,* Their calamity will put them into a great fright. Fear seizes them, and they apprehend that bad will be worse. When public judgments are abroad, the *sinners in Zion are afraid, fearfulness surprises the hypocrites.* Death is the *king of terrors* to them...; this fear will be their continual torment. *Thirdly,* ... Their *fear shall come* (the thing they were afraid of shall befal them); it shall *come as desolation,* as a mighty deluge bearing down all before it; it shall be their *destruction,* their total and final destruction; and it shall come *as a whirlwind,* which suddenly and forcibly drives away all the chaff. ... *Fourthly,* Their fright will then be turned into despair. (Proverbs 1:26-27)

Sooner or later men shall be made sensible that their sin is the cause of all their miseries. (Jeremiah 40:2-3)

*The wages of sin is death.* ... Death is as due to a sinner when he hath sinned as wages are to a servant when he hath done his work. (Romans 6:23)

The condition of sinners is woeful and very deplorable. Note, also, It is the soul that is damaged and endangered by sin. Sinners may prosper in their outward estates, and yet at the same time, there may be a woe to their souls. Note, further, Whatever evils befals sinners it is of their own procuring, Jer. 2:19. (Isaiah 3:9)

Man is a mean creature, and therefore under a law of distance—unprofitable to God, and therefore under a law of disesteem and disregard—guilty and obnoxious, and therefore under a law of death and damnation. (2 Samuel 7:18-20)

The longer men continue in sin the sorer punishments they have reason to expect. It is the Lord that will bring these days upon them, for our times are in his hand, and who can resist or escape the judgments he brings? (Isaiah 7:17)

God himself is this devouring fire, Heb. 12:29. Who is able to stand before him? 1 Sam. 6:20. His wrath will burn those everlastingly that have made themselves fuel for it. It is a fire that shall never be quenched, nor will ever go out of itself; for it is the wrath of an everlasting God preying upon the conscience of an immortal soul. (Isaiah 33:14)

This destruction will be everlasting. They shall always be dying, and yet never die. Their misery will run parallel with the line of eternity. The chains of darkness are everlasting chains, and the fire is everlasting fire. It must needs be so, since the punishment is inflicted by an eternal God, fastening upon an immortal soul, set out of the reach of divine mercy and grace. (2 Thessalonians 1:9)

## 11: Judgment and Retribution

The triumphing of the wicked is short, Job 20:5. They are *exalted for a little while*, that their fall and ruin may be the sorer, Job 24:24. See how easily, how quickly, the scale turns against those that have not God on their side. (Joshua 8:21-22)

1. That which is to be dreaded by us more than any thing else is the wrath of God; for that is the spring and bitterness of all present miseries and will be the quintessence and perfection of everlasting misery. 2. It is the *evil of our doings* that kindles the fire of God's wrath against us. The consideration of the imminent danger we are in of falling and perishing under this wrath should awaken us with all possible care to *sanctify ourselves to God's glory* and to see to it that we be *sanctified by his grace*. (Jeremiah 4:3-4)

Those that most fear God's wrath are least likely to feel it. (2 Kings 23:19)

There is a hell in the other world, out of which there is no crying to God with any hope of being heard; but, whatever hell we may be *in the belly of* in this world, we may thence *cry to God*. (Jonah 2:2)

[I]t is *on earth* only that there is occasion for *faith;* for sinners in hell are *feeling* that which they would not believe, and saints in heaven are *enjoying* that which they did believe. (Luke 18:7-8)

What is the fire of hell but the wrath of God? Seared consciences will feel it hereafter, but do not fear it now. Enlightened consciences fear it now, but shall not feel it hereafter. (Job 19:11)

What is hell, that external excision, by which damned sinners are for ever cut off from God and all happiness, but God's terrors fastening and preying upon their guilty consciences? (Psalm 88:16)

The soul, as soon as it leaves the body, goes either to heaven or hell, to comfort or torment, immediately, and does not sleep, or go into purgatory. (Luke 16:25)

In hell there will be great grief, floods of tears shed to no purpose; anguish of spirit preying eternally upon the vitals, in the sense of the wrath of God, is the torment of the damned. (Matthew 8:12)

Damned sinners will be to eternity accusing, condemning, and upbraiding, themselves with their own follies, which, how much soever they are in love with them, will at the last *bite like a serpent,* and *sting like an adder.* (Mark 9:47-48)

Damned sinners are said to be tormented *in the presence of the Lamb,* intimating that he does not interpose on their behalf, Rev. 14:10. ... Thus those that hate to be refined by the fire of divine grace will undoubtedly be ruined by the fire of divine wrath. (Leviticus 10:2)

*Hell* is the destruction both of *soul and body;* not of the *being* of either, but the *well*-being of both; it is the ruin of the whole man; if the soul be lost, the body is lost too. They sinned together; the body was the soul's tempter to sin, and its tool in sin, and they must eternally suffer together. (Matthew 10:28)

It concerns us all to make it sure to ourselves that we shall be hid in the great day of God's wrath; and, if we hide ourselves in the chambers of duty, God will hide us in chambers of safety, Isa. 26:20. If we prepare an ark, that shall be our hiding-place, Gen. 7:1. (Zephaniah 2:3)

The sorrows of death are great sorrows, and the pains of hell great pains. Let us *therefore* give diligence to prepare for the former, that we may escape the latter. (Psalm 116:3)

That evil counsel or deed to which we have not consented shall not be reckoned our act. (Luke 23:50-51)

God is pleased to give warning of his judgments beforehand, that sinners may be awakened to meet him by repentance, and so *turn away his wrath,* and that, if they do not, they may be left inexcusable. (Jeremiah 1:16)

The removal of useful men by death, in the midst of their usefulness, is a very threatening symptom to any people. (Isaiah 3:1-3)

A public loss must be every man's grief, for every man shares in it. (2 Samuel 3:38)

The falls of the wise and good into sin, and the falls of the rich and great into trouble, are loud alarms to those that are every way their inferiors not to be secure. (Zechariah 11:2)

The wickedness of those that profess religion, and enjoy the means of grace, is the most unreasonable unaccountable thing in the world, and the whole blame of it must lie upon the sinners themselves. "*If thou scornest, thou alone shalt bear it,* and shalt not have a word to say for thyself in the judgment of the great day." God will prove his own ways equal and the sinner's ways unequal. (Isaiah 5:3-4)

Wherever sin has gone before judgment will follow after; and though *judgment begins at the house of God,* yet it shall not end there. The holy city shall be no more a protection to the wicked people than the holy house was to the wicked priests. (Ezekiel 9:6-7)

Those that are shameless are graceless and their case is hopeless. But those that will not submit to a penitential shame, nor take that to themselves as their due, shall not escape an utter ruin;… [W]hen God visits the nation in wrath, they shall be sure to be cast down and made to tremble, because they would not blush. (Jeremiah 6:15)

See the power of God's anger; there is no resisting it, no escaping it. See the mischief that sin makes; it provokes God to anger against a people, and so kindles a universal conflagration, sets all on fire. (Isaiah 42:25)

# 11: Judgment and Retribution

The judgments of God sometimes make quick work with a sinful people. A month devours more, and more portions, than many years can repair. (Hosea 5:7)

Very great changes, both for the better and for the worse, often happen in a very little time, so sudden are the revolutions of the wheel of nature. (Genesis 40:20-22)

Extraordinary judgments are rare things, and seldom happen, which is an instance of God's patience. When God had drowned the world once he promised never to do it again. (Joel 2:2)

When God's judgments are abroad they make a great noise; and it is necessary for the awakening of a secure and stupid world that they should do so. (Joel 2:5)

From the harms and falls of others it is good for us to infer that which will be of caution to us. (Matthew 19:23-24)

God's judgments upon others should affect us with a holy fear, Ps. 119:120. (1 Samuel 3:12-13)

It is an evidence of great stupidity and security when we are not awakened to a holy fear by the judgments of God upon others. (Jeremiah 3:8)

It will not always secure men from suffering wrong to be able to say they have done no wrong; not to have given offence will not be a defence against such men as Nebuchadnezzar. (Jeremiah 49:30)

*If a soul sin* (that is, a person, for the soul is the man), ... if in such a case, for fear of offending one that either has been his friend or may be his enemy, he refuses to give evidence, or gives it but in part, *he shall bear his iniquity*. And that is a heavy burden, which, if some course be not taken to get it removed, will sink a man to the lowest hell. (Leviticus 5:1)

Omissions are sins which will come into judgment, as well as commissions. He that does not the good he knows should be done, as well as he who does the evil he knows should not be done, will be condemned. (James 4:17)

Sinners will be condemned, at the great day, for the omission of that good which it was in the power of their hand to do. (Matthew 25:42-43)

Those will have a great deal to answer for who, though they have a secret kindness for good people, dare not own it in a time of need, nor will do what they might do to prevent mischief designed them. (Jeremiah 38:5)

As there is a day of the Lord's patience, so there will be a day of his vengeance; for, though he bear long, he will not bear always. (Isaiah 34:8)

Thus the righteous God sometimes, in his providence, makes the punishment to answer the sin, and observes an equality in his judgments; the spoiler

Part I: Folly (Damnation)

shall be spoiled, and the *treacherous dealer dealt treacherously* with, Isa. 33:1. And those that *showed no mercy*, shall have *no mercy shown them*, Jam. 2:13. (Judges 1:7-8)

The righteous God often pays sinners in their own coin. (Isaiah 33:1)

Those that spoil others must expect to be themselves spoiled (*ch.* 33:1); for the Lord is righteous, and those that are troublesome shall be troubled. (Isaiah 8:4)

Those who pursue and prosecute the sins of their predecessors must expect to be pursued and prosecuted by their plagues; if they do as they did, let them fare as they fared. (Jeremiah 50:17-18)

[T]hose who thirst for blood shall have enough of it. Those who love to be destroying shall be destroyed; for we know who has said, *Vengeance is mine, I will repay.* (Exodus 15:9-12)

Those who, when they are in power, turn and toss others, will be justly turned and tossed themselves when their day shall come to fall. Many who have thought themselves fastened like a nail, may come to be tossed like a ball;… (Isaiah 22:18-19)

Those will have a great deal to answer for who, when they should be the patrons of the oppressed, are their greatest oppressors. (Isaiah 1:23)

Such brethren there are in the world, who have no sense at all either of *natural equity* or *natural affection,* who make a prey of those whom they ought to patronize and protect. They who are so wronged have God to go to, who will *execute* judgment and justice for *those that are oppressed.* (Luke 12:13)

The justice of God is the refuge and comfort of oppressed innocence. If men wrong us, God will right us, at furthest, in the judgment of the great day. (1 Samuel 24:15)

It is sad for any to live so that, when they die, none will be sorry to part with them. (Jeremiah 22:18-19)

Whatever injuries are done us, we must not study to avenge ourselves, but must leave it to God to do it *to whom vengeance belongs,* and who hath said, *I will repay.* (Jeremiah 20:12)

Whatever injuries bad men do us (which we are not to wonder at; he that lies among thorns must expect to be scratched), yet we must not return them; never render railing for railing. Though *wickedness proceed from the wicked,* yet let it not therefore proceed from us by way of retaliation. Though the dog bark at the sheep, the sheep does not bark at the dog. (1 Samuel 24:13)

This is a good reason why we should not avenge ourselves; for, if vengeance be God's, then, *First,* We may not do it. We step into the throne of God if we do and take his work out of his hand. *Secondly,* We need not do it. For God will, if we meekly leave the matter with him; he will avenge us as far as there is rea-

## 11: Judgment and Retribution

son or justice for it, and further we cannot desire it. (Romans 12:19)

The more patiently men bear injuries that are done them the greater is the sin of those that injure them, and the more occasion they have to expect that God will give them redress, and take vengeance for them. (Amos 2:6-7)

The fire of our anger against our brethren kindles the fire of God's anger against us. (Amos 1:12)

Those that imagine an evil thing, though it prove a vain thing (Ps. 2:1), will be reckoned with for the imagination. (Hosea 7:15)

Let not us then be *overcome of evil, but overcome evil with good.* ... The most glorious victory over an enemy is to turn him into a friend. (2 Kings 6:22-23)

We should consider, to our terror and caution, that God knows all the revengeful thoughts we have in our minds against others, and therefore we should not allow of those thoughts nor harbour them, and that he knows all the revengeful thoughts others have causelessly in their minds against us, and therefore we should not be afraid of them, but leave it to him to protect us from them. (Lamentations 3:59)

Injuries to men are affronts to God, the righteous God, that loveth righteousness and hateth wickedness; and, as the Judge of all the earth, he will give redress to those that suffer wrong and take vengeance on those that do wrong. (Obadiah 10)

Those that will not submit to God's government shall not be able to escape his wrath. There is no fleeing from his justice, no avoiding his cognizance. Evil pursues sinners and entangles them in snares out of which they cannot extricate themselves. (Jeremiah 11:11)

Evil doers must expect to be destroyed: *Evil shall hunt the violent man,* as the blood-hound hunts the murderer to discover him, as the lion hunts his prey to tear it to pieces. Mischievous men will be brought to light, and brought to ruin; the destruction appointed shall run them down and overthrow them. *Evil pursues sinners.* (Psalm 140:11)

[T]he just punishment of iniquity ... is an intimation that evil pursues impenitent sinners beyond death, greater evil than that, and that they shall *rise to everlasting shame and contempt.* (Isaiah 14:20-21)

"Some sinners live long, to aggravate their judgment, others die soon, to hasten it;" but is certain that evil pursues sinners, and sooner or later, it will overtake them.... (2 Kings 1:17)

Those that escape punishment from men, yet shall not escape the righteous judgments of God; so wretchedly do those deceive themselves that promise themselves impunity in sin. (Leviticus 20:3)

Hope of impunity is a great encouragement to iniquity. (2 Samuel 11:6)

Impunity hardens sinners in impiety, and the patience of God is shamefully abused by many who, instead of being led by it to repentance, are confirmed by it in their impenitence. (Ecclesiastes 8:11)

Their sin shall be their punishment: "You will flee … you will be upon the full speed, and therefore so shall those be that pursue you." The dogs are most apt to run barking after him that rides fast. (Isaiah 30:16)

God will make thorough work of it; for, as he will perform what he has purposed, so he will perfect what he has begun. (Jeremiah 51:40)

God's anger is ready to fall upon sinners, as a lion falls on his prey, and there is none to deliver, as a mountain of lead falling on them, to sink them past recovery into the lowest hell. But if they repent, it shall be turned away, Isa. 12:1. (Jeremiah 3:12-14)

God will severely reckon with those that strengthen the hands of the wicked in their wickedness. (Exodus 9:11)

# Part II

## Wisdom (Salvation)

# -1-

## Repentance and Forgiveness

... Those that have already by a holy contempt of this world stripped themselves can easily bear to be stripped when trouble and death come.

Matthew Henry
on Isaiah 32:11

[W]hen the calamity comes ... God's judgments would strip them and make them bare, but, (1.) That the best prevention of the trouble would be to repent and humble themselves for their sin, and lie in the dust before God in true remorse and godly sorrow, which will be the lengthening out of their tranquility. This is meeting God in the way of his judgments, and saving a correction by correcting our own mistakes. Those only shall break that will not bend. ... Those that have already by a holy contempt of this world stripped themselves can easily bear to be stripped when trouble and death come. (Isaiah 32:11)

Sin will, without doubt, find out the sinner sooner or later. It concerns us therefore to find our sins out, that we may repent of them and forsake them, lest our sins find us out to our ruin and confusion. (Numbers 32:23)

The consideration of the judgment to come, and of the great hand Christ will have in that judgment, should engage us all to repent of our sins and turn from them to God. This is the only way to make the Judge our friend in that day, which will be a terrible day to all who live and die impenitent; but true penitents will then *lift up their heads with joy, knowing that their redemption draws nigh.* (Acts 17:31)

(1.) Reformation is absolutely necessary to salvation. There is no other way of preventing judgments, or turning them away when we are threatened with them, but taking away the sin by which we have procured them to ourselves. (2.) No reformation is saving but that which reaches the heart. (Jeremiah 4:14)

The language of true penitents is, *Let the righteous smite me; it shall be a kindness;* and the law is *therefore* good, because, being spiritual, in it sin appears sin, and exceedingly sinful. ... Those that see the evil of sin, and what it deserves, will justify God in all that is brought upon them for it, and own that he punishes them less than their iniquities deserve. (Isaiah 39:5-8)

It is necessary to our repentance for sin that we be acquainted with the evil of it, as it is necessary to the cure of a disease to know its nature, causes, and malignity. ... It well becomes penitents to say the worst they can of sin, for the truth is we can never speak ill enough of it. (Ecclesiastes 7:25)

The more we see of the heinousness of our sins the better qualified we are to find mercy with God. When we confess sin we must aggravate it. (Psalm 25:11)

True penitents lay a load upon themselves, do not extenuate, but aggravate, their sins, and own that they have exceeded in them. (Job 36:8-10)

True penitents take shame to themselves, not honour;... (2 Kings 21:18)

[M]ay ... our penitent reflection [be]: *Other lords besides God, have had dominion over us;* every lust has been our lord, and we have been led captive by it; and it has been long enough, and too long,

# 1: Repentance and Forgiveness

that we have thus wronged both God and ourselves. The same therefore must be our pious resolution, that henceforth we will make mention of God's name only and by him only, that we will keep close to God and to our duty and never desert it. (Isaiah 26:13)

Let us return from our evil ways, into which we have gone aside, and rest and settle in the way of God and duty, and that is the way to be saved. (Isaiah 30:15-17)

[T]he methods prescribed for the healing of the leprosy of sin are so plain that we are utterly inexcusable if we do not observe them. It is but, "Believe, and be saved" — "Repent, and be pardoned" — "Wash, and be clean." (2 Kings 5:13)

[R]epent and become wise ... *Turn you at My reproof.* ... Turn, that is, return to your right mind, turn to God, turn to your duty, turn and live. (Proverbs 1:23)

"When you shall have abandoned your idols, *then shall God give the rain on your seed.*" When we return to God in a way of duty, he will meet us with his favours. (Isaiah 30:23)

When we return to God in a way of duty he will return to us in a way of mercy; take away the cause, and the effect will cease. (Exodus 4:26)

When one sin is sincerely parted with all sin is abandoned too, for he that hates sin, as sin, will hate all sin. And those that are cured of their spiritual idolatry, their inordinate affection to the world and the flesh, that no longer make a god of their money or their belly, have a happy blow given to the root of all their transgressions. (Ezekiel 37:23)

Repentance, if it be true, strikes at the root, and washes the heart from wickedness. We must alter our judgments concerning persons and things, dislodge the corrupt imaginations and quit the vain pretences under which an unsanctified heart shelters itself. Note, it is not enough to break off from evil practices, but we must enter a caveat against evil thought. (Isaiah 55:7)

It is necessary, in repentance, that we not only *cease to do evil, but learn to do well,* not only do no wrong to any, but do good to all. (Daniel 4:27)

It is not enough to know well, and speak well, and profess well, and promise well, but we must do well; do that which is good, not only for the matter of it, but for the manner of it. We must do it well. (Romans 2:10)

Penitents should be preachers. Solomon was so, and blessed Paul. ... The great thing to be aimed at in teaching transgressors is their conversion to God; that is a happy point gained, and happy are those that are instrumental to contribute towards it, Jam. 5:20. (Psalm 51:13)

Works of charity are so far from impoverishing us that they are the proper means truly to enrich us, or make us truly rich. (2 Corinthians 9:11)

Therefore we should be forward to give, because we know not but we ourselves may some time be in want, Eccl. 11:2. *And he that watereth shall be watered also himself*, Prov. 11:25. (2 Samuel 9:5-7)

Our doing good to others will do none to us, if it be not well done, namely, from a principle of devotion and charity, love to God, and good-will to men. Note, If we leave charity out of religion, the most costly services will be of no avail to us. If we give away all we have, while we withhold the heart from God, it will not profit. (1 Corinthians 13:3)

Here are four necessary duties that we are called to, all amounting to the same:—1. We must repent; we must change our mind and change our ways; we must be sorry for what we have done amiss and be ashamed of it, and go as far as we can towards the undoing of it again. 2. We must *turn ourselves from all our transgressions,…* 3. We must *cast away from us all our transgressions;* we must abandon and forsake them with a resolution never to return to them again, give sin a bill of divorce, break all the leagues we have made with it, throw it overboard, as the mariners did Jonah (for it has raised the storm), cast it out of the soul, and crucify it as a malefactor. 4. We must *make us a new heart and a new spirit.* (Ezekiel 18:30-32)

In reflecting upon ourselves it is good to compare what we have done with what we should have done, our practice with the rule, that we may discover wherein we have done amiss, have *done those things which we ought not to have done.* … Sin thus looked upon, in the glass of the commandment, will appear exceedingly sinful. (Obadiah 10:12-14)

Those that do things with self-will reflect upon them afterwards with self-reproach. (Esther 7:7)

We often do that, through inconsideration, which afterwards we see cause a thousand times to wish undone again, which is good reason why we should *ponder the path of our feet*, for then *all our ways will be established.* (Daniel 6:14)

Those that have said and done amiss must, as far as they can, unsay it and undo it again by repentance. (Acts 8:22)

The guilt of sin is not removed if the gain of sin be not restored. (Job 11:14)

We should often put this question to ourselves, Is it well to say thus, to do thus? Can I justify it? Must I not unsay it and undo it again by repentance, or be undone forever? Ask, 1. Do I well to be angry? (Jonah 4:4)

See here what sin is; it is an *abomination*, a loathsome thing, that abominable thing which the Lord hates. See what is the first step towards repentance; it is *remembering our own evil ways*, reflecting seriously upon the sins we have committed and being particular in recapitulating them. (Ezekiel 36:31)

## 1: Repentance and Forgiveness

God remembers former iniquities against those only who by the present discoveries of their wickedness show that they do not repent of them. (Ezekiel 21:23)

Note, [a.] *Evil doers*, whatever they pretend, will be treated in the day of judgment as *evil men*. [b.] The resurrection will be to evil-doers, who did not by repentance undo what they had done amiss, a *resurrection* of damnation. They shall come forth to be publicly convicted of rebellion against God, and publicly *condemned* to everlasting punishment; to be *sentenced* to it, and immediately *sent* to it without reprieve. (John 5:28-30)

People are ruined, not so much by doing what is amiss, as by doing it and not repenting of it, doing it and standing to it. (Genesis 25:34)

It is not sinning that ruins men, but sinning and not repenting, falling and not getting up again. (1 Samuel 13:10-13)

The sin of sinners is never forgotten till it is forgiven. It is ever before God, till by repentance it comes to be ever before us. (Jeremiah 17:1-2)

God sees the sins of his people and is displeased with them; but, upon their repentance, he turns away his wrath. (Isaiah 27:4-5)

Sin is a fall; and it concerns those that have fallen by sin to get up again by repentance. ... The ancient Jews had a saying grounded on this, *Repentance is a great thing, for it brings men quite up to the throne of glory.* (Hosea 14:1-2)

Bring down your spirits to repentance and faith, and that is the way to bring up your spirits to heaven and glory. (Jeremiah 27:12)

Wherever God designs to give life he gives repentance; for this is a necessary preparative for the comforts of a sealed pardon and a settled peace in this world, and for the seeing and enjoying of God in the other world. (Acts 11:17-18)

Repentance and faith prepare people for the blessings of the kingdom of heaven, which Christ gives. (Matthew 11:1-6)

Both these must go together; we must not think either that reforming our lives will save us without trusting in the righteousness and grace of Christ, or that trusting in Christ will save us without the reformation of our hearts and lives. Christ hath joined these two together, and let no man think to put them asunder. They will mutually assist and befriend each other. Repentance will quicken faith, and faith will make repentance evangelical; and the sincerity of both together must be evidenced by a diligent conscientious obedience to all God's commandments. (Mark 1:15)

God is long-suffering with provoking sinners, because he is not willing that *any should perish, but that all should come to repentance,* 2 Pet. 3:9. (Daniel 4:29)

"Does your Lord delay his coming? Do not think this is to give more time to make provision for your lusts, to gratify them; it is so much space to repent and work out your salvation...." (2 Peter 3:11-18)

God gives notice of danger, and space to repent, that sinners may *flee from the wrath to come*. (Judges 8:7-9)

Divine patience has kept us out of hell, that we might have space to repent, and get to heaven. (Romans 3:24-26)

Observe, *First*, Repentance is necessary to prevent a sinner's ruin. *Secondly*, Repentance requires time, a course of time, and time convenient; it is a great work, and a work of time. *Thirdly*, Where God gives space for repentance, he expects fruits meet for repentance. *Fourthly*, Where the space for repentance is lost, the sinner perishes with a double destruction. (Revelation 2:20-21)

God does not begin with the sorest judgments, to show that he is patient, and delights not in the death of sinners; but, if they repent not, he will proceed to the sorest, to show that he is righteous, and that he will not be mocked or set at defiance. (Leviticus 26:28)

It is certain that God has no delight in the ruin of sinners, nor does he desire it. If they will destroy themselves, he will glorify himself in it, but he has no pleasure in it, but would rather they should *turn and live*, for his goodness is that attribute of his which is most his glory, which is most his delight. He would rather sinners should turn and live than go on and die. (Ezekiel 33:11)

Though the damnation of all that perish will be intolerable, yet the damnation of those who had the fullest and clearest discoveries made them of the power and grace of Christ, and yet repented not, will be of all others the most intolerable. (Matthew 11:22)

The slavery of sin is foolishly preferred by many to the glorious liberty of the children of God, only because they apprehend some present difficulties attending that necessary revolution of the government in the soul. (Matthew 2:3)

Christ does not take refusers at their first word, but repeats his offers to those who have often repulsed them. (Matthew 13:53-54)

See here what method God takes to bring sinners to repentance. He leads them, not drives them like beasts, but leads them like rational creatures, allures them (Hos. 2:14); and it is goodness that leads, bands of love, Hos. 11:4. ... The consideration of the goodness of God, his common goodness to all (the goodness of his providence, of his patience, and of his offers), should be effectual to bring us all to repentance; and the reason why so many continue in impenitency is because they do not know and consider this. (Romans 2:4)

Wilful impenitency is the great damning sin of multitudes that enjoy the

## 1: Repentance and Forgiveness

gospel, and which (more than any other) sinners will be upbraided with to eternity. ... The stronger inducements we have to repent, the more heinous is the impenitency and the severer will the reckoning be, for Christ keeps account of the *mighty works done* among us, and of the gracious works done for us too, by which we should be *led to repentance,* Rom. 2:4. (Matthew 11:20)

The devils believe and tremble, but they never believe and repent. Note, There may be the terror of strong convictions, where there is not the truth of a saving conversion. (Matthew 14:8-9)

The greatest calamities that can befal men will not bring them to repentance without the grace of God working with them. (Revelation 16:21)

Till the heart is renewed by the grace of God, the impressions made by the force of affliction do not abide; the convictions wear off, and the promises that were extorted are forgotten. Till the disposition of the air is changed, what thaws in the sun will freeze again in the shade. (Exodus 8:15)

When we have received special mercy from God, we ought to be quick and speedy in our returns of praise to him, before time and the deceitfulness of our own hearts efface the good impressions that have been made. David sang his triumphant song in the day that the Lord delivered him, 2 Sam 22:1. ... *He gives twice who gives quickly.* (Exodus 15:1)

If convictions be not speedily prosecuted, it is a thousand to one but in a little time they will be quite lost and forgotten. (Daniel 4:9)

As soon as ever God by his Spirit convinces our consciences of any sin or duty we must immediately set in with the conviction, and prosecute it, as those that are not ashamed to own our former mistake. (Leviticus 5:2-3)

Poverty and disgrace sometimes prove a happy means of making great sinners true penitents. (Hosea 3:2)

If men's dignity and power do not, as they ought, keep them from sin, they will not serve to exempt them from reproof, to excuse their repentance, or to secure them from the judgments of God if they do not repent. (Ezekiel 34:2)

God can soon awaken the most secure and make the heart of the stoutest sinner to tremble; and there needs no more to do it than to let loose his own thoughts upon him; they will soon play the tyrant, and give him trouble enough. (Daniel 5:5-6)

Guilty consciences are apt to take good providences in a bad sense, and to put wrong constructions even upon those things that make for them. They flee when none pursues. (Genesis 42:28)

Where there is an *idle faith,* there is commonly a *working fancy.* ... A guilty conscience needs no accuser or tormentor but itself. ... [T]hose therefore who would keep an undisturbed peace, must keep an undefiled conscience, Acts 24:16. (Mark 6:16)

[A] wounded conscience makes troubles lie heavily, Ps. 38:4. (2 Samuel 15:30)

Note, the best way to have a good night is to keep a good conscience, then we may lie down in peace. (Daniel 6:18)

A guilty conscience exposes men to continual frights, even where no fear is, and makes them suspicious of everybody, as Cain.... Those that would be fearless must keep themselves guiltless. If our heart reproach us not, then have we confidence both towards God and man. (Genesis 50:15)

Conscience is God's vicegerent, calls the court in his name, and acts for him. ... If conscience condemn us, God does so too: *For, if our heart condemn us, God is greater than our heart, and knoweth all things....* (1 John 3:20-21)

The testimony of conscience for us that we have walked with God in our integrity will be much our support and rejoicing when we come to look death in the face, 2 Cor. 1:12. (2 Kings 10:2)

Thus those that feel their consciences under guilt and wrath must not cover it, nor endeavour to shake off their convictions, but by repentance, and prayer, and humble confession, take the appointed way to peace and pardon. (Deuteronomy 24:8-9)

Those that can lay their heads upon the pillow of a clear conscience, may sleep quietly and sweetly in a storm.... (Matthew 8:24)

When we have finished a day's work, and are entering upon the rest of the night, we should commune with our own hearts about what we have been doing that day; so likewise when we have finished a week's work, and are entering upon the sabbath-rest, we should thus prepare to meet our God; and when we are finishing our life's work, and are entering upon our rest in the grave, that is a time to bring to remembrance, that we may die repenting, and so take leave of it. (Genesis 2:31)

Those only who are thus purged from an evil conscience are prepared *to serve the living God,* Heb. 9:14. The taking away of sin is necessary to our speaking with confidence and comfort either to God in prayer or from God in preaching;... (Isaiah 6:6-7)

Hope of mercy is the great encouragement to repentance and reformation; and though there be but some glimmerings of hope mixed with great fears arising from a sense of our own sinfulness, and unworthiness, and long abuse of divine patience, yet they may serve to quicken and engage our serious repentance and reformation. Let us boldly cast ourselves at the footstool of free grace, resolving that if we perish, we will perish there; yet who knows but God will look upon us with compassion? (Jonah 3:9)

# 1: Repentance and Forgiveness

Calls to repentance are plain indications of mercy designed. ... God has no pleasure in the death of those that die; let them return and repent, and then mercy, which otherwise is at a loss, knows what to do. (Exodus 33:5)

Though God is justly and greatly angry with sinners, yet he is not implacable in his anger; it may be turned away; it shall be turned away, from those that turn away from their iniquity. God will be reconciled to those that are reconciled to him and to his whole will. (Hosea 14:4)

It is wonderful condescending love of the eternal Father, that such as we should be made and called his sons—we who by nature are heirs of sin, and guilt, and the curse of God—we who by practice are children of corruption, disobedience and ingratitude! Strange, that the holy God is not ashamed to be called our Father, and to call us his sons! (1 John 3:1)

(1.) If, in covenanting with God, we make a reservation for any known sin, which we continue to indulge ourselves in, that reservation is a defeasance of his covenant. We must cast away all our transgressions and not except any house of Rimmon. (2.) Though we are encouraged to pray for the remission of sins we have committed, yet, if we ask for a dispensation to go on in any sin for the future, we mock God, and deceive ourselves. ... Those that truly hate evil will make conscience of abstaining from all appearances of evil. (2 Kings 5:18)

Those do not truly, nor acceptably, repent or reform, who only part with the sins that they lose by, but continue their affection to the sins that they get by. (2 Kings 3:2-3)

Many mourn for their sins that do not truly repent of them, weep bitterly for them, and yet continue in love and league with them. (1 Samuel 24:16)

It is no new thing to find the show and profession of repentance where yet the truth and substance of it are wanting. (1 Kings 21:27)

Many pretend to repent of their wrongdoing, when it does not succeed, who, if they had prospered in it, would have justified it and gloried in it. (1 Kings 20:31)

Those that flee to Christ from their sins shall be safe in him, but not those that expect to be sheltered by him in their sins. Salvation itself cannot save such: divine justice will fetch them even from the city of refuge, the protection of which they are not entitled to. (Deuteronomy 19:11-13)

Though Christ is always ready to hear and answer holy desires and prayers, yet he will not gratify corrupt lusts and humours. Those who *ask amiss, ask, and have not*. (Matthew 12:39)

The greatest shall not have their lusts indulged, but the meanest shall have their wants considered. (Matthew 12:3-4)

When we are entering upon any new condition of life our care should be to bring none of the guilt of the sins of our former condition into it. When we are in any imminent peril let us be sure to make our peace with God, and then we are safe: nothing can do us any real hurt. (Ezra 8:21)

The reprieve will not be continued if the repentance be not continued in. If men turn from the good they began to do, they can expect no other than that God should turn from the favour he began to show, Jer. 18:10. (Nahum 1:1)

1. True penitents will forsake both open sins, will put away not only the whoredoms that lie in sight, but those that lie in secret *between their breasts*, the sin that is *rolled under the tongue as a sweet morsel*. 2. They will both avoid the outward occasions of sin and mortify the inward disposition to it. (Hosea 2:2)

Those that truly repent of sin will keep themselves as far as possible from the occasions of it. (Acts 19:19)

Besides the first conversion of a soul from a state of nature to a state of grace, there are after-conversions from particular paths of backsliding, which are equally necessary to salvation. Every step out of the way by sin, must be a step into it again by repentance. (Matthew 18:3)

If God has set apart those that are godly for himself, they ought to set themselves apart. (Isaiah 26:20)

To separate ourselves from wicked people is the only way to save ourselves from them; though we expose ourselves to their rage and enmity, we really save ourselves from them;... [I]t is better to have the trouble of swimming against their stream than the danger of being carried down their stream. (Acts 2:40)

[C]onviction must prepare for comfort, and must also separate between the precious and the vile, and mark out those to whom comfort does not belong. (Isaiah 58:1-2)

Christ has said, *I love those that love me*. He is pleased with his people, notwithstanding their weaknesses, when they sincerely repent of them and return to their duty, and commends them as if they had already arrived at perfection. (Song of Solomon 6:5-7)

There is more joy for the sheep that is brought back than there would have been if it had never gone astray. (Ezekiel 36:11)

Greater joy there is in heaven for returning sinners than for remaining angels. (Matthew 18:12-13)

[God] ... infused compassion even into their stony hearts, and made them relent, which is more than any art of man could have done with the utmost force of rhetoric. Note, God can change lions into lambs, and *when a man's ways please the Lord*, will make even *his enemies to pity him* and *be at peace with him*. When God pities men shall. (Psalm 106:45-46)

## 1: Repentance and Forgiveness

Those that thus quit their temporal interests for the securing of their spiritual welfare will be unspeakable gainers at last; for what they lose upon those terms they shall find again to life eternal. (Jonah 1:5)

Those who now own God for theirs, he will then own for his, will publicly confess them before angels and men.... (Malachi 3:16-17)

When men are brought to honour God, particularly by a penitent confession of sin and a believing acknowledgement of his sovereignty, then, and not till then, they may expect that God will put honour upon them, will not only restore them to the dignity they lost by the sin of the first Adam, but *add excellent majesty to them* from the righteousness and grace of the second Adam. (Daniel 4:34)

Those that humble themselves in penitential shame and fear shall soon be encouraged and exalted; those that are struck down with the visions of God's glory shall soon be raised up again with the visits of his grace; he that tears, will heal. (Isaiah 6:6-7)

We ought to act with great tenderness towards those that are overtaken in a fault and are brought into distress by it. (Jonah 1:11)

A good man may be overtaken in a fault, but the grace of God shall recover him to repentance, so that he shall not be utterly cast down. (Psalm 37:24)

Repentance teaches us to be severe in reflections upon ourselves; but charity teaches us to be candid in our reflections upon others. It is only Christ's example that is a copy without a blot. (Acts 15:36-41)

There is a proneness in our corrupt nature to stint ourselves in that which is good, and to be afraid of doing too much in religion, particularly of forgiving too much, though we have so much forgiven us. ... It does not look well for us to keep count of the offences done against us by our brethren. There is something of ill-nature in scoring up the injuries we forgive, as if we would allow ourselves to be revenged when the measure is full. God keeps account (Deut. 32:34) because he is the Judge, and vengeance is his; but we must not, lest we be found stepping into his throne. ... God multiplies his pardons, and so should we, Ps. 77:38, 40. It intimates that we should make it our constant practice to forgive injuries, and should accustom ourselves to it till it becomes habitual. (Matthew 18:21-22)

How dreadful soever Christ may appear to those under convictions of sin, and in terror by reason of it, there is enough in his word to quiet their spirits and make them easy, if they will but attend to it and apply it. (Daniel 10:8)

God's making use of us is the best evidence of his being at peace with us. (Jonah 3:2)

Let all men know that it is nothing but sin that separates between them and

God, and, if it be not sincerely repented of and forsaken, it will separate eternally. (Joshua 7:12)

When we have faithfully put away sin, that accursed thing, which *separates between us and God*, then, and not till then, we may expect to hear from God to our comfort; and God's directing us how to go on in our Christian work and warfare is a good evidence of his being reconciled to us. (Joshua 8:1)

Though God *gives and upbraids not*, it becomes us, when he forgives, to upbraid ourselves with our unworthy conduct towards him. (Ezekiel 43:7)

When God pardons sin he casts it behind his back, as not designing to look upon it with an eye of justice and jealousy. He remembers it no more, to visit for it. The pardon does not make the sin not to have been, or not to have been sin, but not to be punished as it deserves. When we cast our sins behind our back, and take no care to repent of them, God sets them before his face, and is ready to reckon for them; but when we set them before our face in true repentance, as David did when his sin was ever before him, God casts them behind his back. ...The pardoning of the sin is the delivering of the soul from the pit of corruption. (Isaiah 38:17)

[Y]ou shall be delivered from that anger of God which is everlasting, from the wrath to come; but upon what terms? Very easy and reasonable ones. *Only acknowledge thy sins. If we confess our sins, he is faithful and just to forgive them.* This will aggravate the condemnation of sinners, that the terms of pardon and peace were brought so low, and yet they would not come down to them. (Jeremiah 3:13)

# -2-

# Pardon and Redemption

It is the praying remnant that shall be the saved remnant. And it will aggravate the ruin of those who perish that they might have been saved on such easy terms. ... Those only shall be delivered in the great day that are now effectually called from sin to God, from self to Christ, from things below to things above.

Matthew Henry
on Joel 2:32

It is the praying remnant that shall be the saved remnant. And it will aggravate the ruin of those who perish that they might have been saved on such easy terms. ... Those only shall be delivered in the great day that are now effectually called from sin to God, from self to Christ, from things below to things above. (Joel 2:32)

The conversion of a sinner is the translation of a soul into the kingdom of Christ out of the kingdom of the devil. The power of sin is shaken off, and the power of Christ submitted to. The law of the Spirit of life in Christ Jesus makes them free from the law of sin and death;... Those who are not saints on earth will never be saints in heaven. (Colossians 1:13)

Pardoned people are the only blessed people. The sentiments of the world are, Those are happy that have a clear estate, and are out of debt to man; but the sentence of the word is, Those are happy that have their debts to God discharged. O how much therefore is it our interest to make it sure to ourselves that our sins are pardoned! For this is the foundation of all other benefits. (Romans 4:6-8)

Our transgressions and our sins are as a cloud, a thick cloud; they interpose between heaven and earth, and for a time suspend and intercept the correspondence between the upper and lower world (sin *separates between us and God, ch.* 59:2); they threaten a storm, a deluge of wrath, as thick clouds do, which God will rain upon sinners. Ps. 11:6. ... When God pardons sin, he blots out this cloud, this thick cloud, so that the intercourse with heaven is laid open again. God looks down upon the soul with favour; the soul looks up to him with pleasure. The cloud is scattered by the influence of the Sun of righteousness. It is only through Christ that sin is pardoned. When sin is pardoned, like a cloud that is scattered, it appears no more, it is quite gone. ... And the comforts that flow into the soul when sin is pardoned are like the *clear shining after clouds and rain.* (Isaiah 44:22)

The Old-Testament dispensation was the *ministration of death* ... whereas that of the New Testament is the *ministration of life.* The law discovered sin, and the wrath and curse of God. This showed us a God above us and a God against us; but the gospel discovers grace, and *Emmanuel,* God with us. (2 Corinthians 3:7)

When the gospel comes to any place, to any soul, light comes, a great light, a shining light, which will shine more and more. It should be welcome to us, as light is to those that sit in darkness, and we should readily entertain it, both because it is of such sovereign use to us and because it brings its own evidence with it. Truly this light is sweet. (Isaiah 9:2)

Those that receive the Christian covenant ought to receive the Christian baptism. (Acts 2:38)

## 2: Pardon and Redemption

All that are employed for God must be dedicated to him, according as the degree of employment is. Christians must be baptized, ministers must be ordained; we must first give ourselves unto the Lord, and then our services. (Numbers 8:6, 20)

In the solemn dedicating and devoting of ourselves to God, it is good to make haste, and not to delay; for the present time is the best time, Ps. 119:60. Those who have received the thing signified by baptism should not put off receiving the sign. (Acts 8:36)

*Then* we may see heaven opened to us, when we perceive the Spirit *descending* and working upon us. God's good work in us is the surest evidence of his good will towards us, and his preparations for us. (Mark 1:10)

The reasons why God pardons sin, and keeps not his anger forever, are all taken from within himself; it is *because he delights in mercy,* and the salvation of sinners is what he has pleasure in, not their death and damnation. (Micah 7:18)

Those whom God pardons must be made to know what their sin deserved, and how miserable they would have been if they had been unpardoned, that God's mercy may be the more magnified. (Exodus 33:5)

That such a worm of the earth as man is should be the darling and favourite of heaven is what we have reason forever to admire. (Job 7:17-18)

God's strongest reasons for his sparing mercy are those which are fetched from his own glory. (Ezekiel 20:13-14)

Sometimes the grace of God works upon sinners when they are at the worst, and hotly engaged in the most desperate sinful pursuits, which is much for the glory both of God's pity and of his power. (Acts 9:3)

And many times those that have been great sinners before their conversion prove more eminently and zealously good after, of which Paul is an instance, and therefore in him God was greatly *glorified,* Gal. 1:24. (Luke 15:10)

Some that are eminently good after their conversion have been as remarkably wicked before. ... *How glorious a change does grace make!* It changes the vilest of men into saints and the children of God. (1 Corinthians 6:11)

[T]he greatness of sin is no bar to pardoning mercy if it be truly repented of in time. We read of publicans and harlots entering into the kingdom of the Messiah, and being welcomed to all the privileged of that kingdom, Matt. 21:31, (Joshua 2:1)

Let not great sinners then despair of finding mercy with God if they truly repent; for who is a God like unto him, pardoning iniquity? (2 Samuel 12:13)

Former badness is no bar to God's present grace and mercy. (Romans 9:25)

## Part II: Wisdom (Salvation)

The conversion of sinners ought to be the matter of our joy and praise as it is of the angels'. (Acts 21:19-20)

The calling, the effectual calling, of the Gentiles into the church of God greatly redounded to the glory of the Son of man. The multiplying of the redeemed was the magnifying of the Redeemer. (John 12:23)

Great sin and scandal before conversion, are no barrier to great gifts, graces, and advancements, after; nay, God may be the more glorified. (Mark 2:14)

If those that are grown into years, and have long been accustomed to evil, are cured of their spiritual impotency to good, and thereby of their evil customs, the power of divine grace is therein so much the more magnified. (Acts 4:22)

God's goodness takes occasion from man's badness to appear so much the more illustrious; *therefore* he will sanctify his name by the pardon of sin, because it has been profaned by the commission of sin. (Ezekiel 36:23-24)

Deep convictions of guilt and wrath will put men upon careful enquiries after peace and pardon, and then, and not till then, there begins to be some hope of them. (Micah 6:6)

Those that are convicted of sin would gladly know the way to peace and pardon.... (Acts 2:37)

Those whom Christ designs to admit to the most *intimate acquaintance* with him he first makes sensible that they deserve to be set at the *greatest distance* from him. (Luke 5:8)

The sin of sinners is not forgotten till it is pardoned, but an exact account is kept of it, which will be opened in proper time. (Hosea 13:12)

Time does not wear out the guilt of sin. (Job 13:26)

Those that come to God for the forgiveness of their sins against him, must make conscience of forgiving those who have offended them, else they curse themselves when they say the Lord's prayer. Our duty is to *forgive our debtors;* ... those that *trespass against us,* ... [W]e must forbear, and forgive, and forget the affronts put upon us, and the wrongs done us; and this is a moral qualification for pardon and peace; it encourages to hope, that God will *forgive us;*... (Matthew 6:12)

If our brother has done us an injury, we must not return it upon him, that is avenging; ... It is a most ill-natured thing, and the bane of friendship, to retain the resentment of affronts and injuries, and to let that *word devour for ever.* (Leviticus 19:17-18)

God's compassions towards us should engage our compassions towards our brethren; we must release as we are released, forgive as we are forgiven, and relieve as we are relieved. And this is called a *covenant;* for our performance of the duty required is the condition of the continuance of the favours

## 2: Pardon and Redemption

God has bestowed. ... What God has bound us to by his precept, it is good for us to bind ourselves to by our promise. (Jeremiah 34:13)

God, in forgiving us, has a peculiar respect to our forgiving those that have injured us; and therefore, when we pray for pardon, we must mention our making conscience of that duty, not only to remind ourselves of it, but to bind ourselves to it. (Matthew 6:12)

Those who are forgiven of God should be of a forgiving spirit, and should forgive even as God forgives, sincerely and heartily, readily and cheerfully, universally and for ever, upon the sinner's sincere repentance, as remembering that they pray, *Forgive us our trespasses, as we forgive those who trespass against us.* (Ephesians 4:32)

[T]hose who have wronged us, we must forgive; and those whom we have wronged, we must make satisfaction to.... (Matthew 5:24)

It is the remembering and repeating of matters that separates friends and perpetuates the separation. ... A humble submissive carriage goes a great way towards the turning away of wrath. Many preserve themselves by humbling themselves: the bullet flies over him that stoops. (Genesis 33:3)

When differences happen between near relations, let those be ever reckoned the wisest and the best that are most forward to forgive and forget injuries and most willing to stoop and yield for peace' sake. (Judges 15:1)

[I]t will not justify us in hurting our brother to say that he began, for it is the second blow that makes the quarrel; and when we were injured, we had an opportunity not to justify our injuring him, but to show ourselves the true disciples of Christ, by forgiving him. (Matthew 5:39)

The unkindness of near relations, though by many worst taken, yet should with us, for that reason, because of the relation, be first forgiven. (Deuteronomy 23:7-8)

Satan prevailed first with Eve, and by her with Adam; see what need we have to take heed of being drawn into quarrels by our relations, for we know not how great a matter a little fire may kindle. (Numbers 12:1-2)

Mutual strifes among brethren, if persisted in, are likely to prove a common ruin; those that devour one another are in a fair way to be consumed one of another. Christian churches cannot be ruined but by their own hands.... (Galatians 5:15)

When we are called to vindicate ourselves we should carefully avoid, as much as may be, speaking ill of others. Let us be content to prove ourselves innocent, and not be fond of upbraiding others with their guilt. (Genesis 40:14-15)

These are the lambs of his flock, that

## Part II: Wisdom (Salvation)

shall be sure to want nothing that their case requires. [1.] He will gather them in the arms of his power; his strength shall be made *perfect in their weakness,* 2 Cor. 12:9. He will gather them in when they wander, gather them up when they fall, gather them together when they are dispersed, and gather them home to himself at last; and all this with his own arm, out of which none shall be able to pluck them, John 10:28. [2.] He will carry them in the bosom of his love and cherish them there. ... [3.] He will gently lead them. (Isaiah 40:11)

When believers accept of him as theirs, and join themselves to him in an everlasting covenant, [1.] It is his coronation-day in their souls. Before conversion they were crowning themselves, but then they begin to crown Christ, and continue to do so from that day forward. They appointed him their head; they bring *every thought into obedience to* him; they set up his throne in their hearts, and cast all their crowns at his feet. (Song of Solomon 3:11)

There is that in our sinful hearts that always resists the Holy Ghost, a flesh that lusts against the Spirit, and wars against his motions; but in the hearts of God's elect, when the fulness of time comes, this resistance is overcome and overpowered, and after a struggle the throne of Christ is set up in the soul, and every thought that had exalted itself against it is brought into captivity to it, 2 Cor. 10:4, 5. (Acts 7:51)

Justification by faith lays the foundation of our title to salvation; but by confession we build upon that foundation, and come at last to the full possession of that to which we were entitled. (Romans 10:10)

All that receive the remission of sins *receive the gift of the Holy Ghost.* All that are justified are sanctified. (Acts 2:38)

[O]bserve the nature of sanctification, what it is, and wherein it consists. In general it has two things in it, mortification and vivification—dying to sin and living to righteousness, elsewhere expressed by putting off the old man and putting on the new, ceasing to do evil and learning to do well. (Romans 6:1-4)

Persons, when converted, differ exceedingly from what they were formerly. They are people of another fashion and manner from what they were before; their inward frame, behaviour, speech, and conversation, are much altered from what they were in times past. (1 Peter 1:13-15)

Conversion and sanctification are the renewing of the mind, a change not of the substance, but of the qualities of the soul. It is the same with making a new heart and a new spirit—new dispositions and inclinations, new sympathies and antipathies; the understanding enlightened, the conscience softened, the thoughts rectified; the will bowed to the will of God, and the affections made spiritual and heavenly: so that the man is not what he was—old things are passed away, all things are become new; he acts from

## 2: Pardon and Redemption

new principles, by new rules, with new designs. (Romans 12:2)

Sanctification is the preparation of the soul for glory, making it meet to partake of the inheritance of the saints in light. This is God's work. We can destroy ourselves fast enough, but we cannot save ourselves. Sinners fit themselves for hell, but it is God that prepares saints for heaven; and all those that God designs for heaven hereafter he prepares and fits for heaven now: he works them to the self-same thing, 2 Cor. 5:5. (Romans 9:22-24)

The gospel proclaims liberty to those who were bound with fears and makes it their duty to take hold of their liberty. Let those who have been weary and heavily laden under the burden of sin, finding relief in Christ, shake themselves from the dust of their doubts and fears and loose themselves from those bands; for, *if the Son makes them free, they shall be free indeed.* (Isaiah 52:1-2)

Holy fear prepares the soul for holy joy; the spirit of bondage makes way for the spirit of adoption. God wounds first, and then heals; humbles first, and then lifts up, Isa. 6:5, 6, etc. (Genesis 15:12)

God keeps up his interest in men's souls by giving them a good understanding and a right knowledge of things, Heb. 8:11. (Hosea 2:8)

From whom may we better expect the light of divine revelation than from him who gave us the light of human reason? (John 1:4)

The more conversant we are with God's holiness the more we shall see of the odious nature of sin. There *you shall loathe yourselves in your own sight.* (Ezekiel 20:43)

It is easier to set a man against all the world than against himself, and yet this must be in conversion. (Matthew 7:13)

Sin is defiling, idolatry particularly is so; it renders sinners odious to God and burdensome to themselves. When guilt is pardoned, and the corrupt nature sanctified, then we are cleansed from our filthiness, and there is no other way of being saved from it. (Ezekiel 36:29)

When God pardons sin he cleanses us from it, so that we become acceptable to him, easy to ourselves, and have liberty of access to him. (Psalm 51:2)

Sins leave a stain upon the soul, a stain of guilt and of pollution. Nothing can fetch out this stain but the blood of Christ; and, rather than it should not be washed out, Christ was willing to shed his own blood, to purchase pardon and purity for them. (Revelation 1:5)

[T]here is no piety without purity. A care to keep ourselves unspotted from the world is necessary in order to our acceptance with God. (2 Corinthians 6:6-7)

The way from Babylon to Zion, from the bondage of sin to the glorious liberty of God's children, is a highway; it is right, it is plain, it is safe, it is well-tracked (Isa. 35:8); yet none are likely to walk in it, unless they *set their heart towards it*. (Jeremiah 31:21-22)

*Go, and sin no more*. Impunity emboldens malefactors, and therefore those who are guilty, and yet have found means to escape the edge of the law, need to double their watch, *lest Satan get advantage;* for the fairer the escape was, the fairer the warning was to go and sin no more. (John 8:10-11)

All that have an interest in the new covenant, and a title to the new Jerusalem, have a new heart and a new spirit, and these are necessary in order to their walking in *newness of life*. This is that *divine nature* which believers are by the promises made partakers of. (Ezekiel 36:29)

Whereas, by the guilt of sin, we are bound over to the justice of God, are his lawful captives, sold for sin till payment be made of that great debt, Christ lets us know that he has made satisfaction to divine justice for that debt, that his satisfaction is accepted, and if we will plead that, and depend upon it, and make over ourselves and all we have to him, in a grateful sense of the kindness he has done us, we may by faith sue out our pardon and take the comfort of it; there is, and shall be, *no condemnation to us*. (Isaiah 61:1-3)

The world is God's by right of creation, but the church is his by right of redemption, and therefore it ought to be dear to us, for it was dear to him, because it cost him dear.... (Acts 20:28)

Note, those that belong to Christ have him ready to appear vigorously for them when Satan appears most vehement against them. He does not parley with him, but stops his mouth immediately with this sharp reprimand: *The Lord rebuke thee, O Satan!* ... Christ is ready to make the best of his people, and takes notice of every thing that is pleadable in excuse of their infirmities, so far is he from being extreme to mark what they do amiss. ... A converted soul is a *brand plucked out of the fire* by a miracle of free grace, and therefore shall not be left to be a prey to Satan. (Zechariah 3:1-2)

David ... was brought to the last extremity, dropping into the grave, and ready *to go down into the pit,* and yet rescued and kept alive. ... A life from the dead ought to be spent in extolling the God of our life. (Psalm 30:3)

There is an order among the three persons, though no superiority; they are equal in power and glory, and there is an agreed economy in their works. Thus, in the affair of man's redemption, election is by way of eminency ascribed to the Father, as reconciliation is to the Son and sanctification to the Holy Ghost, though in each of these one person is not so entirely interested as to exclude the other two. Hereby the persons of the Trinity are more clearly discovered to us, and we are taught what obligations we are under to each of them distinctly. (1 Peter 1:2)

In the work of our redemption we ought to take notice how brightly all the divine attributes shine, and give to God the praise of each of them. (Psalm 40:10)

As to Satan, we were a prey in the hand of the mighty, and yet delivered even from him that had the power of death, by him that had the power of life. As to the justice of God, we were lawful captives, and yet delivered by a price of inestimable value. (Isaiah 49:24)

See the power of God over the fiercest creatures, and believe his power to restrain the roaring lion that *goes about continually seeking to devour* from hurting those that are his. (Daniel 6:21-22)

Those that give themselves to God shall be accepted of God, their persons first and then their performances, through the Mediator. (Ezekiel 43:27)

The indwelling of the Spirit is an infallible pledge of the continuance of God's favour. He will hide his face no more from those on whom he has *poured out his Spirit*. When therefore we pray that God would never *cast us away from his presence* we must as earnestly pray that, in order to that, he would *never take his Holy Spirit away from us*, Ps. 51:11. (Ezekiel 39:29)

We have reason to be afraid of approaching to God if we be not clothed and fenced with the righteousness of Christ, for nothing but this will be armour of proof and cover the shame of our nakedness. Let us therefore *put on the Lord Jesus Christ*, and then draw near with humble boldness. (Genesis 3:10)

One of the first symptoms of guilt in our first parents was blushing at their own nakedness. Sin makes us loathsome in the sight of God and utterly unfit for communion with him, and, when conscience is awakened, it makes us loathsome to ourselves too; but, when sin is pardoned, it is covered with the robe of Christ's righteousness, like the coats of skins wherewith God clothed Adam and Eve (an emblem of the remission of sins), so that God is no longer displeased with us, but perfectly reconciled. They are not covered from us (no; *My sin is ever before me*) nor covered from God's omniscience, but from his vindictive justice. (Psalm 32:1)

Those only than can in sincerity call Christ their *beloved*, their *best beloved*, can upon good grounds, desire him to hasten his second coming. As for those whose hearts go a whoring after the world, and who set their affections on the things of the earth, they cannot love his appearing, but dread it rather, because then the earth, and all the things of it, which they have chosen for their portion, will be burnt up. (Song of Solomon 8:14)

Need drives many to God who had set themselves at a distance from him. Those that slighted him in the day of their prosperity will be glad to flee to him in the day of their affliction. (Jeremiah 16:19-21)

When God has remarkably delivered us from the deaths wherewith we were surrounded we must look upon it that for this end, among others, we were spared, that we might glorify God and edify others by making a penitent acknowledgment of our sins. (Ezekiel 12:16)

We should be more thoughtful what will become of us after death than how, or when, or where, we shall die, and more desirous to be told how we may conduct ourselves well in our sickness, and get good to our souls by it, than whether we shall recover from it. (2 Kings 1:2)

It is good for us, when we are sick, to think and speak of death, for sickness is sent on purpose to put us in mind of it; and, if we be duly mindful of it ourselves, we may in faith put God in mind of it…. (Job 7:7)

[A]ll things considered, our going out of the world is a greater kindness than our coming into the world was. … [T]hough … there was joy *when a child was born into the world*, and where there is death there is lamentation, yet, as to ourselves, if we lived so as to merit *a good name, the day of our death*, which will put a period to our cares, and toils, and sorrows, and remove us to rest, and joy, and eternal satisfaction, *is better than the day of our birth*, which ushered us into a world of so much sin and trouble, vanity and vexation. We were born to uncertainty, but a good man does not die at uncertainty. *The day of our birth* clogged our souls with the burden of the flesh, but the *day of our death* will set them at liberty from that burden. (Ecclesiastes 7:1-6)

God would hereby show us the lamentable imperfection of all persons and things under the sun, that we may look for complete holiness and happiness in the other world, and not in this. (Judges Introduction)

Those who know the value of Christ and heaven will readily acknowledge it far better to be in heaven than to be in this world, to be with Christ than to be with any creature; for in this world we are compassed about with sin, born to trouble, born again to it; but, if we come to be with Christ, farewell sin and temptation, farewell sorrow and death, for ever. (Philippians 1:23)

When our dear relations and friends die in Christ, we have no reason to weep for them, who have put off the burden of the flesh, are made perfect in holiness, and have entered into perfect rest and joy, but for ourselves and our children, who are left behind in a world of sins, and sorrows, and snares. (Luke 23:28)

When God's providence removes our relations and friends from us we ought to be humbled for our misconduct towards them while they were with us. (1 Samuel 25:1)

It is good for us to be often thinking and speaking of our death, and of the sufferings which, it is likely, we may meet with betwixt this and the grave; and thus, by making them more famil-

## 2: Pardon and Redemption

iar, they would become less formidable. (Matthew 20:18-19)

When we come to die ourselves, it is good to call to mind the death of our dear relations and friends, that have gone before us, to make death and the grave the more familiar to us. (Genesis 48:7)

If we be at peace with God, and have made a covenant with him, we have in effect made a covenant with death that it shall come in the fittest time, that whenever it comes, it shall be no terror to us, nor do us any real damage.... (Isaiah 28:15)

Those that walk in their uprightness while they live shall enter into peace when they die, Isa. 57:2. (Psalm 37:37)

Death, to a godly man, is like a fair gale of wind to convey him to the heavenly country, but, to a wicked man, it is like an east wind, a storm, a tempest, that hurries him away in confusion and amazement, to destruction. (Job 27:20-21)

[M]oles (they say) open their eyes when they are dying. Sense of unpardoned guilt will make death indeed the king of terrors. Those that have baffled their convictions will perhaps, in their dying moments, be overpowered by them. (2 Samuel 1:9)

[T]here are many who desire to die the death of the righteous, but do not endeavour to live the life of the righteous.

Gladly would they have their end like theirs, but not their way. They would be saints in heaven, but not saints on earth. (Numbers 23:10)

We cannot judge of men's state on the other side death either by the manner of their death or the frame of their spirits in dying. Men may die like lambs, and yet have their place with the goats. (Psalm 73:1-5)

The paths of death are trodden paths, but *vestigial nulla retrorsum—none can retrace their steps*. (1 Chronicles 1:28-54)

"It is true," said that blessed martyr, Bishop Hooper, "life is sweet, and death bitter; but eternal life is more sweet, and eternal death more bitter." (Luke 12:5)

Man is a strange sort of creature, a ray of heaven united to a clod of earth; at death these are separated, and each goes to the place whence it came. ... The soul does not die with the body; it is *redeemed from the power of the grave*.... It goes *to God* as a Judge, to give account of itself, and to be lodged either with the *spirits in prison* (1 Pet. 3:19) or with *the spirits in paradise* (Luke 23:43), according to what was done in the body. This makes death terrible to the wicked ... and comfortable to the godly.... (Ecclesiastes 12:7)

What foolish insignificant projects do proud men fill their heads with! And what care they take about the disposal of their bodies, when they are dead, that have no care at all what shall become of their precious souls! (2 Samuel 18:18)

[T]hink of death as our removal from a world of sense to a world of spirits, the final period of our state of trial and probation, and our entrance upon an unchangeable state of recompense and retribution. (Deuteronomy 32:29)

The soul of a beast is, at death, like a candle blown out—there is an end of it; whereas the soul of a man is then like a candle taken out of a dark lantern, which leaves the lantern useless indeed, but does itself shine brighter. This great difference there is between the spirits of men and beasts; and a good reason it is why men should *set their affections on things above*, and lift up their souls to those things, not suffering them, as if they were the souls of brutes, to cleave to this earth. (Ecclesiastes 3:19-21)

God in judgment remembers mercy; and may yet have good things in store for those whose condition seems most forlorn. There is *hope of a tree, if it be cut down, that it will sprout again, that through the scent of water it will bud,* Job 14:7-9. (Daniel 4:15)

# -3-

# Mercy and Grace

For great is thy mercy towards me. The fountain of mercy is inexhaustibly full; the streams of mercy are inestimably rich. ...Thou hast delivered my soul from the lowest hell, from death, from so great a death ... from eternal death....

Matthew Henry
on Psalm 86:13

*For great is thy mercy towards me.* The fountain of mercy is inexhaustibly full; the streams of mercy are inestimably rich. ...*Thou hast delivered my soul from the lowest hell,* from death, from so great a death ... from eternal death.... (Psalm 86:13)

This is applicable to our redemption by Christ; it was in love to our souls, our poor perishing souls, that he delivered them from the bottomless pit, snatched them as brands out of everlasting burnings. (Isaiah 38:17)

[T]hose who would receive grace and mercy from Christ, must ascribe honour and glory to Christ, and approach to him with humility and reverence. (Mark 1:40)

Those who would find mercy when they are in distress must show mercy when they are in prosperity. (1 Timothy 5:10)

Those that are truly sensible of the mercy they receive from God will without grudging show mercy to the poor. (Leviticus 23:22)

Those are best prepared for the greatest mercies that see themselves unworthy of the least. (Genesis 32:10)

Those that would obtain mercy from Christ, must throw themselves at his feet; must refer themselves to him, humble themselves before him, and give up themselves to be ruled by him. Christ never put any from him, that fell at his feet, which a poor trembling soul may do, that has not boldness and confidence to throw itself into his arms. (Mark 7:26)

Even those that are under the tokens of God's wrath must not despair of his mercy; and mercy, mere mercy, is that which we must flee to for refuge, and rely upon as our only plea. (Habakkuk 3:2)

Some have not yet *grace to repent,* yet it is a mercy to them to have *space to repent*.... (Luke 13:8-9)

God has mercy in store, rich mercy, sure mercy, suitable mercy, for all that in sincerity seek him and submit to him; and the more we are afflicted for sin the better prepared we are for the comforts of that mercy. (Jeremiah 31:18)

The long want of mercies greatly sweetens their return. (Psalm 126:1-3)

It is a great mercy to be delivered from our fears, and to have our doubts resolved, so as to proceed in our affairs with satisfaction. (Matthew 1:20)

Those who desire God's favour as better than life cannot but dread and deprecate his wrath as worse than death. (Psalm 79:4-5)

Of all the bitter fruits and consequences of sin, that which true penitents most lament, and dread most, is God's departure from them. (Exodus 33:4)

There is no fleeing God's justice but by

## 3: Mercy and Grace

fleeing to his mercy. (Jeremiah 19:7)

As the old world was ruined to be a monument of justice, so this world remains to this day, a monument of mercy, according to the oath of God, that the waters of Noah should no more return to cover the earth, Isa. 54:9. ... Sin which drowned the old world, will burn this. (Genesis 9:11)

Gracious souls look down upon the world with a holy disdain and look up to God with a holy desire. (Psalm 63:1-2)

Gracious souls can receive those truths of God with great delight which speak most terror to wicked people. (Ezekiel 3:2-3)

It were well if the disappointment which some have met with in the service of sin, and the pernicious consequences of it to them, might prevail to deter others from treading in their steps. (Jeremiah 16:19-21)

Grace and glory are attainable by all under the gospel: there is an offer, and a promise to those who shall accept the offer. (Hebrews 4:1)

It is just with God to deny his grace to those who have long and often refused the proposals of it, and resisted the power of it. (Matthew 13:15)

The day is coming when those that make light of divine mercy will beg hard for it. O for *mercy, mercy,* when the day of mercy is over, and offers of mercy are no more made. (Luke 16:24)

We are often taught to value mercies by the loss of them which, when we enjoyed them, we did not prize as we ought. (2 Chronicles 35:24-25)

Thus many are taught to lament the loss of those mercies which they would not learn to be thankful for the enjoyment of. (Numbers 20:29)

Grace despised is grace forfeited, like Esau's birthright. They that will not have Christ when they *may* shall not have him when they *would*. Even those that *were bidden,* if they slight the invitation, *shall be for*bidden; when the door is shut, the foolish virgins will be denied entrance. (Luke 14:21)

Miserable is the case of those who have sinned so long against God's mercy that at length they have sinned it away. (Jeremiah 15:6)

We abuse God's mercy when we reckon that his favours countenance and patronize our follies. (Genesis 30:17-19)

God's gifts are upon condition, and revocable upon non-performance of the condition. Mercies abused are forfeited, and it is just with God to take the forfeiture. (Jeremiah 8:13-16)

When the streams of mercy are stopped we can expect no other than that the vials of wrath should be opened. Those whom God will no more have mercy upon shall be utterly taken away, as dross and dung. (Hosea 1:6-7)

God had said ... *I am he that blotteth out thy transgression,* which is the only thing that creates this distance; and when that is taken away the streams of mercy run again in their former channel. The pardon of sin is the inlet of all the other blessings of the covenant. (Isaiah 44:1-2)

"... God is not a man that he should lie. The fountain of life will never be to his people as *waters that fail*." (Jeremiah 15:18)

If God be the fountain of all our mercies, he must be the centre of all our joys. (Psalm 85:6)

*Father sanctify them,* that is, [1.] "Confirm the work of sanctification in them, strengthen their faith, inflame their good affections, rivet their good resolutions." [2.] "Carry on that good work in them, and continue it; let the *light shine more and more*." [3.] "Complete it, crown it with the perfection of holiness; sanctify them throughout and to the end." ... It is the prayer of Christ for all that are his that they may be sanctified.... (John 17:17-19)

Those that have wisdom and grace have that which cannot be taken away from them, whatever else they are robbed of. (Genesis 39:2-3)

None of those shall be lost whom God has marked for life and salvation; for the foundation of God stands sure. (Ezekiel 9:6)

It is God's great mercy to us that we are alive; and the mercy is the more sensible if we have been at death's door and yet have been spared and raised up, just turned to destruction and yet ordered to return. That a life so often forfeited, and so often exposed, should yet be lengthened out, is a miracle of mercy. The deliverance of the soul from spiritual and eternal death is especially to be acknowledged by all those who are now sanctified and shall be shortly glorified. (Psalm 116:8)

Upon a sick-bed, particularly, we should consider our ways and commune with our own hearts about them. (Psalm 4:4)

When God has at any time restored us our health we ought to attend him with solemn praises (Ps. 116:18, 19), and the sooner the better, while the sense of mercy is fresh. ... [F]or it is common for people, when they are sick, to *promise much,* when newly recovered to *perform something,* but after awhile to *forget all*. (John 5:7-8)

When we are desiring and expecting mercy from God we should bind our souls with a bond that we will faithfully do our duty to him, particularly that we will honour him with the mercy we are in the pursuit of. (Numbers 21:2)

When we have received some signal

## 3: Mercy and Grace

mercy from God, it is very fit that we should express our thankfulness by some special act of pious charity. (Genesis 14:20)

It is justly expected that those who have received mercy from God should study to make some suitable returns for the mercies they have received; and, if they do not, their ingratitude will certainly be charged upon them. (2 Chronicles 32:25)

Those that have been dying and yet are living, whose life is from the dead, are in a special manner obliged to praise God, as being most sensibly affected with his goodness. (Isaiah 38:19)

Those whom God designs to exalt and enlarge he first humbles and straitens for a time. (Ezekiel 3:15)

We all owe it to the sparing mercy of God *that we are not consumed*. Others have been consumed round about us, and we ourselves have been in the consuming, and yet *we are not consumed*; we are out of the grave; we are out of hell. Had we been dealt with *according to our sins*, we should have been consumed long ago; but we have been dealt with *according to God's mercies*, and we are bound to acknowledge it to his praise. (Lamentations 3:22)

Distinguishing preservations, in times of general destruction, are special tokens of God's favour, and ought so to be acknowledged. If we are safe when thousands fall on our right hand and our left, are not consumed when others are consumed round about us, so that we are as brands plucked out of the fire, we have reason to say, *It is of the Lord's mercies*, and it is a great mercy. (Matthew 24:40-41)

If, when we are at a loss, we meet seasonably with those that can direct us — if we meet with a disaster, and those are at hand who will help us — we must not say that it was by chance, nor that fortune therein favoured us, but that it was by Providence, and that God therein favoured us. (Genesis 29:1-3)

If our friends be kind to us, it is God that makes them so, that puts it into their hearts, and into the power of their hands, to be so, and we must give him the glory of it. ... [W]e should lift up our hearts to heaven in thanksgiving; blessed be God that there are so many excellent ones on this earth, bad as it is. (Acts 28:15)

In a world of wicked people God could see one righteous Noah; that single grain of wheat could not be lost, no, not in so great a heap of chaff. *The Lord knows those that are his.* (Genesis 7:1)

The best saints must acknowledge themselves indebted to sparing mercy that they are not consumed. ... We must look upon it that for this reason we are spared, that we may do good in our places, may do good by our prayers. (Ezekiel 9:8)

Gracious souls are apt to think lowly of their own good deeds; especially as unworthy to be compared with the glory that shall be revealed. (Matthew 25:37-39)

Lest it should be thought that deliverance was granted for the sake of some worthiness in his [the psalmist's] prayer, he ascribes it to God's mercy. ... "It was not my prayer that fetched the deliverance, but his mercy that sent it." (Psalm 66:19-20)

Misery is the object of mercy. Now both the consequences of sin, by which we have become truly miserable ... and the nature of repentance, by which we are made sensible of our misery and are brought to bemoan ourselves ... both these make us objects of pity, and with God there are tender mercies. ... *He will abundantly pardon*. (Isaiah 55:6-7)

The way to forget the sense of our miseries is to remember the God of our mercies. (Psalm 42:6)

God's mercies to his people have been *ever of old* (Ps. 25:6); and therefore we may hope, even then when he seems to have forsaken or forgotten them, that the mercy which was *from everlasting* will be *to everlasting*. (Lamentations 5:19-22)

We ought to transmit to posterity the memorial of God's judgments as well as of his mercies. (Joel 1:3)

Time is apt to wear out the sense of mercies and the impressions made upon us by them; it should not be so, but so it is. (Genesis 35:1-2)

[T]ime, as it does not wear out the guilt of sin, so it should not wear out the sense of mercy. (Psalm 114:1-2)

God glorifies himself, and we must glorify him, in those mercies that have no miracles in them, as well as in those that have. And, though the favours of God to our fathers must not be forgotten, yet those to ourselves in our own day we must especially give thanks for. (Jeremiah 16:15-16)

When God repeats former mercies we must repeat former praises; we find the song of Moses sung in the New Testament, Rev. 15:3. (Hosea 2:14-15)

A prayer for further mercy is fitly begun with a thanksgiving for former mercy; and when we are waiting upon God to bless us we should stir up ourselves to bless him. (Psalm 144:1)

The receipt of former mercies may encourage us to hope for future mercies; for God is constant in his care for his people, and his compassions are still new. (Isaiah 42:9)

If God gives us not only the word, but the hearing ear, not only the means of grace, but a heart to make a good use of those means, we have reason to say, He is very gracious to us, and reason to hope he has yet further mercy in store for us. (Isaiah 30:21)

## 3: Mercy and Grace

Where there is the truth of grace there will be increase of it. *The path of the just is as the shining light, which shines more and more unto the perfect day.* And where there is the increase of grace God must have all the glory of it. We are as much indebted to him for the improvement of grace, and the progress of that good work, as we are for the first work of grace and the very beginning of it. (2 Thessalonians 1:3)

Grace in the soul is the work of God's own hands, and therefore he will not forsake it in this world (Ps. 138:8), but will have a desire to it, to perfect it in the other, and to crown it with endless glory. (Job 14:15)

Assurances of future mercy must not be interpreted as securities from present troubles. (Jeremiah 32:26-27)

We have our cares at the same time that we have our joys, and they may serve for a balance to each other, that neither may exceed. ... Our calamities serve as foils to our joys. ...[t]hat we may not be secure, but always rejoice with trembling, as those that know not how soon we may be returned into the furnace again, which we were lately taken out of as the silver is when it is not thoroughly refined. (Psalm 60:1-5)

Let us therefore always rejoice with trembling, and never expect a perfect security, nor a perpetual security, till we come to heaven. (Acts 27:14-16)

Many former trials will not supersede nor secure us from further trials; we have not yet put off the harness.... (Genesis 22:1)

It may be of use to be often reminded of our sorrows, that we may always have such thoughts of things as we had in the day of our affliction, and may learn to rejoice with trembling. (1 Chronicles 4:9)

God consults our benefit rather than our desires; for he knows what is good for us better than we do for ourselves, and how long it is fit our restraints should continue and desired mercies should be delayed. (Genesis 8:13-14)

It is a good sign that God is coming towards a people in ways of mercy when they begin to be tenderly affected under his hand. (Jeremiah 50:4-5)

Our sense of private grievances should be drowned in our thanksgiving for public mercies. (Isaiah 33:24)

As God will forgive those that forgive their brethren; so he will not judge those that will not judge their brethren; the *merciful shall find mercy.* It is an evidence of humility, charity, and deference to God, and shall be owned and rewarded by him accordingly. (Matthew 7:1)

When we are receiving any special mercy from God we ought more carefully than ever to watch against all impurity. (Isaiah 52:11)

[There is] ... the constant struggle ... between grace and corruption in the souls of believers; they are in them *as two armies* continually skirmishing.... (Song of Solomon 6:13)

It is a great mercy to be stopped in a sinful way either by conscience or by Providence. (Genesis 16:7-9)

It may be presumed that those willingly yield to a temptation (whatever they pretend) who will not use the means and helps they might be furnished with to avoid and overcome it. (Deuteronomy 22:23-24)

The safety and preservation of the saints are owing, not only to the divine grace in proportioning the strength to the trial, but to the divine providence in proportioning the trial to the strength. (John 18:9)

Those whom God designs for any service his providence shall concur with his grace to prepare and qualify for it. (1 Samuel 16:23)

1. There is a proneness in good men to be over-confident of their own strength and stability. We are ready to think ourselves able to grapple with the strongest temptations, to go through the hardest and most hazardous services, and to bear the greatest afflictions for Christ; but it is because we do not know ourselves. 2. Those often fall soonest and foulest that are most confident of themselves. Those are least safe that are most secure. (Matthew 26:35)

There may be much corruption lurking, nay, and stirring too, in the hearts of good people, and they themselves not be sensible of it. (Luke 9:55)

The carnal mind is very ingenious to *shift off* convictions, and to keep them from fastening, careful to *cover the sin*. (John 4:17-18)

Let him who thinks he stands take heed lest he fall. We see how weak we are of ourselves, without the grace of God; let us therefore live in a constant dependence on the grace. (1 Kings 11:6-8)

Let those therefore that stand take heed lest they fall, and those that have fallen not despair of being helped up again. (Genesis 26:7)

Where grace does not work, corruption will. (Isaiah 5:1)

Those that have the most grace themselves cannot give grace to their children. It has often been the grief of good men to see their posterity, instead of treading in their steps, trampling upon them, and, as Job speaks, *marring their path*. (1 Samuel 8:3)

Grace does not run in the blood, but corruption does. A sinner begets a sinner, but a saint does not beget a saint. (Genesis 5:3)

Sin is that to which naturally we cleave; the design of divine grace is to turn us from it, nay, to turn us against it, that we may not only forsake it, but hate it. The gospel has a direct tenden-

## 3: Mercy and Grace

cy to do this, not only as it requires us, every one of us, to turn from our iniquities, but as it promises us grace to enable us to do so. (Acts 3:26)

Thus there is no way of appeasing God's anger but by mortifying and crucifying our lusts and corruptions. In vain do we expect mercy from God, unless we do justice upon our sins. (2 Samuel 21:9)

Man is not a sincere creature, but partial, blind, and wicked, till he be renewed and sanctified by the regenerating grace of God. (1 Peter 4:3)

We cannot offer unto the Lord any right performances in religion unless our persons be justified and sanctified. Till we ourselves be refined and purified by the grace of God, we cannot do any thing that will redound to the glory of God. God had respect to Abel first, and then to his offering; and *therefore* God purges his people, that they may offer their offerings to him in righteousness, Zeph. 3:9. He makes the tree good that the fruit may be good. (Malachi 3:3)

Nothing goes to God but what comes from him. We must have grace, that holy fire, from the God of grace, else we cannot *serve him acceptably*, Heb. 12:28. (Leviticus 9:23-24)

Jesus Christ is very tender toward those that have true grace, though they are but weak in it, and accepts the willingness of the spirit, pardoning and passing by the weakness of the flesh. (Isaiah 42:1-3)

When we had baptism in the room of circumcision, the Lord's supper in the room of the passover, and a gospel ministry in the room of a Levitical priesthood, we had gold instead of brass. Sin turned gold into brass when Rehoboam made brazen shields instead of the golden ones he had pawned; but God's favour, when that returns, will turn brass again into gold. (Isaiah 60:17)

This teaches us that grace, and not gold, is the best riches, and acquaintance with God and his law, not with arts and sciences, the best knowledge. (2 Chronicles 8:18)

[K]nowledge without grace does but make men the more *ingeniously* wicked. (Luke 23:10-11)

The wonders of grace exceed the wonders of nature; and what is discovered of God by revelation is much greater than what is discovered by reason. (Psalm 138:1-5)

Such is the nature of worldly wealth, plenty of it makes it the less valuable; much more should the enjoyment of spiritual riches lessen our esteem of all earthly possessions. If *gold in abundance* would make silver to seem so despicable, shall not wisdom, and grace, and the foretastes of heaven, which are far better than gold, make earthly wealth seem much more despicable? (1 Kings 10:27)

All the pious workings of our heart towards God are the fruit and consequence of the powerful working of his grace in us. ... The way God takes of converting souls to himself is by opening the eyes of their understandings, and all good follows thereupon.... (Jeremiah 31:19)

So stupid are we that nothing less then the mighty hand of divine grace, known experimentally, can make us know rightly the name of God as it is revealed to us. (Jeremiah 16:21)

Those are best able to speak of the power of divine grace who have themselves experienced it. (2 Kings 5:15)

Those are best able to teach others the grace of God who have themselves had the experience of it: and those who are themselves taught of God ought to *tell others what he has done for their souls* (Ps. 66:16) and so teach them. (Psalm 32:8)

None are ruined by the justice of God but those that hate to be reformed by the grace of God. (Genesis 6:6-7)

None can be delivered out of the hands of God's justice but those that are delivered into the hands of his grace. It is in vain for a man to strive with his Maker. (Hosea 5:11-12)

There can be no true peace where there is not true grace; and, where grace goes before, peace will follow. (Revelation 1:4)

Those that love simplicity find themselves under a moral impotency to change their own mind and way; they cannot turn by any power of their own. To this God answers, *"Behold, I will pour out my Spirit unto you;* set yourselves to do what you can, and the grace of God shall set in with you, and work in you both to will and to do that good which, without that grace, you could not do." ... The author of this grace is the Spirit. ... Our Heavenly Father *will give the Holy Spirit to those that ask him.* (Proverbs 1:23)

It is a sign that God is about to appear remarkably for his people when he raises their believing expectations from him and dependence upon him, and when by his grace he turns them from idols to himself. (Zechariah 9:1)

Renewing grace works as great a change in the soul as the turning of a dead stone into living flesh. (Ezekiel 36:25-28)

Those who are, through grace, heirs of the land of promise, ought to remember what was the land of their nativity, what was their corrupt and sinful nature, the rock out of which they were hewn. (Genesis 11:28)

It is the great privilege which believers have through Christ that they are adopted children of the God of heaven. We who by nature are children of wrath and disobedience have become by grace children of love. (Galatians 4:5-7)

## 3: Mercy and Grace

God is pleased sometimes to favour young converts with such tokens of his love as are very encouraging to them, in reference to the difficulties they meet with at their setting out of the ways of God. (Matthew 2:10)

They who are carried by a holy zeal, to seek Christ diligently, will find the difficulties that lie in their way strangely to vanish, and themselves helped over them beyond their expectation. (Mark 16:3-4)

The work of grace, and its workings, are the same, for substance, in grown Christians that they are in young beginners, only that the former have got so much nearer their perfection. The faith of all the saints is alike precious, though it be not alike strong. There is a great resemblance between one child of God and another; for *all they are brethren* and bear the same image. (Ezekiel 40:27-38)

Note, it is very beneficial and comfortable for those that have a good work of grace begun in their souls, and Christ in the *forming* there, to consult those who are in the same case, that they may communicate experiences one to another; and they will find that, as in water face answers to face, so doth the heart of man to man, of Christian to Christian. (Luke 1:39-42)

Those who possess spiritual blessings in their own souls earnestly desire the communication of the same to others. The grace of God is a generous, not a selfish principle. (1 Peter 1:2)

True grace hates monopolies. Those that have found mercy themselves should endeavour that through their mercy others also may obtain mercy. (Romans 11:25)

Those that have grace have need to be called upon again and again to exercise grace and to improve in it. (Joshua 1:9)

God keeps an account, whether we do or no, how long we have enjoyed the means of grace; and the longer we have enjoyed them the heavier will our account be if we have not improved them. (Jeremiah 25:3)

True grace hates monopolies, and loves not to eat its morsels alone. (John 1:41-42)

The meanest of those that *follow the Lamb* far excel the greatest of those that went before him. Those therefore who live under the gospel dispensation have so much the more to answer for. (Luke 7:29)

Frequently those who are nearest to the means of knowledge and grace, are most negligent. Familiarity and easiness of access breed some degree of contempt. (Matthew 12:46)

Men's pride and envy make them scorn to be instructed by those who once were their school-fellows and play-fellows. Desire of novelty, and of that which is far-fetched and dear-bought, and seems to drop out of the sky to them, makes them despise those persons and things which they have long been used to and know the rise of. (John 4:43-44)

Those are fools indeed who are fools in *their latter end;* ... Those that get grace will be wise *in the latter end,* will have the comfort of it in death and the benefit of it to eternity.... (Jeremiah 17:11)

A holy heart will be a comfort to us when the holy flesh has passed from us; an inward principle of grace will make up the want of the outward means of grace. But woe unto us if the departure of the holy flesh be accompanied with the departure of the Holy Spirit. (Jeremiah 11:15)

The means of grace are moveable things; and the candlestick, when we think it stands most firmly, may be removed out of its place (Rev. 2:5); and those that now slight the *days of the son of man* may wish in vain to see them. (Amos 8:12-13)

The calling in of the Gentiles was accompanied with the rejection of the Jews; it was their fall, and the *diminishing of them, that was the riches of the Gentiles;* and the casting *off of them* was *the reconciling of the world*.... (Isaiah 2:6)

At the first planting of Israel in Canaan, the *fall of the Gentiles was the riches of Israel,* (Ps. 135:10, 11), so, at their extirpation, the fall of Israel was the riches of the Gentiles, Rom. 11:12. It shall go to *a nation bringing forth the fruits thereof.* (Matthew 21:41)

As Jews and Gentiles, if they believe, are equally acceptable to God and good men; so, if they do not, they are equally abominable. (Acts 13:50-51)

It were ill with us if God did not sometimes graciously thrust upon us those means of grace and salvation which we have foolishly thrust from us. (Ezekiel 1:1-3)

The Christian religion is a revealed religion, has its rise in heaven; it is a religion from above, given by inspiration of God, not the learning of philosophers, nor the politics of statesmen. (Matthew 16:17)

Sometimes more of the power of religion is found in those places and families that have made little show of it, and have enjoyed but little of the means of grace, than in others that have distinguished themselves by a flourishing profession; and then more are the children of the desolate, more the fruits of their righteousness, than those of the married wife; so the last shall be first. (Isaiah 54:9)

Seeking the Lord is to be every day's work, but there are some special occasions given by the providence and grace of God when it is, in a particular manner, time to seek him. (Hosea 10:12)

Gospel times are the last days. For 1. They were long in coming, were a great while waited for by the Old-Testament saints, and came at last. 2. We are not to look for any dispensa-

## 3: Mercy and Grace

tion of divine grace but what we have in the gospel, Gal. 1:8, 9. 3. We are to look for the second coming of Jesus Christ at the end of time, just as the Old-Testament saints did for his first coming; *this is the last time....* (Isaiah 2:2)

# -4-

# Patience and Faith

[Jesus] is a precious stone, for such are the foundations of the New Jerusalem (Rev. 21:19), a corner stone, in whom the sides of the building are united, the head-stone of the corner. And he that believes these promises, and rests upon them, shall not make haste, shall not run to and fro in a hurry, as men at their wit's end, shall not be shifting hither and thither for his own safety...

Matthew Henry
on Isaiah 28:16

[Jesus] is a precious stone, for such are the foundations of the New Jerusalem (Rev. 21:19), a corner stone, in whom the sides of the building are united, *the head-stone of the corner*. And *he that believes* these promises, and rests upon them, *shall not make haste*, shall not run to and fro in a hurry, as men at their wit's end, shall not be shifting hither and thither for his own safety, nor be driven to his feet by any terrors, as the wicked man is said to be (Job 18:11), but with a fixed heart shall quietly wait the event, saying *Welcome the will of God*. He *shall not make haste* in his expectations, so as to anticipate the time set in the divine counsels, but, though it tarry, will wait the appointed hour.... (Isaiah 28:16)

We must wait with patience for the full discovery of that which to us seems intricate and perplexed, acknowledging that we *cannot find out the work that God makes from the beginning to the end*, and therefore must judge nothing before the time. We are to believe that God has made all beautiful. Every thing is done well, as in creation, so in providence, and we shall see it when the end comes, but till then we are incompetent judges of it. While the picture is in drawing, and the house in building, we see not the beauty of either; but when the artist has put his last hand to them, and given them their finishing strokes, then all appears very good. We see but the middle of God's works, not from the beginning of them (then we should see how admirably the plan was laid in the divine counsels), nor to the end of them, which crowns the action (then we should see the product to be glorious), but we must wait till the veil be rent, and not arraign God's proceedings nor pretend to pass judgment on them. *Secret things belong not to us*. (Ecclesiastes 3:11)

We may be sure of the righteousness, when we cannot see the reasons, of God's proceedings. (Judges 20:25)

God sees his work from the beginning to the end, but we do not .... How admirable are the projects of Providence! (Genesis 45:5-7)

God's providences often seem to contradict his promises, and to go cross to them; and yet, when the mystery of God shall be finished, we shall see that all was for the best, and that cross providences did but render the promises and accomplishment of them the more illustrious. (Genesis 28:1-5)

Providence may change, but the promise cannot. (Job 5:24)

God often works by contraries. ... [T]hose that put Christ to death were many of them saved by his death. (Genesis 45:7-8)

Often is the devil out-shot with his own bow. (1 Samuel 19:11-12)

The intentions of Providence commonly do not appear till a great while after the event, perhaps *many years* after. The sentences in the book of providence are sometimes *long*, and you must read a

## 4: Patience and Faith

great way before you can apprehend the sense of them. (John 9:3)

The methods of Providence are often intricate and perplexing, and such as the wisest and best of men know not what to say to; but *they shall know hereafter,* John 13:7. (Joshua 7:7-8)

Events that seem inconsiderable, and purely accidental, afterwards appear to have been designed by the wisdom of God for very good purposes, and of great consequence to his people. A casual transient occurrence has sometimes occasioned the greatest and happiest turns of a man's life. (Exodus 2:16-22)

Many a great affair is brought about by a little turn, which seemed fortuitous to us, but was directed by Providence with design. (Ruth 2:3)

The glory and goodness, the beauty and harmony, of God's works, both of providence and grace, as this of creation, will best appear when they are perfected. When the top-stone is brought forth we shall cry, *Grace, grace, unto it,* Zech. 4:7. Therefore judge nothing before the time. (Genesis 1:31)

The glory of the Lord will shortly be present. We now look upon it as distant, and too many look upon it as uncertain, but it will come, and it will be manifest and apparent. *Every eye shall see him,* Rev. 1:7. This is now the object of our faith, but hereafter (and surely it cannot *now* be long) it will be the object of our sense; whom we now believe in, him we shall shortly see, to our unspeakable joy and comfort or inexpressible terror and consternation. (Jude 24)

Promised salvations, though they always come surely, yet often come slowly. (John 11:17)

He that believeth will not make haste, or conclude that the promise will never be performed because it is not performed so soon as he expected. (Joshua 10:1-6)

True Christian fortitude consists more in a gracious security and serenity of mind, in patiently bearing and patiently waiting, than in daring enterprises with sword in hand. (Psalm 3:1-3)

[W]hile the cause is in trying between the kingdom of God and the kingdom of Satan it becomes all people silently to expect the issue, not to object against God's proceedings, but to be confident that he will carry the day. (Isaiah 41:1)

Suggestions that reflect dishonour upon God and his justice and holiness are rather to be startled at than parleyed with. Get thee behind me, Satan; never entertain such a thought. *For then how shall God judge the world?* (Romans 3:17-18)

God sometimes raises up very bad men to honour and power, spares them long, and suffers them to grow insufferably insolent, that he may be so much the more glorified in their destruction at last. (Exodus 9:16)

Part II: Wisdom (Salvation)

God has wise and holy ends in permitting the enemies of his glory to carry on their impious projects a great way, and to prosper long in their enterprises. (Genesis 11:5-9)

Even those duties that are most unpleasant to flesh and blood, are *profitable for us;* and our Master requires nothing from us but what he knows to be for our advantage. (Matthew 5:29-30)

Strong faith is often exercised with strong trials and put upon hard services. (Genesis 22:1)

Tribulation works patience in those that are sanctified. The more we bear the better able we should be to bear still more; what tries our patience should improve it. The more we are inured to trouble the less we should be surprised at it, and not think it strange. (2 Samuel 16:11)

Those that rejoice in hope are likely to be patient in tribulation. It is a believing prospect of the joy set before us that bears up the spirit under all outward pressure. (Romans 12:12)

We may be in the way of our duty and yet meet with trouble and danger. God orders it so for the trial of our confidence in him and the manifestation of his care concerning us. (2 Chronicles 32:1-2)

God brings his people into trouble, that they may experience his power and mercy in protecting and sheltering them, and may have occasion to praise him. (Psalm 59:16)

[A]ll things come ordinarily alike to all, and good men are oftentimes greatly afflicted in this life, for the exercise and improvement of their faith and patience. (Acts 28:4-5)

If we do imitate the faith and patience of good men in their afflictions, we may hope to partake of their consolations here and their salvation hereafter. (2 Corinthians 1:6)

Poor people must not demand kindness as a debt, but humbly ask it, and take it as a favour, though in ever so small a matter. (Ruth 2:2)

He make some poor, to exercise their patience, and contentment, and dependence upon God, and others rich, to exercise their thankfulness and beneficence. (Proverbs 22:2)

Acknowledging the wisdom of God in appointing us to poverty, we must be easy in it, patiently bear the inconveniences of it, be thankful for what we have, and make the best of that which is. It is to sit loose to all worldly wealth, and not set our hearts upon it.... (Matthew 5:3)

Providence sometimes favours those that deal in the world, and prospers them, that people may be encouraged to set their hands to worldly business; at other times Providence crosses them, that people may be warned not to set their hearts upon it. Events are thus

## 4: Patience and Faith

varied, that we may learn both how to want and how to abound. (Acts 28:11)

It is good for us to accommodate ourselves to the place and condition which God, in his providence, has put us in. (Matthew 3:4)

Man proposes, but God disposes, and in his disposal we must acquiesce, and set ourselves to follow providence. (Exodus 13:17-18)

After we have been admitted into the communion of God, we must expect to be set upon by Satan. The enriched soul must double its guard. *When thou has eaten and art full, then beware.* (Matthew 4:1)

Trouble of soul sometimes follows after great enlargements of spirit. In this world of mixture and change we must expect damps upon our joy, and the highest degree of comfort to be the next degree to trouble. When Paul had been in the third heavens, he had a *thorn in the flesh.* (John 12:27)

God sometimes reserves the sharpest trials of his people by affliction and temptation for the latter end of their days. (Joshua 11:21-22)

When we have had the most comfortable communion with God, and the clearest discoveries of his favour to us, we may expect that Satan will set upon us (the richest ship is the pirate's prize), and that God will suffer him to do so, that the power of his grace may be manifested and magnified. (Luke 4:1-2)

The more sinners the more sin; and the multitude of offenders emboldens men. Infectious diseases are most destructive in populous cities; and sin is a spreading leprosy. (Genesis 6:1-2)

Note, 1. The more sinners there are the more sin there is: *When the wicked*, being countenanced by authority, grow numerous, and walk on every side, no marvel if *transgression increases,* as a plague in the country is said to increase when still more and more are infected with it. *Transgression* grows more impudent and bold, more imperious and threatening, when there are many to keep it in countenance. ... 2. The more sin there is the nearer is the ruin threatened. Let not *the righteous* have their faith and hope shocked by the increase of sin and sinners. Let them not say that they have *cleansed their hands in vain,* or that *God has forsaken the earth,* but wait with patience; the transgressors shall fall, the measure of their iniquity will be full, and then they shall fall from their dignity and power, and fall into disgrace and destruction, and *the righteous shall* have the satisfaction of *seeing their fall* (Ps. 37:34), perhaps in this world, certainly in the judgment of the great day, when the fall of God's implacable enemies will be the joy and triumph of glorified saints. (Proverbs 29:16)

When the mirth of carnal worldlings ceases the joy of the saints is as lively as ever; when the merry-hearted do sigh because the vine languishes the upright-hearted do sing because the covenant of grace, the fountain of their

## Part II: Wisdom (Salvation)

comforts and the foundation of their hopes, never fails. Those that rejoice in the Lord can rejoice in tribulation, and by faith may be in triumphs when all about them are in tears. (Isaiah 24:13-15)

Though the greatest part of mankind have all their comfort ruined by the emptying of the earth, and the making of that desolate, yet there are some few who understand their interests better, who have laid up their treasure in heaven and not in things below, and therefore can keep up their comfort and joy in God even *when the earth mourns and fades away*. (Isaiah 24:13-15)

There are those that are incensed against God's people, that *strive with them* ... that war against them ... that hate them, that seek their ruin, and are continually picking quarrels with them. But let not God's people ... render evil for evil; but wait God's time, and believe ... [t]hat they shall be quite ruined and undone. (Isaiah 41:11-12)

The malignant world thought they had seen enough of him, and *cried, Away with him; crucify him;* and so shall their doom be; they shall see him no more. Those only that see Christ with an eye of faith shall see him for ever. (John 14:19-20)

A good man may with an eye of faith see the same that Jacob saw with his bodily eyes, by believing that promise (Ps. 91:11), *He shall give his angels charge over thee*. (Genesis 32:1-2)

We look with an eye of faith further than we see with an eye of sense. (Psalm 4:6)

Note, (1.) Those that have the honour of age must therewith be content to take the burden of it. (2.) The eye of faith may be very clear even when the eye of the body is very much clouded. (Genesis 48:10)

Those that will be found faithful have need to be very bold. Those that are resolved to please God must not be afraid to displease any man. (Romans 10:19)

They who truly fear God, need not fear man; and they who are afraid of the least sin, need not be afraid of the greatest trouble. (Matthew 10:26-28)

Whenever there is an awful fear of God, there may be a cheerful faith in him: those that reverence his word may rely upon it. (Psalm 115:10)

Note, (1.) Where there is great faith, yet there may be many fears, 2 Cor. 7:5. (2.) God takes cognizance of his people's fears though ever so secret, and *knows their souls*, Ps. 31:7. (3.) It is the will of God that his people should not give way to prevailing fears, whatever happens. (Genesis 15:1)

(1.) It is the duty and interest of the people of God not to *be afraid of evil tidings*, not to be afraid of hearing bad news; and, when they do, not to be put into confusion by it and into an amazing expectation of worse and worse,

## 4: Patience and Faith

but whatever happens, whatever threatens, to be able to say, with blessed Paul, *None of these things move me,* neither will I *fear, though the earth be removed,* Ps. 46:2. (2.) The fixedness of the heart is a sovereign remedy against the disquieting fear of evil tidings. (Psalm 112:7-8)

*Fear not.* Unbelieving fears are enemies to spiritual joys; if they be cured, if they be conquered, joy will come of course; Christ comes to his people to *silence* their fears. (John 12:15)

Those that are faithful in well-doing need not fear those that are spiteful in evil-doing, for they have a God to trust to who has well-doers under the hand of his protection and evil-doers under the hand of his restraint. (Jeremiah 20:13)

*The Lord is round about his people* on every side. There is no gap in the hedge of protection which he makes round about his people, at which the enemy, who goes about them, seeking to do them a mischief, can find entrance, Job 1:10. (Psalm 125:2)

Those who have been sharers with each other in afflictions and mercies, dangers and deliverances, ought in consideration thereof to unite for their joint and mutual safety and protection; ... [T]hen, whatever difficulties there may be in the way of return of the dispersed, the Lord shall find out some way or other to remove them, as when he brought Israel out of Egypt he dried up the Red Sea and Jordan ... and led them to Canaan through the invincible embarrassments of a vast howling wilderness,... (Isaiah 11:13-16)

While trouble is prolonged, and deliverance is deferred, we must patiently wait for God and his gracious returns to us. While we *wait for him* by faith, we must *seek him* by prayer: our *souls* must *seek him,* else we do not seek so as to find. Our seeking will help to keep up our waiting. And to those who thus wait and seek God will be gracious; he will show them his *marvelous lovingkindness.* (Lamentations 3:25)

To all that by faith and prayer ask, seek, and knock, these doors shall at any time be opened; for the God of heaven is rich in mercy to all that call upon him. He not only keeps a good house, but keeps open house. (Psalm 78:23-25)

All patience includes all the kinds of it; not only bearing patience, but waiting patience. ... This is even unto long-suffering, that is, drawn out to a great length; not only to bear trouble awhile, but to bear it as long as God pleases to continue it. (Colossians 1:11)

[W]hen God keeps his people long waiting for mercy he sometimes is pleased to recompense them for their patience by *doubling* the worth of it when it comes. (Luke 1:7)

Affectionate professions of faith in Christ, and resignations to him, are the most prevailing petitions for mercy from him, and shall speed accordingly. (Mark 2:40-41)

## Part II: Wisdom (Salvation)

While promised mercies are delayed our unbelief and impatience are apt to conclude them denied. ... True believers sometimes find it hard to reconcile God's promises and his providences, when they seem to disagree. (Genesis 15:2-4)

Unbelieving hearts will gladly take any occasion to quarrel with the equity of God's proceedings, and to condemn him that is most just, Job 34:17. (Romans 3:5)

Note, (1.) If faith be kept up in an hour of temptation, though we may fall, yet we shall not be utterly cast down. Faith will quench Satan's fiery darts. (2.) Though there may be many failings in the faith of true believers, yet there shall not be a total and final failure of their faith. It is their seed, their root, remaining in them. (3.) It is owing to the mediation and intercession of Jesus Christ that the faith of his disciples, though sometimes sadly shaken, yet is not sunk. (Luke 22:31-32)

It is not the perfect faith that is required to justification (there may be acceptable faith where there are remainders of unbelief), but the prevailing faith, the faith that has the upper hand of unbelief. (Romans 4:3)

Weak believers, in their despondency, are ready to say, "God has forsaken his church and forgotten the sorrows of his people." But we have no more reason to question his promise and grace than we have to question his providence and justice. He is as sure a rewarder as he is a revenger. Away therefore with these distrusts and jealousies, which are the bane of friendship. (Isaiah 49:14)

See to what a low ebb the profession of religion may sometimes be brought, and how much the face of it may be eclipsed, that the most wise and observing men may give it up for gone. ... Things are often much better with the church of God than wise and good men think they are. They are ready to conclude hardly, and to give up all for gone, when it is not so. (Romans 11:1-5)

Weak and tender spirits are influenced more by fear than hope, and are more apt to receive impressions that are discouraging than those that are encouraging. (Genesis 45:26)

When God gives us the mercies we began to despair of we ought to remember with sorrow and shame our sinful distrusts of God's power and promise, when we were in pursuit of them. (Genesis 21:3)

Past experiences are great encouragements to faith and hope, and they lay great obligations to trust in God for time to come. We reproach our experiences if we distrust God in future straits, who hath delivered as in former troubles. (2 Corinthians 1:10)

God's house lies in the midst of an enemy's country, and his church is as a lily among thorns; and therefore God's power and goodness are to be observed in the special preservation of it. (Zechariah 9:8)

## 4: Patience and Faith

To know and believe in Jesus Christ, in the midst of a world that persists in ignorance and infidelity, is highly pleasing to God, and shall certainly be crowned with distinguishing glory. Singular faith qualifies for singular favours. (John 17:24-26)

Among men we say, "He that trusts another, gives him credit, and honours him by taking his word;" thus Abraham gave glory to God by trusting him. We never hear our Lord Jesus commending any thing so much as great faith (Matt. 8:10 and 15:28): therefore God gives honour to faith, great faith, because faith, great faith, gives honour to God. (Romans 4:20)

Doubting of the power and promise of God is the great thing that spoils the efficacy and success of faith. (Matthew 21:21-22)

*The righteous are bold as a lion.* Difficulties that lie in the way of salvation dwindle and vanish before a lively active faith in the power and promise of God. *All things are possible,* if they be but promised, *to him that believes.* (Numbers 13:30)

God looks down upon those with an eye of favour who sincerely look up to him with an eye of faith. (Genesis 6:8-10)

For by faith we stand firmly, and live safely and comfortably. Our strength and ability are owing to faith, and our comfort and joy must flow from faith. (2 Corinthians 1:24)

The perplexing, disquieting fears of good people, arise from their mistakes and misapprehensions concerning Christ, his person, offices, and undertaking; the more clearly and fully we know his name, with the more assurance we shall trust in him, Ps. 9:10. ...A little thing frightens us in a storm. ...If Christ's disciples be not cheerful in a storm, it is their own fault, he would have them so. ... The sinking of our spirits is owing to the weakness of our faith; we are upheld (but it is as we are saved) *through faith* (1 Pet. 1:5); and therefore, when our *souls are cast down and disquieted,* the sovereign remedy is, *to hope in God,* Ps. 43:5. ... When faith is weak, prayer should be strong. (Matthew 14:22-33)

A cheerful resignation to God is the way to obtain a cheerful satisfaction and confidence in God. (Psalm 3:4-8)

In our spiritual conflicts, we must look up to heaven for strength; and it is the believing prayer that will be the prevailing prayer. (1 Chronicles 5:20)

Good Christians often perplex themselves about that with which they should comfort and encourage themselves. (Luke 24:2-4)

When we are magnifying the causes of our fear we ought to possess ourselves with clear, and great, and high thoughts of God and the invisible world. *If God be for us,* we know what follows, Rom. 8:31. (2 Kings 6:16)

Even true and great believers some-

## Part II: Wisdom (Salvation)

times find it hard to trust God under the discouragements of second causes, and *against hope to believe in hope.* (Numbers 11:21-22)

Christ's disciples are often sad and sorrowful even when they have reason to rejoice, but through the weakness of their faith they cannot take the comfort that is offered to them. (Luke 24:17)

It is hard to take comfort from former smiles under present frowns. (Jeremiah 31:3)

Whatever hard things we suffer, we must never entertain any hard thoughts of God, but must still be ready to own that he is both kind and faithful. (Lamentations 3:21-23)

We are to be fully persuaded of the truth of all God's promises and threatenings, such a faith being of great use against temptations. Consider faith as it *is the evidence of things not seen and the substance of things hoped for,* and it will appear to be of admirable use for this purpose. (Ephesians 6:16)

Faith demonstrates to the eye of the mind the reality of those things that cannot be discerned by the eye of the body. Faith is the firm assent of the soul to the divine revelation and every part of it, and sets to its seal that God is true. (Hebrews 11:1-3)

We should think twice before we speak once…. (Job 2:13)

An offended conscience can find a time to speak when it will be heard, (Esther 6:1-3)

It is matter of comfort to us that the troubles which oppress our spirits are open before God's eye. (Lamentations 1:20)

God sometimes sends comforts to his people very seasonably, and, what time they are most afraid, encourages them to trust in him. (Isaiah 7:3)

What strange steps God sometimes takes in delivering his people; he often brings them to the utmost straits when he is just ready to appear for them. The lowest ebbs go before the highest tides; and very cloudy mornings commonly introduce the fairest days, Deut. 32:36. God's time to help is when things are at the worst; and Providence verifies the paradox, *The worse the better.* (Exodus 5:13-14)

God is preparing for his people's deliverance, when their way is darkest, and their distress deepest. (Acts 7:20)

God brings us into straits that he may bring us to our knees. (Exodus 14:10)

Man's extremity is God's opportunity of magnifying his own power; his time to appear for his people is when *their strength is gone,* Deut. 32:36, (2 Kings 7:1-2)

God often brings his people into great straits, that they may apprehend their own insufficiency to help themselves,

## 4: Patience and Faith

and may be induced to place their trust and hope in his all-sufficiency. Our extremity is God's opportunity. (2 Corinthians 1:9)

Thus are God's people sometimes made *to sow in tears* that they may *reap in* so much the more *joy*. (Esther 8:16-17)

A sight of Christ's glory, while we are here in this world, is a good preparative for our sufferings with him, as these are preparatives for the sight of his glory in the other world. Paul, who had abundance of trouble, had abundance of revelations. (Matthew 17:1-2)

[I]t is promised, 1. That God will strengthen their hands, that is, will help them: *"I will hold thy right hand,* go hand in hand with thee" (so some): he will take us by the hand as our guide, to lead us in our way, will help us up when we are fallen or prevent our falls; when we are weak he will hold us up—wavering, he will fix us—trembling, he will encourage us, and so *hold us by the right hand,* Ps. 73:23. (Isaiah 41:13)

The grace of faith is absolutely necessary to the quieting and composing of the mind in the midst of all the tosses of this present time.... (Isaiah 7:9)

They are *blessed* who *believe* the word of God, for that Word will not fail them; ... The inviolable certainty of the promise is the undoubted felicity of those that build upon it and expect their all from it. The faithfulness of God is the blessedness of the faith of the saints. (Luke 1:45)

Though it is a great privilege to hear the word of God, yet those only are truly blessed, that is, blessed of the Lord, that hear and *keep* it, that keep it in memory, and keep to it as their way and rule. (Luke 11:28)

Let us know then these seven things concerning the Lord Jehovah, with whom we have to do in all the acts of religious worship: — 1. *That the Lord he is God,* the only living and true God—that he is a Being infinitely perfect, self-existent, and self-sufficient, and the fountain of all being; he is God, and not a man as we are. He is an eternal Spirit, incomprehensible and independent, the first cause and last end. ... We worship him that made us and all the world; he is God, and all other pretended deities are vanity and a lie, and such as he has triumphed over. 2. That he is our Creator: *It is he that has made us, and not we ourselves.* I find that I am, but cannot say, *I am that I am,* and therefore must ask, Whence am I? Who made me? *Where is God my Maker?* And it is the Lord Jehovah. He gave us being, he gave us this being; he is both the former of our bodies and the Father of our spirits. We did not, we could not, make ourselves. ... 3. That therefore he is our rightful owner. ... He has an incontestable right to, and property in, us and all things. His we are, to be actuated by his power, disposed of by his will, and devoted to his honour and glory. 4. That he is our sovereign ruler: *We are his people* or subjects, and he is our prince, our rector or governor, that gives law to us as moral agents, and will call us to an account for what we do. *The Lord is our judge; the Lord is our lawgiver.* We are not at liberty to do what we will, but must always make conscience of doing as we are bidden. 5. That he is our bountiful benefactor. We are not only his sheep, whom he is entitled to, but *the sheep of his pasture,* whom he takes care of; ... He that made us maintains us, and gives us all good things richly to enjoy. 6. That he is a God of infinite mercy and goodness: ... *his mercy is everlasting*; it is a fountain that can never be drawn dry. ... 7. That he is a God of inviolable truth and faithfulness: *His truth endures to all generations,* and no word of his shall fall to the ground as antiquated or revoked. The promise is sure to all the seed, from age to age. (Psalm 100:1-5)

The complete character of a good man: he is one that *worships God,* and *does his will;* he is constant in his devotions at set times, and regular in his conversation at all times. He is one that makes it his business to glorify his Creator by the solemn adoration of his name and a sincere obedience to his will and law; both must go together. (John 9:31)

Thus we see that our persons are justified before God by faith, but our faith is justified before men by works. (James 2:14)

It is the world that lies in our way to heaven, and is the great impediment to our entrance there. But he who believes that Jesus is the Son of God believes therein that Jesus came from God to be the Saviour of the world, and powerfully to conduct us from the world to heaven, and to God, who is fully to be enjoyed there. And he who so believes must needs by this faith overcome the world. (1 John 5:4-5)

The eternal life would assume mortality, would put on flesh and blood (in the entire human nature), and so dwell among us and converse with us, John 1:14. Here were condescension and kindness indeed, that eternal life (a person of eternal essential life) should come to visit mortals, and to procure eternal life for them, and then confer it on them! ... The divine life, or Word incarnate, presented and evinced itself to the very senses of the apostles. (1 John 1:1-3)

The matter of fact, that Jesus did preach such doctrines, and work such miracles, and rise from the dead, is proved, beyond contradiction, by such evidence as is always admitted in other cases, and therefore to the satisfaction of all that are impartial; and then let the doctrine recommend itself, and let the miracles prove it to be of God. (John 21:24)

Jesus Christ is often better than his word, but never worse; often anticipates, but never frustrates, the believing expectations of his people. (Matthew 28:9-10)

True love to Christ will carry us through, to the utmost, in following him. Death itself cannot quench that divine fire, Cant. 8:6, 7. (Matthew 27:57-61)

O what a blessed change would it make in our hearts and lives, did we but firmly believe this truth, that the best way to be comfortably provided for in this world, is to be most intent upon another world! (Matthew 6:33-34)

That which God has to show us is infinitely better and more desirable than any thing that the world has to offer our view. The prospects of an eye of faith are much more rich and beautiful than those of an eye of sense. (Genesis 13:14-15)

But thus we ruin ourselves by giving more credit to the reports and representations of sense than to divine revelation; we walk by sight, not by faith; whereas, *if we* will *receive the witness of men,* without doubt *the witness of God is greater.* (Numbers 13:1-2)

Those that will deal with God must deal upon trust; we must quit the things that are seen for the things that are not seen, and submit to the sufferings of this present time in hopes of a glory that is yet to be revealed.... (Genesis 12:1)

Those that trust in God must have their minds stayed upon him, must trust him at all times, under all events, must firmly and faithfully adhere to him, with an entire satisfaction in him; and such as do so God will keep in perpetual peace, and that peace shall keep them. When evil tidings are abroad *those* shall calmly expect the event, and not be disturbed by frightful apprehensions arising from them, whose hearts are *fixed, trusting in the Lord....* (Isaiah 26:3)

Spiritual growth consists most in the growth of the root, which is out of sight. The more we depend upon Christ and draw sap and virtue from him, the more we act in religion from a principle and the more steadfast and resolved we are in it, the more we *cast forth our roots.* ... The *inward man is renewed day by day.* (Hosea 14:6-7)

In the worst of times God's people have a *nevertheless* to comfort themselves with, something to allay and balance their troubles; they are persecuted, but not forsaken (2 Cor. 4:9), sorrowful yet always rejoicing, 2 Cor. 6:10. And it is matter of comfort to us, when things are at the darkest, that he who *forms the light and creates the darkness* has appointed to both their bounds and set them one over against the other.... (Isaiah 9:1)

If there be those that hate and despise us, let us not be disturbed at that, for there are those also that love and respect us. God hath set the one over against the other, and so must we. (1 Samuel 20:1-3)

[L]et *the righteous man* know that he shall not be lost in the crowd of sinners; the *Judge of all the earth will not slay the righteous with the wicked* (Gen. 18:25); no, assure him, in God's name, that *it shall be well with him.* ... When the whole *stay of bread is taken away,* yet in the *day of famine the righteous shall be satisfied; they shall eat the fruit of their doings*—they shall have the testimony of their consciences for them that they kept themselves pure from the common iniquity, and therefore the common calamity is not the same thing to them that it is to others; they brought no fuel to the flame, and therefore are not themselves fuel for it. (Isaiah 3:10-11)

Those that trust in God, in his power, providence, and promise, are never made ashamed of their hope; but those that put confidence in any creature will sooner or later find it a reproach to them. God is true, and may be trusted, but every man a liar, and must be suspected. The Creator is a rock of ages, the creature a broken reed. We cannot expect too little from man nor too much from God. (Isaiah 30:5)

The consideration of this, that we are strangers and pilgrims, should oblige us to abstain from all fleshly lusts, to live above the things of sense, and look upon them with a generous and gracious contempt. (Jeremiah 35:7)

Satan cannot easily take hold of those who are thus loosened from, and dead to, the *world* and the *flesh*. The more we *keep under the body*, and bring it into subjection, the less advantage Satan has against us. (Luke 4:2)

Those that have their hearts full of the world … have their ears deaf to the gospel invitation. … [B]oth intimate a preference given to the body above the soul, and to the things of time above those of eternity. (Luke 14:18)

# -5-

# Obedience and Perseverance

[T]he way to have the comfort of what God allows us is to forbear what he forbids us. No man shall lose by his self-denial; let God have his dues first, and then all will be clean to us and sure....

Matthew Henry
on Joshua 8:1

[T]he way to have the comfort of what God allows us is to forbear what he forbids us. No man shall lose by his self-denial; let God have his dues first, and then all will be clean to us and sure.... (Joshua 8:1)

Those who have not grace enough to keep their temper in temptation should have wisdom enough to keep out of the way of temptation. (Jeremiah 51:45-46)

Those that would not eat the forbidden fruit must not come near the forbidden tree. *Avoid it, pass not by it,* Prov. 4:15. (Genesis 3:3)

*The beginning* of lust, as *of strife, is like the letting forth of water;* it is therefore wisdom to leave it off before it be meddled with. The foolish fly fires her wings, and fools away her life at last, by playing about the candle. (2 Samuel 11:3)

Those that would avoid sin must not parley with temptation. (Daniel 3:16-17)

It is a dangerous thing to treat with a temptation, which ought at first to be rejected with disdain and abhorrence. The garrison that sounds a parley is not far from being surrendered. (Genesis 3:1-5)

It is our wisdom to avoid the places where we have been overcome by temptations to sin, not to remain in them, or return to them, but to *save ourselves* out of them, as we would out of infected places.... (Ezekiel 37:23)

Though Providence, for a time, may cast us into bad places, yet we ought to tarry there no longer than needs must; we may *sojourn* where we may not *settle.* (Genesis 12:10)

There are many temptations, to which solitude gives great advantage; but the communion of saints contributes much to their strength and safety. (Genesis 3:1)

Those are in danger of being estranged from God who please themselves with those who are strangers to him, for we soon learn the ways of those whose company we love. (Isaiah 2:6)

Bad company and conversation are likely to make bad men. Those who would keep their innocence must keep good company. Error and vice are infectious: and, if we would avoid the contagion, we must keep clear of those who have taken it. *He that walketh with wise men shall be wise; but a companion of fools shall be destroyed,* Prov. 13:20. (1 Corinthians 15:33)

It is strange if those that associate themselves with wicked people, and grow intimate with them, come off without guilt, or grief, or both. (1 Samuel 29:2)

Those whom God has marked for himself must not mingle with evildoers.... (Exodus 12:22)

It is a dangerous thing to associate with evil-doers; we may be entangled both in guilt and misery by it. (2 Kings 9:27-28)

## 5: Obedience and Perseverance

Those that will not be companions with sinners in their mirth, nor eat of their dainties, may in faith pray not to be companions with them in their misery, nor to drink of their cup, their cup of trembling. (Psalm 26:8-10)

Better buy wisdom dear than be without it; but experience is therefore said to be the mistress of fools because those are fools that will not learn till they are taught by experience, and particularly till they are taught the danger of associating with wicked people. (1 Kings 22:48-49)

When God's people are in Babylon they have need to take special care that they *partake not in her sins*. (Daniel 1:8)

Though there be a reason for our being in bad places, yet, when reason ceases, we must by no means continue in them. Forced absence from God's ordinances, and forced presence with wicked people, are great afflictions; but when the force ceases, and such a situation is continued of choice, then it becomes a great sin. (Ruth 1:7-8)

Joy is forbidden fruit to wicked people. Those must not rejoice, because they have gone a whoring from God…. (Hosea 9:1)

As nothing is more *courageous* than a well-informed conscience, so nothing is more *outrageous* than a mistaken one. (John 10:33)

It is a good thing to have a heart within us smiting us for sins that seem little; it is a sign that conscience is awake and tender, and will be the means of preventing greater sins. (1 Samuel 24:5)

God does not force men to walk in his statutes by external violence, but causes them to walk in his statutes by an internal principle. (Ezekiel 36:27)

The integrity of an honest man will itself be his guide in the way of duty and the way of safety. His principles are fixed, his rule is certain, and therefore his way is plain; his sincerity keeps him steady, and he needs not tack about every time the wind turns, having no other end to drive at than to keep a good conscience. *Integrity and uprightness* will *preserve* men, Ps. 25:21. (Proverbs 11:3)

Obedient believers will be sure to inherit the blessing. (Genesis 12:2)

The foundation of all acceptable obedience is laid in a sincere dedication of ourselves, as servants to Jesus Christ as *our Lord,* Ps. 16:2. (Joshua 6:14)

The giving of the Holy Ghost to obedient believers, not only to bring them to the obedience of faith, but to make them eminently useful therein, is a very strong proof of the truth of Christianity. (Acts 5:32)

God's favours to us lay strong obligations upon us to be obedient to him. This we must render, Ps. 116:12. (1 Samuel 15:1)

The more God gives us the more cheerfully we should serve him; our abundance should be oil to the wheels of our obedience. (Deuteronomy 28:47)

Though we are bound to follow God with an implicit obedience, yet we should endeavour that it may be more and more an intelligent obedience. We must never dispute God's statutes and judgments, but we may and must enquire, *What mean these statutes and judgments? Deut. 6:20* (Jeremiah 32:25)

We have no reason to expect God should perform his part of the covenant if we do not make conscience of performing ours. (Malachi 2:9)

Note, 1. The vows we have made we must conscientiously perform. 2. Praising God and paying our vows to him must be our constant daily work; every day we must be doing something towards it, because it is all but little in comparison with what is due, because we daily receive fresh mercies, and because, if we think much to do it daily, we cannot expect to be doing it eternally. (Psalm 61:8)

[T]he vows we have made when we are in pursuit of a mercy must be carefully and conscientiously kept when we have obtained the mercy, though they were made against our interest. (Genesis 14:22)

God by his word puts life, and strength, and spirit into his people; for if he says *Be strong,* power goes along with the word. (Daniel 10:19)

Even those that are espoused to God may yet seem to be refused and forsaken, and may be grieved in spirit under the apprehensions of being so. Those that shall never be forsaken and left in despair may yet for a time be perplexed and in distress. ... When God continues his people long in trouble he seems to forsake them; so their enemies construe it (Ps. 71:11); so they themselves misinterpret it. ...When they are comfortless under their troubles, because their prayers and expectations are not answered, God hides his face from them, as if he regarded them not nor designed them any kindness. ... This arose indeed from his displeasure. It was in wrath that he forsook them and hid his face from them; ... yet it was but in a little wrath: ... little in comparison with what they had deserved, and what others justly suffer, on whom the full vials of his wrath are poured out. ... But God's people, though they be sensible of ever so small a degree of God's displeasure, cannot but be grieved in spirit because of it. (Isaiah 54:6-8)

When troubles continue long, hopes have been often frustrated, and all creature-confidences fail, it is not strange if the spirits sink; and nothing but an active faith in the power, promise, and providence of God will keep them from quite dying away. (Ezekiel 37:11)

The *God of Israel*, the *Saviour,* is sometimes *a God that hideth himself* (Isa. 45:15), but never a God that absenteth himself; sometimes *in the dark,* but never *at a distance.* (Matthew 28:20)

## 5: Obedience and Perseverance

Those that are careful not to do iniquity need not be afraid of any calamity, for it cannot hurt them, and therefore should not terrify them. (Zephaniah 3:13)

(1.) There is a proneness in the best of men to be frightened at threatening clouds, especially when fears are epidemic. We are all too apt to walk in the way of the people we live among, though it be not a good way. (2.) Those whom God loves and owns he will instruct and enable to swim against the stream of common corruptions, particularly of common fears. He will find ways to teach his own people not to walk in the way of other people, but in a sober singularity. ... Those that truly fear God shall not need to fear any evil. (Isaiah 8:11-14)

Those that resolve to serve God must not mind being singular in it, nor be drawn by the crowd to forsake his service. Those that are bound for heaven must be willing to swim against the stream, and must not do as the most do, but as the best do. (Joshua 24:15)

Those that would find the way to heaven must look up to God, must take direction from his word and beg direction from his Spirit. (Psalm 15:1-2)

Those that have given up themselves to the direction of God's word and Spirit steer a steady course, even when they seem to be bewildered. While they are sure they cannot lose their God and guide, they need not fear losing their way. (Numbers 10:13)

[F]or *the dragon is cast out into the earth* (Rev. 12:9) and not yet confined to his place of torment. While we are on this earth we are within his reach, and with so much subtlety, swiftness, and industry, does he penetrate into all the corners of it, that we cannot be in any place secure from his temptations. (Job 1:7)

If we basely yield to temptations, the devil will continually follow us; but if we *put on the whole armour of God,* and stand it out against him, he will be gone from us. Resolution shuts and bolts the door against temptation. (James 4:7)

The way to prevent God's fiery darts of trouble is with the shield of faith to quench Satan's fiery darts of temptation. (Job 6:4)

We must set a *watch before the door of our lips,* that we offend not with our tongue. ... Our hearts being naturally corrupt, out of them a great deal of corrupt communication is apt to come, and therefore we must conceive a great dread and detestation of all manner of evil words, cursing, swearing, lying, slandering, brawling, filthiness, and foolish talking, all which come from a *froward mouth and perverse lips,* that will not be governed either by reason or religion, but contradict both, and which are as unsightly and ill-favoured before God as a crooked distorted mouth drawn awry is before men. All manner of tongue sins, we must, by constant watchfulness and steadfast resolution, *put from us,* put *far from us,* abstaining from all words that have an appearance of evil and fearing to learn any such words. (Proverbs 4:24)

All evil speakings come forth from the heart, and are defiling; from the corrupt heart comes the corrupt communication. (Matthew 15:18)

A malignant tongue makes men like the old serpent; and poison in the lips is a certain sign of poison in the heart. (Psalm 140:3)

No good man can take pleasure in bringing evil tidings.... (1 Samuel 3:15)

Filthy and unclean words and discourse are poisonous and infectious, as putrid rotten meat: they proceed from and prove a great deal of corruption in the heart of the speaker, and tend to corrupt the minds and manners of others who hear them; and therefore Christians should be aware of all such discourse. (Ephesians 4:29)

It is bad to think ill, but it is worse to speak it, for that is giving the evil thought an *imprimatur—a sanction;* it is allowing it, giving consent to it, and publishing it for the infection of others. But it is a good sign that we repent of the evil imagination of the heart if we suppress it, and the error remains within ourselves. If therefore thou hast been so foolish as to think evil, be so wise as to *lay thy hand upon thy mouth,* and let it go no further, Prov. 30:32. (Psalm 73:15)

When the heart is hot, let the tongue be bridled.... (Jeremiah 20:14-18)

The persons, or actions, we can say no good of, we had best say nothing of. (1 Chronicles 20:1-3)

To those that may say any thing it is wisdom to say nothing that is provoking. (Ecclesiastes 10:11)

Sinful words are more offensive to the God of heaven than they are commonly thought to be. (Malachi 2:17)

The purifying of the language in common conversation is necessary to the acceptableness of the words of our mouth and the meditation of our heart on our devotion; for how can *sweet waters and bitter* come *out of the same fountain?* James 3:9-12. (Zephaniah 3:9-10)

[T]hose that have God's law in their heart should have it in their mouth, and be often speaking of it, the more to affect themselves and to instruct others. (Exodus 13:9)

Our tongue is our glory, and never more so than when it is employed in praising God. (Psalm 108:1)

Those who most use their wisdom see most of their need of it, and *ask it of God,* who has promised to *give it liberally,* Jam. 1:5. He *will guide his words with judgment* ... and there is nothing in which we have more occasion for wisdom than in the government of the tongue; blessed is he to whom God gives that wisdom. (Psalm 112:5)

*Even a fool, when he holds his peace, is accounted wise,* because nothing appears to the contrary, Prov. 17:28. (Job 13:5)

As the helm is a very small part of the ship, so is the tongue a very small part of the body: but the right governing of the helm or rudder will steer and turn the ship as the governor pleases; and a right management of the tongue is, in a great measure, the government of the whole man. ... And hence we should learn to make the due management of our tongues more our study, because, though they are little members, they are capable of doing a great deal of good or a great deal of hurt. (James 3:4-5)

Converting grace refines the language, not by making the phrases witty, but the substance wise. ... An air of purity and piety in common conversation is a very happy omen to any people; other graces, other blessings, shall be given where God gives a pure language to those who have been a *people of unclean lips.* (Zephaniah 3:9)

It ill becomes us to be rash and hasty in our censures of others, and to be forward to believe people guilty of bad things, while either the matter of fact on which the censure is grounded is doubtful and unproved or is capable of a good construction. Charity commands us to hope the best concerning all, and forbids censoriousness. (1 Samuel 1:13-15)

When we see others do that which looks suspicious, instead of contending with them, we should enquire of them what ground they went upon; and, if we have not an opportunity to do that, should ourselves put the best construction upon it that will bear, and *judge nothing before the time.* (Acts 11:4)

We have often found more of virtue, honour, and conscience, in some people than we thought they possessed; and it ought to be a pleasure to us to be thus disappointed.... Charity teaches us to hope the best. (Genesis 12:18-20)

*Charity believes all things, hopes all things,* believes and hopes the best, and is very loth to give the lie to any. (Joshua 22:30)

We should take notice of that which is commendable even in bad people. (Romans 10:2)

*Hear the other side* .... This rule we ought to be governed by in our private censures in common conversation; we must not give men bad characters, nor condemn their words and actions, till we have heard what is to be said in their vindication. See John 7:51. (Acts 25:16)

We often create a great deal of uneasiness to ourselves by misinterpreting the words and actions of others that are well intended: it is charity to ourselves to think no evil. (2 Kings 5:7)

The rectifying of mistakes and misunderstandings, and the setting of misconstrued words and actions in a true light, would be the most effectual way to accommodate both private and pub-

## Part II: Wisdom (Salvation)

lic quarrels, and bring them to a happy period. (Joshua 22:13-16)

A good word, well and wisely spoken, may do more good than perhaps we think of. (Job 4:3-4)

We cannot judge what men are by what they have been formerly, nor what they will do by what they have done: age and experience may make men wiser and better. ... The worst may mend in time. (Genesis 44:16-17)

It is a hard thing, and requires more application and resolution than is ordinarily met with, to keep up a good opinion of persons and things that are *every where* run down, and spoken against. Every one is apt to say as the most say, and to throw a stone at that which is put into an ill name. (Matthew 27:39)

Some people, when they have fastened a censure upon a person, will stick to it, though afterwards it appear ever so plainly to be unjust and groundless. (Acts 11:17-18)

Charity teaches us to put the best construction upon every thing that it will bear, especially upon the words and actions of those that are *zealously affected in doing a good thing*, though we may think them not altogether so discreet in it as they might be. It is true, there may be over-doing in well-doing; but thence we must learn to be cautious ourselves, lest we run into extremes, but not to be censorious of others; because that which we may impute to the want of prudence, God may accept as an instance of abundant love. We must not say, Those do too much in religion, that do more than we do, but rather aim to do as much as they. (Matthew 26:8-9)

Such expressions of pious and devout affections as to some may seem indecent and imprudent ought not to be hastily censured and condemned, much less ridiculed, because, if they come from an upright heart, God will accept the strength of the affection and excuse the weakness of the expressions of it. (Psalm 47:1)

It is our duty to be affected both with the iniquities and with the calamities of the church of God and of the times and places wherein we live; but we must take heed lest we grow peevish in our resentments, and carry them too far, so as to entertain any hard thoughts of God, or lose the comfort of our communion with him. (Habakkuk 1:12)

*Sin is a reproach to any people*, but especially to God's people, that have more eyes upon them and have more honour to lose than other people. (Daniel 9:15)

The heinous sins of professed Christians are quickly noted and noised abroad. We should walk circumspectly, for many eyes are upon us, and many mouths will be opened against us if we fall into any scandalous practice. (1 Corinthians 5:1)

The body must be *kept under and brought into subjection*. Nature is content with a little, grace with less, but lust

## 5: Obedience and Perseverance

with nothing. It is good to stint ourselves of choice, that we may the better bear it if ever we should come to be stinted by necessity. (Ezekiel 4:11)

Men's characters appear in their choices and desires. What wouldst thou *have?* tries a man as much as, What wouldst thou *do?* Thus God tried whether Solomon was one of the *children of this world,* that say, *Who will show us any good,* or of the children of light, that say, *Lord, lift up thy countenance upon us.* As we choose we shall have, and that is likely to be our portion to which we give the preference, whether the wealth and pleasure of this world or spiritual riches or delights. ... Like a genuine son of David, he chose spiritual blessings rather than temporal. His petition here is *Give me wisdom and knowledge.* (2 Chronicles 1:6)

But, if we thus seek the things of this world, it is just in God to deny them; whereas, if we seek any thing that we may serve God with it, we may expect he will either give us what we seek or give us hearts to be content without it, and give opportunities of serving and glorifying him some other way. (James 4:3)

Those that would preserve the purity of their souls must keep a strict guard upon the senses of their bodies, must stop their ears to temptations, and turn away their eyes from beholding vanity. (Isaiah 33:15)

Willing minds will do more, and hold out longer, in that which is good, than one would expect from them. (Mark 6:35-36)

A holy war is better than the peace of the devil's palace .... [i]n the hearts of believers. No sooner is Christ formed in the soul than immediately there begins a conflict between the flesh and the spirit, Gal. 5:17. The stream is not turned without a mighty struggle, which yet ought not to discourage us. It is better to have a conflict with sin than tamely to submit to it. (Genesis 25:22-23)

Though sin may remain as an outlaw, though it may oppress as a tyrant, yet let it not reign as a king. Let it not make laws, nor preside in councils, nor command the militia; let it not be uppermost in the soul, so that we should obey it. (Romans 6:12)

When we resolutely resist, and so overcome, our spiritual enemies, then our hearts shall rejoice. But we ruin our own joy if our resistance be feeble and we yield to the temptations of Satan. (Zechariah 10:7)

To those that are sincere in their religion God will give grace to persevere in it: those that follow God faithfully will be divinely strengthened to continue following him. (1 Samuel 12:14)

Those that are unresolved, and go in religious ways without a stedfast mind, tempt the tempter, and stand like a door half open, which invites a thief; but resolution shuts and bolts the door, resists the devil, and forces him to flee. (Ruth 1:18)

Those who are grave and sober, and live by rule and with consideration, thereby make it appear that by the power of Christ the devil's power is broken in their souls. (Mark 5:16)

Draw the lines from the circumference to any other point but the centre, and they will cross. (Matthew 6:23-24)

There is an aptness in us to misinterpret providential discouragements in our duty, as if they amounted to a discharge from our duty, when they are only intended for the trial and exercise of our courage and faith. It is bad to neglect our duty, but it is worse to vouch Providence for the patronizing of our neglects. (Haggai 1:2-8)

The boldness of the attacks which profane people make upon religion should sharpen the courage and resolution of its friends and advocates. ... The blustering wind makes the traveller gather his cloak the closer about him and gird it the faster. Those that are truly wise and good will be continually growing wiser and better. Proficiency in religion is a good sign of sincerity in it. (Job 17:8-9)

Those who act honestly may act boldly; and those who are sure that they have a commission from God need not be afraid of opposition from men. (Micah 3:8)

If men's commands be any way contrary to the commands of God, we must obey God and not man. (Exodus 1:17)

It is not the *suffering*, but the *cause*, that makes the *martyr*. (Mark 10:28)

Many a good cause, when it is distressed by its enemies, is deserted by its friends. (John 16:32)

Despair of success hinders many a good enterprise. No one is willing to venture alone, forgetting that those are not alone who have God with them. (1 Kings 19:9-10)

Those that are partners with God's people in their obedience and sufferings shall be sharers with them in their joys and comforts, Isa. 66:10. (Genesis 13:5)

[W]e must keep our spirits calm and sedate by a continual dependence upon God, and his power and goodness; we must retire into ourselves with a holy quietness, suppressing all turbulent and tumultuous passions, and keeping the peace in our own minds. And we must rely upon God with a holy confidence that he can do what he will and will do what is best for his people. And this will be our strength; it will inspire us with such a holy fortitude as will carry us with ease and courage through all the difficulties we may meet with. (Isaiah 30:15-17)

If water have a sediment at the bottom, though it may be clear while it stands still, yet, when shaken, it grows muddy; so it is with our affections: but pure

## 5: Obedience and Perseverance

water in a clean glass, though ever so much stirred, continues clear; and so it was with Christ. (Mark 14:33)

We must study to answer God's end in all his providences, which is in general to make us religious. *God does all, that men should fear before him,* to convince them that there is a God above them that has a sovereign dominion over them, at whose disposal they are and all their ways, and in whose hands their times are and all events concerning them, and that therefore they ought to have their eyes ever towards him, to worship and adore him, to acknowledge him in all their ways, to be careful in every thing to please him, and afraid of offending him in any thing. (Ecclesiastes 3:11-15)

Those shall never have enough in God (who alone is all-sufficient) that never know when they have enough of this world, which at the best is insufficient. (Isaiah 2:6)

For our instruction in the things of God it is requisite that we have precept upon precept, and line upon line ... the precept of justice must be upon the precept of piety, and the precept of charity upon that of justice. (Isaiah 28:10)

Truths appear in the clearest light when they are taken in their due order; the resolving of the *previous* questions will be a key to the *main* question. (Matthew 21:24)

To convince sinners of the evil of sin, and of their misery and danger by reason of it, there is need of *line upon line,* so loth we are to know the worst of ourselves. (Ezekiel 23:1)

Many of our foolish frets and foolish fears would vanish before a strict enquiry into the causes of them. (Isaiah 40:27-28)

Note, causeless fears would soon vanish, if we would not yield to them, and lie down under them, but get up, and do what we can against them. ... Christ's errand into the world was to give comfort to good people, that, being delivered out of the hands of their enemies, they might *serve God without fear,* Luke 1:74, 75. (Matthew 17:7)

When our condition is not to our mind, we must bring our mind to our condition; and then we are easy to ourselves and all about us; then our souls are *as a weaned child.* (Psalm 131:1-3)

If our desires be towards God, we must give evidence that they are so by diligently seeking him, and seeking him early, as those that desire to find him, and dread the thoughts of missing him. (Isaiah 26:9)

One good means to prevent either our real falling short or seeming to fall short is to maintain a holy and religious fear lest we should fall short. This will make us vigilant and diligent, sincere and serious; this fear will put us upon examining our faith and exercising it; whereas presumption is the high road to ruin. (Hebrews 4:1-2)

## Part II: Wisdom (Salvation)

A holy fear of coming short is an excellent means of perseverance. (Philippians 3:11)

Those that would see Christ must go to his temple; for there *The Lord, whom ye seek, shall suddenly come to meet you,* and there you must be ready to *meet him.* (Luke 2:27)

True believers love and seek Christ, not only *though* he was crucified, but *because* he was so. (Matthew 28:5-6)

They who will have an interest in the great salvation are carried out towards it with a strong desire, will have it *upon any terms,* and not think them hard, nor quit their hold without a blessing, Gen. 32:26. (Matthew 11:12-15)

Note, 1. Those that set out for heaven must persevere to the end, still reaching forth to those things that are before. 2. That which we undertake in obedience to God's command, and a humble attendance upon his providence, will certainly succeed, and end with comfort at last. (Genesis 12:4-5)

The saving truths of the gospel must be fixed in our mind, revolved much in our thoughts, and maintained and held fast to the end, if we would be saved. They will not save us, if we do not attend to them, and yield to their power, and continue to do so to the end. *He only that endureth to the end shall be saved,* Matt. 10:22. (1 Corinthians 15:1-2)

Those who would aright pursue the interests of their souls must beat down their bodies, and keep them under. They must combat hard with fleshly lusts, and not indulge a wanton appetite.... (1 Corinthians 9:24-25)

And when the soul is employed in holy exercises, and heart-work is made of them, through the grace of God the strength of our spiritual enemies will be trodden down and will fall before us. (Judges 5:21)

The Christian life is a warfare against sin, Satan, the world, and the flesh. It is not enough that we engage in this warfare, but we must pursue it to the end, we must never yield to our spiritual enemies, but fight the good fight, till we gain the victory, as all persevering Christians shall do; and the warfare and victory shall have a glorious triumph and reward. (Revelation 2:7)

We in our spiritual warfare must *stand against the wiles of the devil,* remembering that he is a subtle serpent as well as a roaring lion. (Joshua 9:7)

Thus in the conquest of a soul, by the grace of the Son of David, what stands in opposition to God must be destroyed, every lust mortified and crucified, but what may glorify him must be dedicated and the property of it altered. (2 Samuel 8:11-12)

The work of creation not only proceeded gradually from one thing to another, but rose and advanced gradually from that which was less excellent to that which was more so, teaching us to press towards perfection and endeav-

## 5: Obedience and Perseverance

our that are last works may be our best works. (Genesis 1:20-23)

... a dwarf upon a mountain sees further than a giant in the valley. (Matthew 11:11)

Let not dwarfs despair, with good help, by aiming high to reach high. (Luke 19:3-4)

Those that will be wise when they are old must be inquisitive when they are young. (Joshua 4:21)

Those that would improve in knowledge, must be made sensible of their ignorance. (Mark 4:13)

Those that have been left in ignorance, or led into error, by any infelicities of their education, should not therefore be despised nor rejected by those who are more knowing and orthodox, but should be compassionately instructed, and better taught.... (Acts 19:3-5)

Those that would learn must see their need to be taught. ... The way to receive good instructions is to ask good questions. (Acts 8:31-35)

The beginning is small, but the progress is to perfection. Dawning light grows to noonday, a grain of mustard seed to a great tree. Let us not therefore despise the day of small things, but hope for the day of great things. (Job 8:7)

Those that know much should covet to know more, and what they know to know it better, pressing forward towards perfection. (Acts 19:24-28)

What we hear from the mouth of Christ, we must give all diligence to understand. Not only scholars, but even the multitude, the ordinary people, must apply their minds to understand the words of Christ. (Matthew 15:10)

Christ's scholars never learn *above their bibles* in this world; but they need to be learning still more and more *out of their bibles*, and to grow more *ready* and *mighty* in the scriptures. That we may have right thoughts of Christ, and have our mistakes concerning him rectified, there needs no more than to be made to understand the scriptures. (Luke 24:44-45)

Christians are utterly to blame who do not endeavour to grow in grace and knowledge. (1 Corinthians 3:1-4)

We should covet earnestly to know the true *in*tent, and full *ex*tent, of the word we hear, that we may be neither mistaken nor defective in our knowledge. (Luke 8:9)

By mutual converse about divine things we both borrow the light of others and improve our own. (John 16:18)

When we are puzzled with scripture difficulties, we must apply ourselves to Christ by prayer for his Spirit to open our understandings and to lead us into all truth. (Matthew 17:10)

Those that read the scriptures, should labour to understand the scriptures, else their reading is to little purpose; we cannot use that which we do not understand. (Matthew 24:15)

[B]etter be wise late, and buy wisdom by experience, than never wise. (Judges 4:24)

God is often found of those who seek him not, much more will he be found of those who seek him diligently. He speaks comfort to many who not only are not worthy of it, but do not so much as enquire after it. (Isaiah 7:3)

Where a weak head doubts concerning any word of Christ, an upright heart and a willing mind will seek for instruction. (Matthew 15:15)

Note, 1. Christ's people are, and ought to be, a willing people. 2. If they continue seeking Christ and longing after him, even when he seems to withdraw from them, he will graciously return to them in due time, perhaps sooner than they think and with a pleasing surprise. No chariots sent for Christ shall return empty. (Song of Solomon 6:11-13)

What we know of the things of God should be carefully laid up, that hereafter, when there is occasion, it may be faithfully laid out; and what we have not now any use for, yet we may have another time. Divine truths should be sealed up among our treasures, that we may find them again after many days. (Daniel 8:26)

Those meet with an inconceivable loss who let gospel truths, which they had received, slip out of their minds; they have lost a treasure far better than thousands of gold and silver; the seed is lost, their time and pains in hearing lost, and their hopes of a good harvest lost; all is lost, if the gospel be lost. (Hebrews 2:1)

Those that have grown up, nay, those that have grown old, ought often to reflect upon the goodness of God to them in their childhood. (Hosea 11:1)

Christ will be sought while he may be found; if we slip our time, we may lose our passage. (Song of Solomon 5:2)

Seek the Lord ... *While he may be found—while he is near.* ... [I]t shall not be in vain to seek him and call upon him. Now his patience is waiting on us, his word is calling to us, and his Spirit striving with us. Let us now improve our advantages and opportunities; for now is the accepted time. Mercy is now offered, but then judgment without mercy will take place. (Isaiah 55:6)

# -6-

# Communion and Prayer

We should always make it our morning's work to bring our offerings unto the Lord; even the spiritual offerings of prayer and praise, and a broken heart surrendered entirely to God. This is that which the duty of every day requires.

Matthew Henry
on Exodus 36:3

We should always make it our morning's work to bring our offerings unto the Lord; even the spiritual offerings of prayer and praise, and a broken heart surrendered entirely to God. This is that which the duty of every day requires. (Exodus 36:3)

This is that which we should aim at in all our prayers and services, to be accepted of the Lord; this must be the summit of our ambition, not to have the praise of men, but to please God. (Job 42:7-9)

[A] shame to those who say the true God is their God, and yet, in the morning, direct no prayer to him, nor look up. (Judges 6:28-30)

No time is amiss for meditating on the word of God, nor is any time unseasonable for those visits. We must not only set ourselves to meditate on God's word morning and evening, at the entrance of the day and of the night, but these thoughts should be interwoven with the business and converse of every day and with the repose and slumbers of every night. *When I awake I am still with thee.* (Psalm 1:2)

Those that think three meals a day little enough for the body ought much more to think three solemn prayers a day little enough for the soul, and to count it a pleasure, not a task. As it is fit that in the morning we should begin the day with God, and in the evening close it with him, so it is fit that in the midst of the day we should retire awhile to converse with him. ... Let us not be weary of praying often, for God is not weary of hearing. (Psalm 55:16-17)

When the light of nature teaches us that the providence of God has the ordering and disposing of all our affairs does not the law of nature oblige us by prayer to acknowledge God and seek to him? (Daniel 6:7)

If we would know the mind of God, we must apply to Jesus Christ, who lay in the bosom of the Father, and *in whom are hidden all the treasures of wisdom and knowledge,* not hidden from us, but hidden for us. (Daniel 8:13)

A gracious soul, though still desiring more of God, never desires more than God. The gifts of Providence so far satisfy them that they are content with such things as they have. *I have all, and abound,* Phil. 4:18. (Psalm 36:8)

Communion with Christ is that which all that are sanctified earnestly breathe after; and the clearer discoveries he makes to them of his love the more earnestly do they desire it. Sensual pleasures pall the carnal appetite, and soon give it surfeit, but spiritual delights whet the desires, the language of which is, *Nothing more than God,* but still, *more and more of him.* (Song of Solomon 7:11-12)

The pleasures of sense seem right to the carnal appetite, and go down smoothly, but they are often wrong, and compared with the pleasure of communion with God, they are harsh and rough. Nothing *goes down so sweet-*

*ly* with a gracious soul as the wine of God's consolations. ... It is a great cordial. (Song of Solomon 7:9)

Whenever we enter into communion with God it becomes us to have a due sense of the vast distance and disproportion that there are between us and the holy angels, and of the infinite distance, and no proportion at all, between us and the holy God, and to acknowledge that we cannot *order our speech by reason of darkness*. How shall we that are dust and ashes speak to the Lord of glory? (Daniel 10:17)

*I bow my knees*. Note, When we draw nigh to God, we should reverence him in our hearts, and express our reverence in the most suitable and becoming behaviour and gesture. (Ephesians 3:14)

We must come to God, as children to a *Father in heaven*, with reverence and confidence. (Matthew 7:7-11)

It is the folly and infirmity of some good people that they lose much of the pleasantness of their religion by the fretfulness and uneasiness of their natural temper, which they humour and indulge, instead of mortifying it. (Jeremiah 15:17-18)

When any thing disturbs us, it is our interest, as well as our duty, to show before God our trouble, and he gives us leave to be humbly free with him. (1 Samuel 8:6)

Prayer is a salve for every sore. Whatever is a burden to us, we may by prayer cast it upon the Lord and then be easy. (Jeremiah 36:16)

God can by a whirlwind clear the sky and air, and produce that serenity of mind which is necessary to our communion with Heaven. (Ezekiel 1:4)

Those that would converse with Christ must go forth from the world and the amusements of it, must avoid every thing that would divert the mind and be a hindrance to it when it should be wholly taken up with Christ; we must contrive how to *attend upon the Lord without distraction*.... (Song of Solomon 7:11-12)

Those that expect communion with Christ above should study communion with him here in the utmost purity. (1 John 3:5)

[W]hen we are most retired from the world, and taken off from the things of sense, we are most fit for communion with God. (Daniel 7:1)

The satisfaction we have in communion with the saints in this world is but partial; we are but somewhat filled. It is partial compared with our communion with Christ; that, and that only, will completely satisfy, that will fill the soul. (Romans 15:27-28)

Those are not Christ's followers that do not care for being alone; that cannot enjoy themselves in solitude, when they have none else to converse with, none else to enjoy, but God and their own hearts. (Matthew 14:23)

## Part II: Wisdom (Salvation)

[S]olitude gives a good opportunity for communion with God; those that would meet with him must retire from the world, and the business and conversation of it, and love to be private, reckoning themselves never less alone than when alone, because the Father is with them. Enter therefore into thy closet, and shut the door, and be assured that God will meet thee if thou *seek him in due order*. (Numbers 23:3)

God often manifests himself to his people when they are out of the noise and hurry of this world. Silence and solitude befriend our communion with God. (Judges 6:14-16)

A good man is never less alone than when alone with God. (Mark 6:46)

The more we withdraw from the hurry of the world the more likely we are to have acquaintance with Christ, who took his disciples into a garden. Christ's church is a garden enclosed.... (Song of Solomon 6:2)

Wherever we are, we may keep up our communion with God, if it be not our own fault, for he is always at our right hand, his eye always upon us, and both his word and his ear always nigh us. By going about our worldly affairs with heavenly holy hearts, mixing pious thoughts with common actions, and having our eyes ever towards the Lord, we may take Christ along with us whithersoever we go. Nor should we go whither where we cannot in faith ask him to go along with us. ... Those that will go abroad with Christ ... must begin every day with him, seek him early, seek him diligently. (Song of Solomon 7:10-13)

Devotion is a thing we ought to be constant in; other duties are in season now and then, but we must *pray always*. (Luke 2:37)

The more we retreat from the world, and retire into our own hearts, the better frame we are in for communion with God: those that sit down to consider what they have learned shall be taught more. (Ezekiel 8:1)

Those that are entering into covenant and communion with God themselves should bring as many as they can along with them. ... God's ways are to be learned in his church, in communion with his people, and in the use of instituted ordinances—the ways of duty which he requires us to walk in, the ways of grace in which he walks towards us. It is God that teaches his people, by his word and Spirit. It is worth while to take pains to go up to his holy mountain to be taught his ways, and those who are willing to take those pains shall never find it labour in vain. (Isaiah 2:3)

To walk with God is to set God always before us, and to act as those that are always under his eye. It is to live a life of communion with God both in ordinances and providences. It is to make God's word our rule and his glory our end in all our actions. It is to make it our constant care and endeavour in every thing to please God, and nothing to offend him. It is to comply with his will, to concur with his designs, and to be workers together with him. It is to be *followers of him as dear children*. (Genesis 5:21-24)

Those who glorify Christ by coming to him themselves, should further glorify him by bringing all they have, or have influence upon, to him likewise. (Matthew 19:13)

Those reap no benefit by their religion that are not entire and sincere in it; nor can we have any comfortable communion with God in ordinances of worship unless we be inward and upright with him therein. We make nothing of our profession if it be but a profession. (Ezekiel 20:31)

We must not only be devout, but honest, else our devotion is but hypocrisy. (Matthew 7:12)

… God's eye is upon men, and … he takes cognizance of what they do when they are employed in their worldly business, not only when they are at church, praying and hearing, but when they are in their markets and fairs, and upon the exchange, buying and selling, which is a good reason why we should in all our dealings *keep a conscience void of offence*, and have our eye always upon him whose eye is always upon us. (Ezekiel 27:3-6)

The first day of the week is to be religiously observed by all the disciples of Christ; and it is a sign between Christ and them, for by this it is known that they are his disciples; and it should be observed in solemn assemblies…. (Acts 20:7)

The solemn observance of one day in seven, as a day of holy rest and holy work, to God's honour, is the indispensable duty of all those to whom God has revealed his holy sabbaths. (Genesis 2:3)

*The disciples came together,* … Though they read, and meditated, and prayed, and sung psalms, apart, and thereby kept up their communion with God, yet that was not enough; they must come together to worship God in concert, and so keep up their communion with one another, by mutual countenance and assistance, and testify their spiritual communion with all good Christians. (Acts 20:7)

It is good to keep sabbaths in solemn assemblies. (Luke 4:16)

Those are strangers to God, and enemies to themselves, that love market days better than sabbath days, that would rather be selling corn than worshipping God. (Amos 8:4-6)

The sabbath is a market day for our souls, but not for our bodies. (Nehemiah 10:31)

It is our wisdom and duty so to manage our religious exercises as that they may befriend our worldly business, and so to manage our worldly business as that it may be no enemy to our religious exercises. (Luke 5:4)

Part II: Wisdom (Salvation)

The profanation of the sabbath day is an inlet to all impiety; those who pollute holy time will keep nothing pure. (Ezekiel 20:16)

Sabbaths are signs; it is a sign that men have a sense of religion, and that there is some good correspondence between them and God, when they make conscience of keeping holy a sabbath day. (Ezekiel 20:13)

Sabbath days and sabbath work are a burden to carnal hearts, that are always afraid of doing too much for God and eternity. Can we spend our time better than in communication with God? And how much time do we spend pleasantly with the world? Will not the sabbath be gone before we have done the work of it and reaped the gains of it? Why then should we be in such haste to part with it? (Amos 8:4-6)

Note, 1. The sabbath day must be a day, not only of holy rest, but of holy work, and the rest is in order to the work. 2. The proper work of the sabbath is praising God; every sabbath day must be a thanks-giving day.... (Psalm 92:1-2)

It is good to do a full sabbath day's work, to abound in the work of the day, in some good work or other, even till sunset; as those that call the sabbath, and the business of it, *a delight.* (Luke 4:40)

[T]he streams of all religion run either deep or shallow according as the banks of the sabbath are kept up or neglected. (Jeremiah 17:27)

But when we *take hold of God* it is as the boatman with his hook takes hold on the shore, as if he would pull the shore to him, but really it is to pull himself to the shore; so we pray, not to bring God to our mind, but to bring ourselves to him. (Isaiah 64:7)

To pray is to *take hold of God*, by faith to take hold of the promises and the declarations God has made of his goodwill to us and to plead them with him.... (Isaiah 64:7)

We have enough to take hold of, in our wrestling with God by prayer, if we can but plead that his glory is interested in our case, that his name will be profaned if we are run down and glorified if we are relieved. Thence therefore will our most prevailing pleas be drawn: "Do it for thy glory's sake." (Isaiah 37:20)

It becomes us in prayer to show ourselves concerned more for God's glory than for our own comfort. (Jeremiah 14:9)

It will help very much to reconcile us to our troubles, and to make us patient under them, to consider that they are what God has appointed us to. *I opened not my mouth, because thou didst it.* (Jeremiah 29:7)

[T]hose who receive messages of terror from men with patience, and send messages of faith to God by prayer,

## 6: Communion and Prayer

may expect messages of grace and peace from God for their comfort, even when they are most cast down. (Isaiah 37:21-22)

Times of public distress and danger should be praying times with the church; we must pray always, but then especially. (Acts 12:12)

The church's cause is, commonly, more or less successful according as the church's friends are more or less strong in faith and fervent in prayer. (Exodus 17:11)

Those that expect to receive comforts from God must continue instant in prayer. We must call upon him, and then he will answer us. ... Promises are given, not to supersede, but to quicken and encourage prayer. (Jeremiah 33:3)

When the answers of prayer are deferred, God is thereby teaching us to pray more, and to pray better. (Matthew 15:25-28)

[T]his we may be sure of, that, when our prayers are rather the language of our lusts than of our graces, they will return empty. (James 4:3)

Prayers of faith are *filed* in heaven, and are not *forgotten*, though the thing prayed for is not presently *given* in. Prayers made when we were young and coming into the world may be answered when we are old and going out of the world. (Luke 1:7)

The grace of God often with favour accepts the sincere intention, when the providence of God in wisdom prohibits the execution. (Romans 15:24)

God often gives gracious answers to the prayers of his people, not in the thing itself that they pray for, but in something better. Abraham prays, *O that Ishmael may live before thee;* and God hears him for Isaac. So Paul here prays that he may be an instrument of converting souls at Jerusalem: "No," says Christ, "but thou shalt be employed among the Gentiles, and *more shall be the children of the desolate than those of the married wife.*" (Acts 22:21)

In following Christ with our prayers, we must expect to meet with hindrances and manifold discouragements from within and from without, something or other that bids us hold our peace. Such rebuke are permitted, that faith and fervency, patience and perseverance, may be tried. (Matthew 20:31)

Thanksgiving is a proper answer to dark and disquieting thoughts, and may be an effectual means to silence them. Songs of praise are sovereign cordials to drooping souls, and will help to cure melancholy. *I thank thee, O Father;* let us bless God that it is not worse with us than it is. (Matthew 11:25-26)

The world's comforts give but little delight to the soul when it is hurried with melancholy thoughts; they are songs to a heavy heart. But God's comforts will reach the soul, and not the

## Part II: Wisdom (Salvation)

fancy only, and will bring with them that peace and that pleasure which the smiles of the world cannot give and which the frowns of the world cannot take away. (Psalm 94:21-22)

When we are in distress we ought to desire the prayers of our ministers and Christian friends, for thereby we put an honour upon prayer, and an esteem upon our brethren. Kings themselves should look upon their praying people as the strength of the nation.... (Jeremiah 37:3)

Communion in sufferings helps to work compassion towards those that do suffer. (Genesis 40:7)

Those that help us by their prayers at one time should be helped by us with ours at another time. This is the *communion of saints*. (John 21:20-25)

This is one way by which the communion of saints is kept us, not only by their praying together, or with one another, but by their praying for one another when they are absent one from another. (2 Thessalonians 3:1)

We must study to be grateful to those that have prayed for us. (Luke 4:40)

We are really doing our business when we are praying for our friends, if we pray in a right manner, for in those prayers there is not only faith, but love. (Job 42:10-17)

The best way of manifesting our affection to our friends is by praying and giving thanks for them. It is one branch of the communion of saints to give thanks to God mutually for our gifts, graces, and comforts. (1 Corinthians 1:4)

Thanksgiving ought to be part of every prayer; and whatever is the matter of our rejoicing ought to be the matter of our thanksgiving. (Colossians 1:1)

It is common for those to desire to be prayed for who will not be advised; but herein they put a cheat upon themselves, for how can we expect that God should hear others speaking to him for us if we will not hear them speaking to us from him and for him? Many who despise prayer when they are in prosperity will be glad of it when they are in adversity. (Jeremiah 37:3)

Many that prayed not at all, or did but whisper prayer, when they were in prosperity, are brought to pray, nay, are brought to cry, *by reason of their affliction*; and it is for this end that afflictions are sent, and they are in vain if this end be not answered. Those *heap up wrath* who *cry not when God binds them*, Job 36:13. (Jonah 2:2)

*See if there be any sorrow like unto my sorrow....* This might perhaps be truly said of Jerusalem's griefs; but we are apt to apply it too sensibly to ourselves when we are in trouble and more than there is cause for. (Lamentations 1:12)

Grief for a dead child is great, but for a bad child often greater. (1 Samuel 2:34)

Sorrow for the loss of children cannot but be great sorrow, especially if we so far mistake as to think *they are not*. ... Though we mourn, we must not murmur, nor must we resolve, as Jacob did, to go to the grave mourning. In order to repress inordinate grief, we must consider that *there is hope in our end*, hope that there will be an end (the trouble will not last always), that it will be a happy end—the end will be peace. ... We shall see reason to repress our grief for the death of our children that are taken into covenant with God when we consider the hopes we have of their resurrection to eternal life. They are not lost, but gone before. (Jeremiah 31:15-17)

God often takes those soonest whom he loves best, and the time they lose on earth is gained in heaven, to their unspeakable advantage. (Genesis 5:24)

Better is the fruit that drops from the tree before it is ripe than that which is left to hang on till it is rotten. (Ecclesiastes 6:3)

We must live under a constant apprehension of the shortness and uncertainty of life and the near approach of death and eternity. (Psalm 90:12)

When our friends are separated from us by death, this is the consideration with which we raise up our mourning, that we shall see their faces no more; but we complain of this as those that have no hope, for if our friends died in Christ, and we live to him, they are gone to see God's face, to behold his glory, with the reflection of which their faces shine, and we hope to be with them shortly. Though we shall see their faces no more in this world, we hope to see them again in a better world, and to be there together for ever and with the Lord. (Acts 20:36-38)

[T]here is a reason common to all that sleep in Jesus, which is of equal force against inordinate and excessive grief for their death—that they shall rise again, shall rise in glory; and therefore we must *not sorrow as those that have no hope*.... (Luke 7:13)

In affliction we should sit alone to consider our ways (Lam. 3:28), but not sit alone to indulge an inordinate grief. (Psalm 102:4-7)

When sorrow, in such cases, is in danger of growing excessive, we should rather study how to divert and pacify it than to humour and gratify it. (2 Samuel 21:10)

*Is any afflicted? Let him pray.* Weeping must never hinder worshipping. (2 Samuel 12:16)

Weeping must quicken praying, and not deaden it. (Psalm 61:2)

A serious address to our work is the best remedy against inordinate grief. (John 11:34)

The obstinacy of sinners in their sinful ways is altogether their own fault; if their necks are hardened, it is their own act and deed, they have hardened them; if they are deaf to the word of God, it is because they have stopped their own ears. We have need therefore to pray that God, by his grace, would deliver us *from hardness of heart and contempt of his word and commandments.* (Jeremiah 20:15)

Those are not only heated with sin, but hardened in sin, that continue to live without prayer even when they are in trouble and distress. (Hosea 7:6-7)

It is folly to think that God should do for us while we hold fast our iniquity as he did for those that held fast their integrity. (Jeremiah 21:2)

We do not trust God, but tempt him, if, when we pray to him for help, we do not second our prayers with our endeavours. (Isaiah 39:21)

Our prayers must be seconded with our serious endeavours, else we mock God. (Nehemiah 2:1-8)

Prayer to God for grace to turn us is necessary in order to our turning; and those that are convinced by the word of God of the necessity of returning to him will present their supplications to him for that grace. And the consideration of this, that *great is the anger which God has pronounced against us* for sin, should quicken both our prayers and our endeavours. (Jeremiah 36:7)

When we offer up our requests to God it must be with a readiness to receive instructions from him; for, if we turn away our ear from hearing his law, we cannot expect that our prayers should be acceptable to him. We must therefore desire to dwell in the house of the Lord all the days of our life *that we may enquire* there (Ps. 27:4), asking, not only, Lord, what wilt thou do for me? but, Lord *what wilt thou have me to do?* (Zechariah 7:1-7)

Those who would have direction from God must *think on things* themselves, and consult with themselves. It is the *thoughtful,* not the *unthinking,* whom God will guide. (Matthew 1:20)

When we come to God we should consider what we have to say to him; for, if we come without an errand, we are likely to go without an answer. (Hosea 14:2)

Those that would be acquainted with the things of God must be inquisitive concerning those things. Ask, and you shall be told. ... If satisfactory answers be not given to our enquiries and requests quickly, we must renew them, and repeat them, and continue instant and importunate in them, and the vision shall at length *speak, and not lie.* (Zechariah 4:12)

The further we look into the things of God, and the more we converse with them, the more we shall see of those things, and still new discoveries will be made to us; those that know much, if they improve it, shall know more. (Daniel 12:5-6)

When we are speaking to God we must be willing to hear from him; and there-

## 6: Communion and Prayer

fore, on days of fasting and prayer, it is requisite that the word be read and preached. *Hearken unto me, that God may hearken unto you.* (Jeremiah 36:10)

Those that expect to hear from God must withdraw from the world, and get above it, must raise their attention, fix their thought, study the scriptures, consult experiences and the experienced, continue instant in prayer, and thus set themselves *upon the tower.* (Habakkuk 2:1)

It is our wisdom and duty, when we are going to worship God, to lay aside all those thoughts and cares which may divert us from the service, leave them at the bottom of the hill, that we may attend on the Lord without distraction. (Genesis 22:5)

In order to the keeping up of our communion with God we must not only be forward to speak to God, but as forward to hear what he has to say to us; when we have prayed we must look up, must look after our prayers, must set ourselves upon our watchtower. (Daniel 9:21)

Those that act cautiously, and are afraid of sin and snares, if they apply themselves to God for direction, may expect to be led in the right way. (Matthew 2:12)

In every difficult doubtful case our eye must be up to God for direction. (Jeremiah 42:2-3)

The soul may be at liberty when the body is in captivity; for when we are bound, the Spirit of the Lord is not bound. (Daniel 8:2)

When we have but a few breaths to draw we should spend them in the holy gracious breathings of faith and prayer, not in the noisome noxious breathings of sin and corruption. Better die praying and praising than die complaining and quarrelling. (Job 7:11)

As long as we continue living we must continue praying. This breath we must breathe till we breathe our last, because then we shall take our leave of it, and till then we have continual occasion for it. (Psalm 116:1-4)

It is good to die praying; then we need help—strength we never had, to do a work we never did—and how can we fetch in that help and strength but by prayer? (Acts 7:56)

A man may die in a prison and yet *die in peace.* ... It is better to live and die penitent in a prison than to live and die impenitent in a palace. (Jeremiah 34:5)

As in the dark, so out of the depths, we may cry unto God. No place, no time, amiss for prayer, if the heart be lifted up to God. (Acts 16:25)

No confinement can deprive God's people of his presence; no locks nor bars can shut out his gracious visits; nay, oftentimes *as their afflictions abound their consolations much more abound,* and they have the most reviving communications of his favour when the world

## Part II: Wisdom (Salvation)

frowns upon them. Paul's sweetest epistles were those that bore date out of a prison. (Jeremiah 33:1)

When at any time we are perplexed about the particular methods and dispensations of Providence it is good for us to have recourse to our first principles, and to satisfy ourselves with the general doctrines of God's wisdom, power, and goodness. (Jeremiah 32:17-19)

We must, in our prayers, dutifully attend the course of Providence; we must ask for mercies in their proper time, and not expect that God should go out of his usual way and method for us. But, since sometimes God denied rain in the usual time as a token of his displeasure, they must pray for it then as a token of his favour, and they shall not pray in vain. *Ask and it shall be given you.* (Zechariah 10:1)

Miracles are not to be expected when ordinary means are to be used. (Acts 12:10-11)

The mercies we have received must be improved, both for direction what to pray for, and for our encouragement in prayer. The first light and the first grace are given in a preventing way, further degrees of both which must be daily prayed for. (Matthew 13:36)

In every prayer we must make confession, not only of the sins we have been guilty of (which we commonly call *confession*), but of our faith in God and dependence upon him, our sorrow for sin and our resolutions against it. It must be our confession, must be the language of our own convictions and that which we ourselves do heartily subscribe to. (Daniel 9:4-19)

Our prayers may and must agree with God's word; and what day God has here called we are to call for, and no other. And though we are bound in charity to forgive our enemies, and to pray for them, yet we may in faith pray for the accomplishment of that which God has spoken against his and his church's enemies, that will not repent to give him glory. (Lamentations 1:21-22)

When God intends great mercy for his people the first thing he does is to set them a praying; thus he seeks to destroy their enemies by stirring them up to seek to him that he would do it for them; because, though he has proposed it and promised it ... it is for his own glory to do it, ... And it is a happy presage to the distressed church of deliverance approaching, and is, as it were, the dawning of its day, when his people are stirred up to cry mightily to him for it. (Zechariah 12:10)

The surest way to have our deliverances continued and completed is to give God the glory of what he has done for us. (Revelation 19:3)

When we are praising God for what he has done we must call upon him for the future favours which his church is in need and expectation of; and in praying to him we really praise

## 6: Communion and Prayer

him and give him glory; he takes it so. (Jeremiah 31:7)

No God like the God of Israel. ... When we are expecting that God should bless us in doing well for us we must bless him by speaking well of him: and one of the most solemn ways of praising God is by acknowledging that there is none like him. (Deuteronomy 33:26)

Those that have received distinguishing favours from God ought to be most forward and zealous in praising him. (Isaiah 12:4-6)

It is good, at least sometimes, upon special occasions, and when we find our hearts enlarged, to continue long in secret prayer, and to take full scope in *pouring out our hearts before the Lord*. We must not *restrain prayer*, Job 15:4. (Matthew 14:23)

Masters of families should use their authority for the promotion of religion in their families. Not only we, but our houses also, should serve the Lord, Josh. 24:15. (Genesis 35:2-3)

Little children must learn betimes to *minister to the Lord*. Parents must train them up to it, and God will accept them. Particularly let them learn to pay respect to their teachers, as Samuel to Eli. None can begin too soon to be religious. (1 Samuel 2:18)

Little ones, as they come to the exercise of reason, must be trained up in the exercises of religion. (Nehemiah 8:1-2)

*Train up children* in that age of vanity, to keep them from the sins and snares of it, in that learning age, to prepare them for what they are designed for. ... Ordinarily the vessel retains the savour with which it was first seasoned. Many indeed have departed from the good way in which they were trained up; Solomon himself did so. But early training may be a means of their recovering themselves, as it is supposed Solomon did. (Proverbs 22:6)

In all the instructions and informations parents give their children, they should have this chiefly in their eye, to teach and engage them to *fear God for ever*. Serious godliness is the best learning. (Joshua 4:24)

Those that are of kin to each other should, as much as they can, be acquainted with each other; and the bonds of nature should be improved for the strengthening of the bonds of Christian communion. (Numbers 2:2)

Masters of families must not only pray for daily bread for their families, and food convenient, but must lay out themselves with care and industry to provide it. (Genesis 42:2)

Every house not only may be, but ought to be, a house of prayer; where we have a tent God must have an altar, and on it we must offer spiritual sacrifices. (Daniel 6:10)

[T]he law itself was ceremonial, and is now no longer in force: the blood of

Christ who has come (and we are to look for no other) is that alone which makes atonement for the soul, and of which the blood of the sacrifices was an imperfect type: the coming of the substance supersedes the shadow. (Leviticus 17:11)

Praise and thanksgiving are our spiritual sacrifice, and, if they come from an upright heart, shall please the Lord *better than an ox or bullock,* Ps. 69:30, 32. (Hosea 14:2)

The families of good people, in their family capacity, may apply to God and stay themselves upon him as their God. If we and our houses serve the Lord, we and are houses shall be protected and blessed by him. Prov. 3:33. (Jeremiah 31:1)

# -7-

# Humility

The foundation of all other graces is laid in humility. Those who would build high must begin low; ... Those who thus humble themselves, and comply with God when he humbles them, shall be thus exalted.

Matthew Henry
on Matthew 5:3-5

The foundation of all other graces is laid in humility. Those who would build high must begin low; ... Those who thus humble themselves, and comply with God when he humbles them, shall be thus exalted. (Matthew 5:3-5)

Those who seek not their own glory shall have the honour that comes from God; it is reserved for the humble. (Matthew 1:18)

Those that are exalted above others in the world must humble themselves before God, who is higher than the highest, and to whom kings and queens are accountable. (Jeremiah 13:18)

Crowns are at God's disposal; no head wears them but God sets them there, whether in judgment to his land or for mercy the event will show. (Psalm 21:1-6)

Those that would in any office serve the Lord acceptably to him, and profitably to others, must do it with all humility of mind, Matt. 20:26, 27. (Acts 20:19)

Great gifts appear most graceful and illustrious when those that have them use them humbly, and take not the praise of them to themselves, but give it to God. To such God gives more grace. (Genesis 41:16)

Though civility teaches us to call others by their highest titles, yet humility and wisdom teach us to call ourselves by the lowest. (Genesis 16:8)

Though we must aim to be better than others, yet we must, *in lowliness of mind, esteem others better than ourselves;* for we know more evil of ourselves than we do of any of our brethren. (John 21:15)

[W]hat an amazing condescension was it for the Son of God to come from heaven to earth and take our nature upon him, that he might *seek and save those that were lost!* Herein indeed he humbled himself. (Psalm 113:1-9)

Christ's gracious condescensions to us, should make us the more humble and self-abasing before him. (Matthew 8:10-11)

It well becomes those whom God has highly favoured and honoured to be very humble and low in their own eyes, to lay aside all opinion of their own wisdom and worthiness, that God alone may have all the praise of the good they are, and have, and do, and that all may be attributed to the freeness of his good-will towards them and the fulness of his good work in them. ... Humble men will be always ready to think that what God does for them and by them is more for the sake of others than for their own. (Daniel 2:30)

The glory of all that is at any time well done, by ourselves or others, must be humbly and thankfully transmitted to God, who works all our good works in us and for us. (Genesis 9:26)

[W]e must be forward to meet God with our thanksgivings when he is

# 7: Humility

coming towards us with his mercies. (Isaiah 26 Introduction)

Those whom God puts honour upon, are thereby made very humble and low in their own eyes; willing to be abased, so that Christ may be magnified; to be any thing, to be nothing, so that Christ may be all. (Matthew 3:11)

The highest honour of the greatest apostle, and most eminent ministers, is to be the servants of Jesus Christ; not the masters of the churches, but the servants of Christ. (Philippians 1:1)

On the head of Christ God never set a crown of gold, but of thorns first, and then of glory. (Psalm 21:3)

The disciples of Christ, and especially his ministers, should hold fast their integrity, and keep a good conscience, whatever opposition of hardships they meet with from the world. Whatever they suffer from men, they must follow the example, and fulfil the will and precepts, of their Lord. They must be content, with him and for him, to be despised and abused. (1 Corinthians 4:12-13)

[I]t becomes inferiors to bear with meekness and silence the contempts put upon them in wrath and passion. *When thou art the anvil lie thou still.* (1 Samuel 20:34)

Let us acknowledge God's right to rule us, and our own obligations to be ruled by him; and never allow any will of our own in contradiction to, or competition with, the holy will of God. (Genesis 2:16-17)

It is a great affront to God, and an abuse of his goodness, when the more mercies we receive from him the more sins we commit against him, and when the more wealth men have the more mischief they do. Should not we be thus abundant in the service of our God, as they were in the service of their idols? As we find our estates increasing, we should proportionably abound the more in works of piety and charity. (Hosea 10:1)

When men's outward condition rises their minds commonly rise with it; and it is very rare to find a humble spirit in the midst of great advancements. (Ezekiel 31:10)

The world's smiles are more dangerous than its frowns. (2 Samuel 16:5)

It very well becomes the greatest and best of men, even in the midst of the highest advancements, to have low and mean thoughts of themselves; for the greatest of men are worms, the best are sinners, and those that are highest advanced have nothing but what they have received…. (2 Samuel 7:18)

It is an excellent thing to have a lowly spirit in the midst of high advancements; and those who abase themselves shall be exalted. (2 Corinthians 12:6-7)

A well-grounded assurance of heaven and happiness, instead of puffing a man up with pride, will make and keep him very humble. Those that would be found conformable to Christ, and partakers of his Spirit, must study to keep their minds low in the midst of the greatest advancements. (John 13:4-5)

*Knowledge puffeth up*; it is hard to know much and not to know it too well and to be elevated with it. He [the prince of Tyrus] that was *wiser than Daniel* was prouder than Lucifer. Those therefore that are knowing must study to be humble and to evidence that they are so. (Ezekiel 28:3)

Many can so readily affirm the truth, that they think they have knowledge enough to be proud of, who, when they are called to confirm the truth, and to vindicate and defend it, show they have ignorance enough to be ashamed of. (Matthew 22:43-45)

Many ask good questions with a design rather to *justify themselves* than to *inform themselves*, rather proudly to show what is good in them than humbly to see what is bad in them. (Luke 10:25-28)

Humility is a lesson so hardly learned, that we have need by all ways and means to be taught it. (Matthew 18:2)

Humility is one of the brightest ornaments of youth, and one of the best omens. (Ruth 2:1-3)

When the estate rises, the mind is apt to rise with it, in self-conceit, self-complacency, and self-confidence. Let us therefore strive to keep the spirit low in a high condition; humility is both the ease and the ornament of prosperity. (Deuteronomy 8:13-14)

Many have been undone by coming too soon to their honours and estates. (2 Kings 21:2)

Holy fear of ourselves, and not presumptuous confidence, is the best security from apostasy from God, and final rejection by him. (1 Corinthians 9:27)

[I]t is better to be low and in the church than high and out of it…. (Genesis 48:5)

It should be a satisfaction to them who are in a low condition, that they are not exposed to the temptations of a high and prosperous condition…. (Matthew 19:23)

It is hard for good men to compare themselves with others, and not to have too great a conceit of themselves; to prevent which, we should consider that our preference to others is no achievement of our own, but the free gift of God's grace to us, and not to others; so that we have nothing to boast of, Ps. 115:1; Cor. 4:7. (Matthew 16:17)

If we would compare ourselves with others who excel us, this would be a good method to keep us humble; we should be pleased and thankful for what we have of gifts or graces, but never pride ourselves therein, as if there were none to be compared with us or that did excel us. (2 Corinthians 10:12)

We should reckon nothing below us

## 7: Humility

but sin, and be willing to condescend to the meanest offices, if there be occasion, for the good of our brethren. ... Those that receive benefit by the fire should help to carry fuel to it. (Acts 28:3)

If we be not so bold as to lead, yet we must not be so proud and sullen as not to follow even our inferiors in a good work. (Judges 5:14)

Those that would be *placed alone in the midst of the earth* while they were above ground, and obliged all about them to keep their distance, must lie with the multitude when they are underground, for there are innumerable before them. (Jeremiah 19:11)

Those who lie in Christ's bosom may often learn from those who lie at his feet something that will be profitable for them, and be reminded of that which they did not of themselves think of. (John 13:25)

In our best state in this world we have need of one another's help; for we are members one of another, and *the eye cannot say to the hand, I have no need of thee*, 1 Cor. 12:21. We must therefore be glad to receive help from others, and give help to others, as there is occasion. (Genesis 2:18)

Every branch of the tree is not a top branch; but, because it is a lower branch, is it therefore not of the tree? (Genesis 47:1-3)

Munificence recommends a man more than magnificence. ... [Be] such a saint as not to avenge affronts, yet ... not such a fool as not to take notice of them. (1 Samuel 30:31)

If a man cheat and abuse me once, it is his fault; if twice, it is my own. (Matthew 18:17)

Christian prudence and humility teach us, in many cases, to recede from our right, rather than give offence by insisting upon it. We must never decline our duty for fear of giving offence ... but we must sometimes deny ourselves in that which is our secular interest, rather than give offence; as Paul, 1 Cor. 8:13; Rom. 14:13. (Matthew 17:27)

*Answer not a fool according to his folly.* But, if it be answered, let reason and grace have the answering of it, not pride and passion. (Job 11:2-3)

Though Christ did not think fit to answer him [Pilate] when he was impertinent (then *answer not a fool according to his folly, lest thou also be like him*), yet he did think fit to answer him when he was imperious; then *answer a fool according to his folly, lest he be wise in his own conceit*, Prov. 26:4, 5. (John 19:8-11)

*Be not wise in your own conceits.* It is good to be wise, but it is bad to think ourselves so; for there is more hope of a fool than of him that is wise in his own eyes. (Romans 12:3)

Those that climb so fast have need of good heads and good hearts. It is more difficult to know how to abound than how to be abased. (1 Samuel 18:5)

## Part II: Wisdom (Salvation)

Those who would rise high must begin low. *Before honour is humility.* ... God has further honours in reserve for those whose spirits continue low when their reputation rises. (Matthew 3:13-15)

Those whose latter end greatly increases ought, with humility and thankfulness, to remember how small their beginning was. (Genesis 32:10)

Those whom God has built up into families, whose beginning was small, but whose latter end greatly increases, should use that as an argument with themselves why they should serve God. (Deuteronomy 11:6)

Those that are comfortably fixed ought often to call to mind their former unsettled state, when they were but little in their own eyes. (Leviticus 24:43)

Those whom God has endued with abilities for his service ought not to be despised nor laid aside for the meanness either of their origin or of their beginnings. Though Amos himself is not ashamed to own that he was a herdsman, yet others ought not to upbraid him with it nor think the worse of him for it. (Amos 1:1-2)

If old people be upbraided with their infirmities, and laid aside for them, let them not think it strange; Samuel himself was so. (1 Samuel 8:4-5)

Let not those that are great in the world be ashamed to own their kindred that are mean and despised, lest they be found therein proud, scornful, and unnatural. (Ruth 2:1)

It is the wisdom of those that would rise fast, and stand firm, to take their friends along with them. (2 Kings 9:14-15)

The more fit any person is for service commonly the less opinion he has of himself.... (Exodus 3:11)

Sometimes there is most of the *power* of religion where there is least of the *pomp* of it: *the poor receive the gospel.* (Matthew 13:1-3)

It is a bad thing to speak of good men with disdain because they are poor. (Matthew 12:24)

The value of good people ought not to be estimated by their present external condition. (1 Peter 1:1-2)

But he who thus *reproaches the poor despises his Maker,* in whose hands *rich and poor meet together.* (Amos 8:4-6)

Ignorance is the cause of our rash and uncharitable censures of our brethren. (Matthew 12:7)

Many of our mistakes would be rectified, and our unjust censures of others corrected, if we would but recollect what *we have read* in the scripture; appeals to that are most convincing. (Mark 2:25-26)

Worldly prosperity, when it feeds men's pride, makes them forgetful of God; for they remember him only

## 7: Humility

when they want him. ... It is sad that those favours which ought to make us mindful of God, and studious what we shall render to him, should make us unmindful of him, and regardless what we do against him. We ought to know that we live upon God when we live upon common providence, though we do not, as Israel in the wilderness, live upon miracles. (Hosea 13:5-6)

See here, 1. That which should make us humble. As we were made out of the earth, so we are maintained out of it. Once indeed men did eat angels' food, bread from heaven; but they died (John 6:49); it was to them but as food out of the earth, Ps. 104:14. (Genesis 1:29)

We must never take the praise of our prosperity to ourselves, nor attribute it to our ingenuity or industry; for bread is not always *to the wise,* nor *riches to men of understanding,* Eccl. 9:11. (Deuteronomy 8:14)

When we look upon our enjoyments, and have occasion to speak of them, it must be with humble acknowledgements of our own unworthiness and thankful acknowledgements of God's goodness, with a just value for the achievements of others and with an expectation of losses and changes, not dreaming that our mountain stands so strong but that it may soon be moved. (Isaiah 39:2)

As, when we are in prosperity, we are ready to think our mountain will never be brought low, so when we are in adversity we are ready to think our valley will never be filled, but, in both, to conclude that *to morrow must be as this day,* which is as absurd as to think, when the weather is either fair or foul, that it will always be so, that the flowing tide will always flow, or the ebbing tide will always ebb. (Job 35:14-16)

See what changes the comforts of this life are subject to. After great plenty may come great scarcity; how strong soever we may think our mountain stands, if God speak the word, it will soon be moved. (Genesis 41:29-31)

When proud sinners are humbled and brought down it is designed that others should take example by them not to lift up themselves in security and insolence when they prosper in the world. (Nahum 3:7)

[T]he greater dignity men are advanced to the greater disgrace they are in danger of falling into. (1 Chronicles 10:8-10)

The fall of proud presumptuous men is intended for warning to others to keep humble. It would have been well for Nebuchadnezzar, who was himself active in bringing down the Assyrian, if he had taken the admonition. (Ezekiel 31:17)

Let not the stout man glory in his courage, any more than the strong man in his strength; for God can weaken both mind and body. (Joshua 2:11)

God often orders it so that that which we most trust to first fails us, and that which was *the chief of our might* proves

## Part II: Wisdom (Salvation)

the least of our help. (Jeremiah 49:34-39)

Those that are written childless must see God's writing them so. God often withholds those temporal comforts from his own children which he gives plentifully to others that are strangers to him. (Genesis 15:2-3)

It is just with God to take that from us which we make the matter of our pride, and on which we build a carnal confidence. (Isaiah 39:6)

None of our comforts are ever lost but what have been a thousand times forfeited. If the wicked are *driven away*, it is *in their wickedness*. (Ezekiel 31:11)

God is able to destroy both soul and body, and therefore we should fear him more than man, who can but kill only the body. Great armies before him are but as great woods, which he can fell or fire when he pleases. (Isaiah 10:18)

Those who are truly humbled for sin will cheerfully submit to the will of God, even in a sentence of death itself. (Jonah 1:12)

Those are in the best frame to meet sufferings who are mortified to the world and live a life of self-denial. (Jeremiah 35:7)

Seasons of deep humiliation require abstinence from lawful pleasures. (1 Corinthians 7:5)

This ... is a warning to us never to be secure in this world. Worse may be yet to come when we think the worst is over; and that end of one trouble, which we fancy to be the end of all trouble, may prove to be the beginning of another, of a greater. ... There is many a ship wrecked in the harbour. We can never be sure of peace on this side heaven. (Jeremiah 41:10)

See the uncertainty of human affairs; such turns are they subject to that the spoke which was uppermost may soon come to be undermost. (1 Kings 20:32)

When we are in the midst of our possessions and enjoyments, we must keep up an expectation of troubles, for our gardens of delight are in a vale of tears. (John 18:1)

The removal of the comforts of others should awaken us to think of parting with ours too; for *are we better than they?* We know not how soon the same cup, or a more bitter one, may be put into our hands, and should therefore weep with those that weep, as being ourselves also in the body. (Ezekiel 24:21)

It is seldom that those who are at ease themselves rightly weigh the afflictions of the afflicted. Every one feels most from his own burden; few feel from other people's. (Job 6:2-3)

As Christians, our duty to God obliges us to frequent sorrow: and our compassion towards the miserable, the dishonour done to God, the calamities of his church, and the destruction of mankind, from their own folly and from divine vengeance, raise, in a generous and pious mind, almost continual sorrow. (1 Peter 1:6)

A good man, in such a bad world as this is, cannot but be a *man of sorrows*. (Jeremiah 4:19)

Tears of tenderness and affection are no disparagement at all, even to great and wise men. (Genesis 29-30)

Let no man think he disparages himself by his humility or charity. (Acts 23:19)

There is nothing more commonly seen *under the sun* than *the tears of the oppressed*, with whom *the clouds return after the rain*, Eccl. 4:1. (Lamentations 1:4)

As long as we are here in this world we must expect that the clouds will return after the rain, and perhaps the sorest and sharpest trials may be reserved for the last. (Job 10:16-17)

It becomes us, while we are here in this vale of tears, to conform to the temper of the climate and to sow in tears. *Blessed are those that mourn, for they shall be comforted* hereafter; but let them expect that while they are here the *clouds will still return after the rain*. While we find our hearts such fountains of sin, it is fit that our eyes should be fountains of tears. (Jeremiah 9:1)

*Weeping may endure for a night, but joy will come in the morning*. If we can but get to heaven at last, *all tears shall be wiped from our eyes*; and the prospect of it now should make us moderate our sorrows and refrain our tears. (1 Corinthians 7:30)

In time of trouble we must not only pray, but cry, must be fervent and importunate in prayer; and to God, from whom both the destruction is and the salvation must be, ought our cry to be always directed. (Joel 1:19)

Even where there is little cry of devotion, the God of pity sometimes graciously hears the cry of affliction. Tears speak as well as prayers. (Genesis 16:11)

Prayers and tears are the weapons with which the saints have obtained the most glorious victories. (Hosea 12:4-6)

[P]rayers and tears are the church's arms; therewith she fights, not only against her enemies, but for her friends: and to these means they have recourse. (Acts 12:5)

[T]ears of devout affection have a voice, a loud prevailing voice, in the ears of Christ; no rhetoric like this. (John 11:31-32)

Observe, (1.) The very different events that befal the children of men. Light and darkness are opposite to each other, and yet, in the course of providence, they are sometimes intermixed, like the morning and evening twilights, *neither day nor night....* There is a mixture of joys and sorrows in the same cup, allays to each other. Sometimes they are counterchanged, as noonday light and midnight darkness. (Isaiah 45:7)

## Part II: Wisdom (Salvation)

By the variety of events that befal us, if we look up to God in all, we may come to acquaint ourselves better with his various attributes and designs. (Ezekiel 40:28)

[L]et them not dare to contend with him who is infinitely above them.... *Shall the clay say to him that forms it, "What makest thou?"* ... "Shall the clay pretend to be wiser than the potter, and therefore to advise him, or mightier than the potter and therefore to control him?" He that gave us being, that gave us this being, may design concerning us, and dispose of us, as he pleases; and it is impudent presumption for us to prescribe to him. Shall we impeach God's wisdom, or question his power, who are ourselves so curiously, so wonderfully made? Shall we say *He has no hands*, whose hands made us, and in whose hands we are? The doctrine of God's sovereignty has enough in it to silence all our discontents and objections against the methods of his providence and grace.... (Isaiah 45:9)

Man is not his own maker, therefore he must not be his own master; but the Author of his being must be the director of his motions and the centre of them. ... Those have little reason to be proud who are so near akin to dust. (Genesis 5:1-2)

Observe, 1. That man was made last of all the creatures, that it might not be suspected that he had been, any way, a helper to God in the creation of the world: that question must be forever humbling and mortifying to him, *Where wast thou, or any of thy kind, when I laid the foundations of the earth?* Job 38:4. (Genesis 1:26)

God cannot be a *gainer* by our services, and therefore cannot be made a *debtor* by them. He has no need of us, nor can our services make any addition to his perfections. (Luke 17:10)

The best men are often much at a loss in their enquiries concerning divine things, and meet with that which they do not *understand*. But the better they are the more sensible they are of their own weaknesses and ignorance, and the more ready to acknowledge them. (Daniel 12:8)

Those that have the least sin are the most sensible of it. (2 Chronicles 20:3)

*Thou art a man, and not God,* a depending creature; thou art *flesh, and not spirit,* Isa. 31:3. Note, Men must be made to know that they are *but men,* Ps. 9:20. The greatest wits, the greatest potentates, the greatest saints, are *men, and not gods.* Only Jesus Christ was both God and man. (Ezekiel 28:2)

It is our wisdom and duty to accommodate ourselves to our place and rank, and not aim to live above it. What has been the lot of our fathers why may we not be content that it should be our lot, and live according to it? *Mind not high things.* ... Humility and contentment in obscurity are often the best policy and men's surest protection. (Jeremiah 35:6-7)

## 7: Humility

As in our *stature*, so in our *state*, it is our wisdom to take *it as it is*, and make the best of it; for fretting and vexing, carping and caring, will not mend it. (Luke 12:25)

If we have for necessity, it is no matter though we have not for delicacy and curiosity. God, in love, gives *meat for our hunger;* but, in wrath, gives *meat for our lusts,* Ps. 78:18. (Mark 6:38)

We may live well enough upon plain food without dainties; but we cannot live upon dainties without plain food. Let us thank God that that which is most needful and useful is generally most cheap and common. (Genesis 43:11)

In all conditions of life it is our wisdom and duty to make the best of that which is, and not to throw away the comfort of what we may have because we have not all we would have. ... If the *earth be the Lord's*, then, wherever a child of God goes, he does not go off his Father's ground. (Jeremiah 29:4-6)

Our triumphs must not terminate in what God does for us and gives to us, but must pass through them to himself, who is the author and giver of them: *This is our God*. (Isaiah 25:9)

Wise and good men, though they covet to do good, yet are far from coveting to have it talked of when it is done; because it is God's acceptance, not men's applause, that they aim at. (Matthew 12:16)

Good works must be done, not of vainglory to be seen, yet such as may be seen to God's glory and the good of men. (Philemon 6)

Humble saints take more pleasure in doing good than in hearing of it again. (Genesis 30:30)

[H]onour is like a shadow, which flees from those who pursue it *(for a man to seek his own glory is not glory)*, but follows those that decline it, and draw from it. The less good men say of themselves, the more will others say of them. (Luke 5:15)

None will be losers at last by their humility and modesty. Honour, like the shadow, follows those that flee from it, but flees from those that pursue it. (1 Samuel 10:23)

Humble generous souls will give others their due praise without fear of diminishing themselves by it. What we have of reputation, as well as of other things, will not be the less for our giving every body his own. (John 1:34-36)

It well becomes us to speak sparingly of our own good deeds. (Matthew 9:10-13)

It becomes us, when we have any service to do for God, to be afraid lest we mismanage it, and lest it suffer through our weakness and unfitness for it; it becomes us likewise to have low thoughts of ourselves and to be diffident of our own sufficiency. Those that are young should consider that they are

## Part II: Wisdom (Salvation)

so, should be afraid ... and not venture beyond their length. (Jeremiah 1:6)

We must take heed of tempting God by running upon difficulties beyond our strength, and venturing too far in a way of suffering. If our call be clear to expose ourselves, we may hope that God will enable us to honour him; but, if it be not, we may fear that God will leave us to shame ourselves. (John 18:16-27)

[M]any that are feeble in spirit, timorous and faint-hearted, unfit for services and sufferings, are yet strengthened by the grace of God *with all might in the inward man*. To those who are sensible of their weakness, and ready to acknowledge they have no might, God does in a special manner increase strength; for, *when we are weak* in ourselves, *then we are strong in the Lord*. (Isaiah 40:29)

The same power that is engaged against proud sinners is engaged for humble saints, who prevail with God by strength derived from him.... (Job 23:6)

Those who, while their beginning is small, are humble and honest, contented and industrious, are in a likely way to see their latter end greatly increasing. He that is faithful in a little shall be entrusted with more. (Genesis 30:43)

When God is about to give his people the expected good he pours out a spirit of prayer, and it is a good sign that he is coming towards them in mercy. ... Promises are given, not to supersede, but to quicken and encourage prayer: and when deliverance is coming we must by prayer go forth to meet it. (Jeremiah 29:12-14)

Though a sense of our own weakness and insufficiency should make us go humbly about our work, yet it should not make us draw back from it when God calls us to it. God was angry with Moses even for his modest excuses.... (Jeremiah 1:7)

# -8-

# Backsliding and Discipline

The backslidings of those that have professed religion and relation to God are in a special manner provoking to him.

Matthew Henry
on Isaiah 1:2-4

The backslidings of those that have professed religion and relation to God are in a special manner provoking to him. (Isaiah 1:2-4)

It is often so; when some backslide many backslide with them; the disease is infectious. (John 6:66)

As one coward makes many, so does one believer, one sceptic, *making his brethren's heart to faint like his heart*, Deut. 20:8. (John 20:25)

[T]heir backslidings have been their choice and their pleasure, which should have been their shame and pain, and therefore they will be their ruin. (Jeremiah 14:10)

Satan may tempt, but he cannot force; may persuade us to cast ourselves down, but he cannot cast us down, Matt. 4:6. (Genesis 3:6)

Whatever real mischief is done us, it is of *our own doing;* the Devil can but persuade, he cannot compel; he can but say, *Cast thyself down;* he cannot cast us down. Every man is tempted, when he is drawn away of his own lust, and not forced, but enticed. (Matthew 4:6)

When we are tempted to sin we should consider how it will appear in the reflection. Let us never do any thing for which our own consciences will afterwards have occasion to upbraid us, and which we shall look back upon with regret: *My heart shall not reproach me.* (1 Samuel 25:30-31)

Withdrawing from the communion of the faithful is commonly the first overt-act of a backslider, and the beginning of an apostasy. (John 13:30)

God knows how to suit his favours to the wants and necessities of his children. He that has a plaster for every sore will provide one for that first which is most painful. (Genesis 12:2)

Though backslidings from God are the dangerous diseases and wounds of the soul, yet they are not incurable, for God has graciously promised that if backsliding sinners will apply to him as their physician, and comply with his methods, he will heal their backslidings. He will heal the guilt of their backslidings by pardoning mercy and their *bent to backslide* by renewing grace. Their *iniquity* shall *not be their ruin.* (Hosea 14:4)

It is possible that a good man may, not only fall into sin, but relapse into the same sin, through the surprise and strength of temptation and the infirmity of the flesh. Let backsliders repent then, but not despair, Jer. 3:22. (Genesis 20:1-2)

Constant care to abstain from that sin, whatever it be, which most easily besets us, and to mortify the habit of it, will be a good evidence for us that we are upright before God. (Psalm 18:20-21)

One miscarriage should serve as a warning to prevent another; those are

## 8: Backsliding and Discipline

careless indeed that stumble twice at the same stone. (Genesis 28:45)

When we find ourselves either by our outward circumstances or our inward dispositions entering into temptation, it concerns us to *rise and pray*, Lord, help me in this *time of need*. (Luke 22:46)

Those who keep the gospel in a time of peace shall be kept by Christ in an hour of temptation. (Revelation 3:10)

When we are out of the way of our duty we are in the way of temptation. (2 Samuel 11:1)

In our repentance we ought to lament not only our backslidings, but our *bent to backslide*, not only our actual transgressions, but our original corruption, the sin that dwells in us, the carnal mind. (Hosea 11:7)

Though our sins have been very great and very many, and though we have often backslidden and are still prone to offend, yet God will repeat his pardon, and welcome even backsliding children that return to him in sincerity. (Isaiah 55:7)

God suffers those that are out of the way to wander awhile, that when they see their folly, and what a loss they have brought themselves to, they may be the better disposed to return. (Genesis 16:7-9)

God can make his call to reach those that are ever so far off, and none come but those whom he calls. (Acts 2:39)

Those who, upon their repentance, are received by the church into communion again may take the comfort of their absolution in heaven, if their hearts be upright with God. As suspension is for the terror of the obstinate, so absolution is for the encouragement of the penitent. (Matthew 18:18)

Those that have backslidden from God, if they do in sincerity return to him, are admitted as freely as any to all the privileges and comforts of the everlasting covenant.... (Jeremiah 24:7)

Those that are in a sinful state are concerned to make all possible haste out of it. ... Those who leave their sins, and turn to God, will themselves be unspeakable gainers by the change, Prov. 9:12 (Genesis 12:1)

When we have stepped aside into any disagreeable frame or way our care must be to return and compose ourselves into a right temper of mind again; and *then* we may expect God will help us, if thus we endeavour to help ourselves. (Jeremiah 15:19)

It is of good use to oblige ourselves to our duty with all possible solemnity, and this is especially seasonable after notorious backslidings to sin and decays in that which is good. He that bears an honest mind does not shrink from positive engagements: fast bind, fast find. (2 Kings 23:1-3)

Thus, when backsliders return, they must *do their first works*, must renew the covenant they first made; and it must be a *perpetual covenant*, that must never be broken; and, in order to that, must never be forgotten; for a due remembrance of it will be the means of a due observance of it. (Jeremiah 50:5)

*Faithful are the reproofs of a friend*, though for the present they are painful as *wounds*. It is a sign that our friends are faithful indeed if, in love to our souls, they will not suffer sin upon us, nor let us alone in it. The physician's care is to cure the patient's disease, not to please his palate. ... It is dangerous to be caressed and flattered by *an enemy* whose *kisses are deceitful*. (Proverbs 27:6)

The greatest kindness we can do to one that is going a dangerous way is to tell him of his danger. (1 Kings 22:18)

*Rebuke a wise man, and he will be yet wiser*, and will take warning, Prov. 9:8, 9. (2 Chronicles 19:1-4)

It is possible for a man to be in the way of duty, and in the way to happiness, and yet meet with great troubles and disappointments. (Genesis 12:10)

Sometimes God makes his people's troubles contribute to the increase of their greatness, and their sun shines the brighter for having been under a cloud. (Psalm 71:21)

If we suffer ill for doing well, provided we suffer it well, and as we should, we ought to rejoice in that grace which enables us so to do. (Acts 5:40)

Suffering in a good cause should rather sharpen than blunt the edge of holy resolution. (1 Thessalonians 2:2)

We must not wonder if, when we are doing well, God sends afflictions to quicken us to do better, to do our best, and to press forward towards perfection. (Isaiah 36:1)

Afflictions are God's threshing-instruments, designed to loosen us from the world, to separate between us and our chaff, and to prepare us for use. (Isaiah 28:28-29)

When God's hand is lifted up, and men will not see, it shall be laid on, and they shall be made to feel.... (Jeremiah 12:12)

When God afflicts his people, it is with a gracious design to mollify and reform them; it is but when need is and when he knows it is the best method he can use. The rest shall be ruined.... (Jeremiah 9:9)

God is sometimes angry with his own people; yet it is to be complained of, not as a sword to cut off, but only as a rod to correct; it is to them *the rod of his wrath*, a chastening which, though grievous for the present, will in the issue be advantageous. (Lamentations 3:1)

God's people, when they are cast down, are tempted to think themselves cast off and forsaken of God; but it is a mistake. ... The people of God, being greatly afflicted and oppressed ...

though they suffered hard things, yet they kept close to God and to their duty. ... When the heart turns back the steps will soon decline; for it is the evil heart of unbelief that inclines to depart from God. (Psalm 44:17)

The distresses of God's people sometimes prevail to such a degree that they cannot find any footing for their faith, nor keep their head above water, with any comfortable expectation. (Lamentations 3:54)

Where there is true faith, yet there may be a mixture of unbelief. The best are not always alike strong. (Matthew 11:1-6)

The grievance and the grief sometimes may be such that the most prudent patient man cannot forbear complaining. ... It is not for himself, or any affliction in his family that he grieves thus; but it is purely upon the public account, it is his people's case that he lays to heart thus. (Jeremiah 4:19-21)

It is a certain sign that our afflictions are means of much good to us, and earnests of more, when we are kept by the grace of God from being overcome by the temptations of an afflicted state. (Hosea 3:1-3)

Whatever evil is upon us at any time we must conclude *there is a cause* for it; there is evil done by us, or else this evil would not be upon us; there is a ground for God's controversy. (Jonah 1:4-6)

Though Christ's disciples be brought into wants and straits, through their own carelessness and incogitancy, yet he encourages them to trust in him for relief. (Matthew 16:8)

However we may see cause for our own information to plead with God, yet it becomes us to own that, whatever he says or does, he is in the right. (Jeremiah 12:1)

When our services of God are soured with sin his providences will justly be embittered to us. (Amos 6:12)

A humble believing enquiry into the design and tendency of the darkest dispensations of Providence would help to reconcile us to them, and to grieve the less, and fear the less, because of them; it will silence us to ask, Whence came they? but will abundantly satisfy us to ask, Whither go they? for we know they *work for good*, Rom. 8:28. (John 16:1-6)

The afflictions of good people are designed for their trial; but by these trials they are *purified* and *made white*, their corruptions are purged out, their graces are brightened, and made both more vigorous and more conspicuous.... (Daniel 12:12)

It is a gross mistake, but a very common one, to think that whom God afflicts he treats as his enemies; whereas, on the contrary, *as many as he loves he rebukes and chastens;* it is the discipline of his sons. (Job 19:11)

Those that bear the inconveniences of an afflicted state with patience and submission, are humbled by them and prove well under them, are best prepared for better circumstances. (Deuteronomy 8:7-9)

Though afflictions are sent for our spiritual benefit, yet we may pray to God for the removal of them: we ought indeed to desire also that they may reach the end for which they are designed. (2 Corinthians 12:7-8)

When we begin to be at war with sin God will be at peace with us; for he continues the affliction no longer than till it has done its work. (Ezekiel 16:42)

If we have humbled hearts under humbling providences, the affliction has done its work, and it shall either be removed or the property of it altered. (2 Chronicles 12:7-12)

The benefit of affliction; they often prove the happy and effectual means of awakening conscience, and bringing sin to our remembrance, Job 13:26. (Genesis 42:21)

When men begin to complain more of their sins than of their afflictions then there begins to be some hope of them; and this is that which God requires of us, when we are under his correcting hand, that we own ourselves in a fault and justly corrected. (Hosea 5:15)

He does not afflict with pleasure, he delights not in the death of sinners, or the disquiet of saints, but punishes with a kind of reluctance. He comes out of his place to punish, for his place is the mercy seat. (Lamentations 3:33)

We must not rejoice when our enemy falls, as ours; but when Babylon, the common enemy of God and his Israel, sinks, then *rejoice over her, thou heaven, and you holy apostles and prophets*, Rev. 18:20. (Isaiah 14:4)

Those do better for themselves who patiently submit to the rebukes of Providence than those who contend with them. (Jeremiah 38:2)

It is a very wicked thing to fret against God when we are in affliction, and in our distress thus to trespass yet more. If we die, if we perish, it is owing to ourselves, and the blame will lie upon on our heads. (Numbers 18:12-13)

Sins against reproof are doubly sinful, Prov. 29:1. (Hosea 5:2)

[T]hose who cannot bear to be corrected must expect to be destroyed. (Proverbs 15:10)

When I am in affliction I should say, "This is an evil, and I will bear it, because it is the will of God that I should, because his wisdom has appointed this for me and his grace will make it work for good to me." ... But to say, "This is an evil, *and I must bear it*, because I cannot help it," is but a brutal patience, and argues a want of those good thoughts of God which we should always have, even under our afflictions.... (Jeremiah 10:19)

## 8: Backsliding and Discipline

Many are chastised that do not bear chastisement, do not bear it well, and so, in effect, do not bear it at all. Penitents, if sincere, will take all well that God does, and will bear chastisement as a medicinal operation intended for good. (Job 34:31)

We must take heed lest our reverence of God's glory, by which we should be awakened to hear his voice both in his word and in his providence, should degenerate into such a dread of him as will disable or indispose us to hear it. (Daniel 10:8)

Through our ignorance and mistake, and the weakness of our faith, we often apprehend that to be against us which is really for us. We are afflicted in body, estate, name, and relations; and we think all these things are against us, whereas these are really working for us the weight of glory. (Genesis 43:36)

Christ hath still a power over bodily diseases, and heals his people that *need healing*. Sometimes he sees that we need the *sickness* for the good of our souls, more than the *healing* for the ease of our bodies…. (Luke 9:11)

The lower we are brought the more need we have of help from heaven and the more will divine power be magnified in raising us up. (Psalm 79:8)

Note, (1.) We cannot pray in faith that we may never be corrected, while we are conscious to ourselves that we need correction and deserve it, and know that as many as God loves he chastens.

(2.) The great thing we should dread in affliction is the wrath of God. Say not, Lord, *do not correct* me, but Lord, do not correct me *in anger;* … We may bear the smart of his rod, but we cannot bear the weight of his wrath. (Jeremiah 10:24)

To those who know how to value God's favour nothing appears more dreadful than his anger; corrections in love are easily borne, but rebukes in love wound deeply. (Lamentations 2:6)

When God afflicts his people, yet he does not forget them; when he casts them out of their land, yet he does not cast them out of sight, nor out of mind. Even then when God is speaking against us, yet he is acting for us, and designing our good in all; and this is our comfort in our affliction, that *the Lord thinks upon us,* though we have forgotten him. (Jeremiah 31:20)

God in his providence sometimes seems harsh with those he loves, and speaks roughly to those for whom yet he has great mercy in store. (Genesis 42:7)

[E]xtraordinary afflictions are not always the punishment of extraordinary sins, but sometimes the trial of extraordinary graces…. (Job 8:4)

We must not conclude concerning the first and greatest sufferers that they were the worst and greatest sinners; for perhaps it may appear quite otherwise, … Those that went first into captivity were as the son whom the *father loves, and chastens betimes,* chastens while there is hope; and it did well. But those that staid behind were like a child long *left to himself*, who, when afterwards corrected, is stubborn, and made worse by it, Lam. 3:27. ... [T]hey should learn more of God by his providences in Babylon than they had learned by all his oracles and ordinances in Jerusalem.... (Jeremiah 24:1-7)

We should bear our afflictions when they are present as those that know not but Providence may so outweigh them by after-comforts as that we may even forget them when they are past. (Genesis 42:50-52)

[W]e cannot judge of men's *sins* by their *sufferings* in this world; for many are thrown into the furnace as gold to be purified, not as dross and chaff to be consumed. We must therefore not be harsh in our censures of those that are afflicted more than their neighbours, as Job's friends were in their censures of him, lest we condemn *the generation of the righteous*, Ps. 72:14. (Luke 13:2-3)

God is omniscient, and can discover that which is most secret. As the strongest cannot oppose his arm, so the most subtle cannot escape his eye; and therefore, if some are punished either more or less than we think they should be, instead of quarrelling with God, it becomes us to ascribe it to some secret cause known to God only. (Job 34:26)

*Thy way, O God! is in the sea, and thy path in the great waters.* We cannot judge of men by their sufferings, nor of sins by their present punishments; with some the flesh is destroyed that the spirit may be saved, while with others the flesh is pampered that the soul may ripen for hell. (1 Kings 13:30)

We must not think that all who die suddenly are sinners above others; perhaps it is in favour to them, that they have a quick passage: however, it is a forewarning to all to be always ready. (Acts 5:10)

When God punishes the less guilty it is folly for the more guilty to promise themselves impunity; and when judgment begins at God's house it will reach the strangers. (Jeremiah 49:20-21)

Whatever desolations God makes in his church, they are all according to his counsels; he *performs the thing that is appointed for us*, even that which makes most against us. But, when it is done, he has *stretched out a line*, a measuring line, to do it exactly and by measure: hitherto the destruction shall go, and no further; no more shall be cut off than what is marked to be so. (Lamentations 2:7-9)

It is an invisible power that sets bounds to the malice of the church's enemies, and suffers them not to do that which we should think there is nothing to hinder them from. (1 Samuel 14:1)

We must see and acknowledge the hand of God in all the calamities that befal us at any time, whether personal or public.... (Lamentations 3:37-38)

## 8: Backsliding and Discipline

Whenever we speak of any calamity that has befallen us, it is good to add this, "it was for my transgression," that God may be justified and clear when he judges. (1 Chronicles 9:1)

Those who truly repent of their sins, and have them pardoned are yet often made to smart for them in this world. (2 Samuel 24:11-12)

We should never receive from God the evil [of] punishment if we did not provoke him by the evil of sin. God deals fairly with us, never corrects his children without cause, nor causes grief to us unless we give offence to him. (Jeremiah 25:7)

The fondling of children is with good reason commonly called the spoiling of them. Those that are trained up to do nothing are likely to be good for nothing. (Genesis 37:2)

Note, 1. To the education of children in that which is good there is necessary a due correction of them for what is amiss; every child of ours is a child of Adam, and therefore has that foolishness bound up in its heart which calls for rebuke, more or less, the rod and reproof which give wisdom. Observe, it is *his* rod that must be used, the rod of a parent, directed by wisdom and love, and designed for good, not the rod of a servant. 2. It is good to begin betimes with the necessary restraints of children from that which is evil, before vicious habits are confirmed. The branch is easily bent when it is tender. (Proverbs 13:24)

Young people may be allowed a youthful liberty, provided they flee youthful lusts. (Job 1:4-5)

When young people that have been well educated begin to change their company, they will soon change their manners, and lose their good education. (Genesis 38:1)

Let children think of this, and conduct themselves accordingly, remembering that, when they are from under their parents' eye, they are still under God's eye. (1 Samuel 17:17-18)

We must not expect that ... the mercies God showed to our fathers that served him, and kept close to him, should be renewed to us, if we degenerate and revolt from him. (Judges 6:13)

Those children seldom prove either the best or the happiest that are most indulged. (Genesis 34:1-5)

Young people would better consult their own interests if they would less indulge their own will. (Genesis 49:5)

Things never go well when the authority of a parent runs low in a family. Let every man *bear rule in his own house, and have his children in subjection with all gravity.* (Genesis 34:5)

Those that allow and countenance their children in any evil way, and do not use their authority to restrain and punish them, do in effect *honour them more than God,* being more tender of their reputation than of his glory and more desirous to humour them than to honour him. (1 Samuel 2:29)

See how willing tender parents are to believe the best concerning their children, and, upon the least indication of good, to hope, even concerning those that have been untoward, that they will repent and reform. But how easy is it for children to take advantage of their good parents' credulity, and to impose upon them with the show of religion, while still they are what they were! (2 Samuel 15:7-10)

Those are perfectly lost to all virtue, and abandoned to all wickedness, that have broken through the bonds of filial reverence and duty to such a degree as in word or action to abuse their own parents. What yoke will those bear that have shaken off this? Let children take heed of entertaining in their minds any such thought or passions towards their parents as savour of undutifulness and contempt; for the righteous God searches the heart. (Ezekiel 21:15)

[T]he father's correcting his son is not a disinheriting of him. (Lamentations 3:31-32)

Parents that are very fond of a child will not let it be out of their sight; none of God's children are ever from under his eye, but on them he looks with a singular complacency, as well as with a watchful and tender concern. (Psalm 34:15)

Though God will afflict them, yet he will make their afflictions for the good of their souls, and correct them as the father does the child, to drive out foolishness that is bound up in their hearts. This is the design of the affliction ... it shall have this blessed effect. It shall mortify the habits of sin; by this those defilements of the soul shall be purged away. It shall break them off from the practice of sin: *This is all the fruit*, this is it that God intends.... (Isaiah 27:9-11)

The remembrance of former afflictions should bring to mind the workings of our souls under them, Ps. 66:13, 14. (Genesis 35:1)

It is a debt we owe to our brethren, if we have got good by our afflictions, to comfort them by letting them know it. ... When afflictions have done their work, and have accomplished that for which they were sent, then will appear the wisdom and goodness of God in sending them, and God will be not only justified, but glorified in them. (Ezekiel 14:22-23)

The intention of afflictions is to teach us righteousness; and blessed is the man whom God chastens, and thus teaches, Ps. 94:12. (Isaiah 26:9)

## -9-

# Rewards and Blessings

Inward peace ... follows upon the indwelling of righteousness. Those in whom that work is wrought shall experience this blessed product of it. It is itself peace, and the effect of it is quietness and assurance for ever, that is, a holy serenity and security of mind, by which the soul enjoys itself and enjoys its God, and it is not in the power of this world to disturb it in those enjoyments

Matthew Henry
on Isaiah 32:16-17

Inward peace ... follows upon the indwelling of righteousness. Those in whom that work is wrought shall experience this blessed product of it. It is itself peace, and the effect of it is *quietness and assurance for ever*, that is, a holy serenity and security of mind, by which the soul enjoys itself and enjoys its God, and it is not in the power of this world to disturb it in those enjoyments. Note, Peace, and quietness and everlasting assurance may be expected, and shall be found, in the way and work of righteousness. True satisfaction is to be had only in true religion, and there it is to be had without fail. (Isaiah 32:16-17)

They that by faith are healed of their spiritual diseases, have reason to *go in peace*. (Mark 5:34)

A godly man's way may be melancholy, but his end shall be peace and everlasting light. (Isaiah 50:10-11)

The consideration of the end will help to reconcile us to all the difficulties and discouragements of the way. (Proverbs 23:17)

There are many that spend their time in sorrow who yet shall spend their eternity in joy. (Psalm 80:5)

[I]f God be my salvation, if he undertake my eternal salvation, *I will trust* in him to prepare me for it and preserve me to it. I will trust him with all my temporal concerns, not doubting but he will make all to work for my good. ... Those that have God for their salvation may enjoy themselves with a holy security and serenity of mind. (Isaiah 12:2)

All our joy depends upon the will of God. The comfort of the creature is in every thing according to the disposal of the Creator. (Romans 15:32)

Those that show favour to men shall find favour with God. (Genesis 15:1)

Those that have *found favour with God* should not give way to disquieting distrustful fears. Doth God favour thee? Fear not, though the world frown upon thee. Is he for thee? No matter who is against thee. (Luke 1:30)

The consolations of God are strong enough to support his people under their strongest trials. The comforts of this world are too weak to bear up the soul under temptation, persecution, and death; but the consolations of the Lord are neither few nor small. (Hebrews 6:18)

Strength and comfort commonly come by degrees to those that have been long cast down and disquieted; they are first helped up a little, and then more. ... Note, before God *gives strength and power unto his people* he makes them sensible of their own weakness. (Daniel 10:10-11)

Crosses and obstacles in an evil course are great blessings, and are so to be accounted. They are God's hedges, to keep us from transgressing, to restrain us from wandering out of the green pastures, to *withdraw man from his pur-*

## 9: Rewards and Blessings

*pose* (Job 33:17), to make the way of sin difficult, that we may not go on in it, and to keep us from it whether we will or not. We have reason to bless God both for restraining grace and for restraining providences. (Hosea 2:6-7)

It is God that restrains men from doing the ill they would do. It is not from him that there is sin, but it is from him that there is not more sin, either by his influence upon men's minds, checking their inclination to sin, or by his providence, taking away the opportunity to sin. (Genesis 20:6)

Deliverances out of trouble are then comforts indeed when they are the fruits of the forgiveness of sin, Isa. 38:17. (Jeremiah 50:20)

Christ's being born and given to us is the great foundation of our hopes, and fountain of our joys, in times of greatest grief and fear. (Isaiah 9:6)

The cross of Christ is a good Christian's chief glory, and there is the greatest reason why we should glory in it, for to it we owe all our joys and hopes. (Galatians 6:14)

Note, [1.] The happiness of men lies in an acquaintance with God; it *is life eternal,* it is the perfection of rational beings. [2.] Those who would have an acquaintance with God, must apply themselves to Jesus Christ; for the light of the knowledge of the glory of God shines in the face of Christ. ... [T]here is no comfortable intercourse between a holy God and sinful man, but in and by a Mediator, John 14:6. (Matthew 11:25-30)

Those who are saved with the everlasting salvation shall never be ashamed of what they did or suffered in the hopes of it; for it will so far outdo their expectations as to be a more abundant reimbursement. (Isaiah 45:17-18)

The greater pains we take, and the greater hazards we run, in the service of God and our generation, the greater will our recompense be at last; for *God is not unrighteous to forget the work and labour of love.* (Numbers 31:25-47)

The cause of Christ will bear a scrutiny. Satan shows the best, but hides the worst, because his best will not counter-vail his worst; but Christ's will abundantly. (Luke 14:25-27)

It will be found that the longest voyages make the richest returns, and that the charitable will be no losers, but unspeakable gainers, by having their recompense adjourned *till the resurrection.* (Luke 14:13-14)

There is nothing lost by lending to God or losing for him; it shall be repaid *a hundredfold,* Matt. 19:29. (1 Samuel 2:21)

The more we fix our hopes on the recompense of reward in the other world, the more free and charitable shall we be of our earthly treasure upon all occasions of doing good. (Colossians 1:5)

[T]here are *degrees of glory* in heaven; every vessel will be alike *full,* but not alike *large*. And the degrees of glory there will be according to the degrees of usefulness here. (Luke 19:13-19)

The lowest seat in heaven is an abundant recompense for the greatest sufferings on earth. (Matthew 20:23)

God will honour those who are despised for his sake. And the gospel, like the sea, gets in one place what it loses in another. (Matthew 14:1-2)

Sinners would become saints if they would but show themselves men, if they would but support the dignity of their nature and use aright its powers and capacities. (Isaiah 46:8)

It is better to live poorly upon the fruits of God's goodness, than live plentifully upon the products of our own sin. (Matthew 4:3-4)

[R]eligion and piety are the best friends to outward prosperity. (Deuteronomy 28:8)

The surest foundations of lasting prosperity are those which are laid in an early piety, Matt. 6:33. (1 Kings 7:1)

"Forget not God's hand in thy present prosperity.... Remember it is he that giveth thee wealth; for he *giveth thee power to get wealth.*" (Deuteronomy 8:18)

It is God's presence with us that makes all we do prosperous. Those that would prosper must therefore make God their friend; and those that do prosper must therefore give God the praise. (Genesis 39:3)

Whatever degree of outward prosperity any arrive at, they must own that it is of God's giving, not their own getting. Let it never be said, *My might, and the power of my hand, have gotten me this wealth,* this preferment; but let it always be remembered that it is *God that gives men power to get wealth,* and gives success to their endeavours. (Daniel 5:18-19)

It would engage great men to be kind to the people of God if they would but observe, as they easily might, how often such conduct brings the blessings of God upon kingdoms and families. (Isaiah 16:4-5)

God's hand must be eyed and owned in the advancement of the great men of the earth, and therefore we must not envy them; yet that will not secure the continuance of their prosperity, for he that gave them their beauty, if they be deprived of it, knows how to turn it into deformity. (Ezekiel 31:9)

While we cannot but own that we are more *favoured* of God than we deserve, let us by no means envy that others are *more highly* favoured than we are. (Luke 1:39-45)

Those are preparing ruin for themselves who envy those in whom God has put honour upon and usurp the dignities they were never designed for. (Psalm 106:16)

## 9: Rewards and Blessings

It will help to keep us from envying those that are above us duly to consider how many there are below us. Instead of fretting that any are preferred before us in honour, power, estate, or interest, in gifts, graces, or usefulness, we have reason to bless God if we, who are less than the least, are not put among the very last. (Numbers 16:9-10)

Striving to be greatest is a sin which easily besets disciples themselves, and it is exceedingly sinful. Even those that are well preferred are seldom pleased if others be better preferred. Those that excel are commonly envied. (Numbers 12:2)

[O]ver-praising a man makes him the object of envy; every man puts in for a share of reputation, and therefore reckons himself injured if another monopolize it or have more given him than his share. (Proverbs 27:14)

[H]umility of deportment is the best way to remove envy. (Judges 8:1-3)

Envy is grieving at the good of another, than which no sin is more offensive to God, nor more injurious to our neighbour and ourselves. (Genesis 30:1)

It is the unhappiness of those who in any thing excel others that thereby they make themselves the objects of envy; and *who can stand before envy?* (Ezekiel 31:9)

[W]e ought not to envy others God's grace to them because we shall have never the less for their sharing in it. ...

[T]hey that walk in the light and warmth of the sun have all the benefit they can have by it, and yet not the less for others having as much.... (Luke 15:31)

We may thus make the comforts of others our own, by taking pleasure, as God does, in the *prosperity of the righteous*. (Exodus 18:1-6)

Whatever any have of the good things of this world, it is what God sees fit to give them; we ourselves should therefore be content, though we have ever so little, and not envy any their share, though they have ever so much. ... The things of this world are not the best things, for God often gives the largest share of them to bad men, that are rivals with him and rebels against him. ... Dominion is not founded in grace. Those that have not any colourable title to eternal happiness may yet have a justifiable title to their temporal good things. (Jeremiah 27:5)

Such is the nature of worldly wealth, plenty of it makes it the less valuable; much more should the enjoyment of spiritual riches lessen our esteem of all earthly possessions. If *gold in abundance* would make silver to seem so despicable, shall not wisdom, and grace, and the foretastes of heaven, which are far better than gold, make earthly wealth seem much more despicable? (1 Kings 10:21-27)

Spiritual gifts are conferred without money and without price, because no money can be a price for them. Wisdom is likewise a more valuable gift to him that has it, makes him richer and happier, than gold or precious stones. It is *better to get wisdom than gold.* Gold is another's, wisdom our own; gold is for the body and time, wisdom for the soul and eternity. Let that which is most precious in God's account be so in ours. (Job 28:12)

Christ sometimes chooses to endow those with the gifts of grace who have least to show of the gifts of nature. (Matthew 4:18-19)

That gifts may be rightly used, it is proper to know the ends which they are intended to serve. (1 Corinthians 14:22)

What enabled them to leave all to follow Christ, and to continue with him in his temptations? What enabled them to preach the gospel, and work miracles, but the Spirit dwelling in them? The experiences of the saints are the explications of the promises; paradoxes to others are axioms to them. (John 14:15-17)

We are not now to expect any such extraordinary gifts as they had then. The canon of the New Testament being long since completed and ratified, we depend upon that as the most sure word of prophecy. But there are graces of the Spirit given to all believers, which are as earnests to them.... (Acts 19:1-7)

Faith comes by hearing the word of God; miracles do but make way for it. (1 Kings 19:12-13)

We must not expect that the miracles which were wrought when a church was in the forming, and some great truth in the settling, should be continued and repeated when the formation and settlement are completed.... (Judges 6:13)

Among fruitful Christians, some are more fruitful than others: where there is true grace, yet there are degrees of it; some are of greater attainments of knowledge and holiness than others; all Christ's scholars are not in the same form. We should aim at the highest degree, to bring *forth a hundred-fold,* as Isaac's ground did (Gen. 26:12), *abounding in the work of the Lord,* John 15:8. (Matthew 13:23)

The hearing ear, the seeing eye, and the understanding heart, are the gift of God. All that have them have them from him. (Deuteronomy 29:4)

Whatever gifts God confers on any man, he confers them that he may do good with them, whether they be common or spiritual. The outward gifts of his bounty are to be improved for his glory, and employed in doing good to others. No man has them merely for himself. They are a trust put into his hands, to profit withal; and the more he profits others with them, the more abundantly will they turn to his account in the end, Phil. 4:17. (1 Corinthians 12:7)

For where God sows plentifully in the gifts of his bounty he expects to reap accordingly in the fruits of our piety

## 9: Rewards and Blessings

and charity. (Numbers 32:50)

Those that receive courtesies should study to return them; it ill becomes men of God to be ungrateful, or to sponge upon those that are generous. (2 Kings 4:13)

To be able to lend, and not to have need to borrow, we must look upon as a great mercy, and a good reason why we should do good with what we have, lest we provoke God to turn the scales. ... It is a dreadful thing to have the cry of the poor against us, for God has his ear open to that cry, and, in compassion to them, will be sure to reckon with those that deal hardly with them. (Deuteronomy 15:7-8)

The greater the privileges we enjoy the greater is our danger if we do not improve them and live up to them. (Exodus 33:2-3)

Those are most valuable that are most serviceable; and those are the greater lights, not that have the best gifts, but that humbly and faithfully do the most good with them. (Genesis 1:14-19)

A good wife is a great blessing to a man. He that *finds a wife* (that is, a wife indeed; a bad wife does not deserve to be called by the name of so much honour), that finds a help meet for him ... that sought such a one with care and prayer and has found what he sought, he has found a *good thing*, a jewel of great value, a rare jewel; he has found that which will not only contribute more than any thing to his comfort in this life, but will forward him in the way to heaven. (Proverbs 18:22)

Those who would keep up peace and love must return soft answers to hard accusations. Husbands and wives particularly should agree, and endeavour not to be both angry together. (Genesis 16:6)

Husbands and wives, for their common good and benefit, have a joint-interest in their worldly possessions; but if either waste, or unduly spend in any way, it is a robbing of the other. (1 Samuel 25:18-20)

Husbands and wives should not quarrel at all, or should be quickly reconciled. They are bound to each other for life. The divine law allows of no separation. They cannot throw off the burden, and therefore should set their shoulders to it, and endeavour to make it as light to each other as they can. (1 Corinthians 7:10-12)

There is not a greater piece of hard-heartedness in the world, than for a man to be harsh and severe with his own wife. (Matthew 19:8-9)

It is very comfortable when husband and wife agree to go together in the way to heaven. (Genesis 12:5)

Husbands that love their wives will communicate their purposes and intentions to them. Where there is a mutual affection there will be a mutual confidence. And the prudence of the wife should engage the heart of her husband to trust in her, Prov. 31:11. (Genesis 31:4)

Sometimes those that have the smallest estates have the most numerous progeny; but he that sends mouths will be sure to send meat. ... The greatest blessing that can be entailed upon a family is to have the worship of God kept up in it from generation to generation. (Jeremiah 35:18-19)

Our blessing God is only our speaking well of him; his blessing us is doing well for us; those whom he blesses are blessed indeed. (Numbers 6:24-27)

True believers are precious in God's sight; they are his jewels, his peculiar treasure (Exod. 19:5); he loves them, his delight is in them, above any people. His church is his vineyard. And this makes God's people truly honourable, and their name great; for men are really what they are in God's eye. (Isaiah 43:4)

The wisdom of God is both employed and displayed for the honour of the saints—employed from eternity, and displayed in time, to make them glorious both here and hereafter, in time and to eternity. What honour does he put on his saints! (1 Corinthians 2:7)

There are saints in the earth; and saints on earth we must all be, or we shall never be saints in heaven. Those that are renewed by the grace of God, and devoted to the glory of God, are saints on earth. (Psalm 16:3)

Besides the heavenly inheritance prepared for the saints, there is a present inheritance in the saints; for grace is glory begun, and holiness is happiness in the bud. (Ephesians 1:18)

The names of the saints are precious with God, and should be so with us; we cannot have our names recorded in the Bible, but, if God open our hearts, we shall find them *written in the book of life*, and this is better (Phil. 4:3) and more to *be rejoiced in*, Luke 10:20. (Acts 16:14)

The meanest saint under the gospel understands more than the greatest prophets under the law. He who is least in the kingdom of heaven is greater than they. (Colossians 1:26-27)

Whoever they be that God has chosen, and in whom he is well pleased, he will be sure to *put his Spirit upon them*. Wherever he confers his love, he confers somewhat of his likeness. (Matthew 12:18)

Let us observe it, to the honour of the spiritual life above the natural, that though many have cursed the day of their first birth, never any cursed the day of their new-birth, nor wished they never had had grace, and the Spirit of grace, given them. Those are the most excellent gifts, above life and being itself, and which will never be a burden. (Job 3:1-3)

The gift of the Holy Ghost is a gift we are every one of us concerned earnestly and constantly to pray for. (Luke 11:13)

## 9: Rewards and Blessings

The revealing of Christ to us and in us is a distinguishing token of God's good will, and a firm foundation of true happiness; and blessed are they that are thus highly favoured. (Matthew 16:17)

Those are truly rich who have enough to supply their necessities, and know when they have enough. We need not go to the treasures of kings and provinces, or to the cash of merchants, to look for wealthy people; they may be found among shepherds *that dwell in tents*. (Jeremiah 49:31)

Though God loves all his children, yet there are some that are more than the rest *greatly beloved*. Christ had one disciple that lay in his bosom; and that *beloved disciple* was he that was entrusted with the prophetical visions of the New Testament, as Daniel was with the Old. For what greater token can there be of God's favour to any man than for the secrets of the Lord to be with him? (Daniel 9:22)

Those who make a good use of the discoveries God has favoured them with may expect further discoveries; for *to him that hath shall be given*. (Ezekiel 1:15)

God's visits, if gratefully received, shall be graciously repeated. Bid God welcome, and he will come again. (Judges 6:25-26)

To him that has, and to him that asks, shall be given; to him that uses and improves what he has, and that desires and prays for more of the knowledge of Christ, God will give more. (John 8:56)

Those that do good with what they have shall have more to do good with. (Proverbs 3:9-10)

When it is well with us, we are apt to be mindless of others, and in the fulness of our *enjoyments* to forget the *necessities* of our brethren.... (Mark 9:5-6)

What favours God bestows on us are intended not only to make us cheerful ourselves, but also that we may be useful to others. (2 Corinthians 1:4)

A cheerful spirit is a great blessing; it makes the yoke of our employments easy and the burden of our afflictions light. (Ecclesiastes 5:20)

Those who follow their business, and get abundance by it with a great deal of ease, should think with compassion of those who cannot follow theirs but with a great fatigue, and hardly get a bare livelihood by it. When we have *rested all night*, let us not forget those who have *toiled all night*.... (Luke 5:5)

Those that are the *blessed of the Lord* must study to make themselves blessings to the world. He that is good, let him do *good*; he that has received the gift, the grace, let him minister the same. (Ezekiel 34:30-31)

The accomplishments of the promises he had formerly made concerning his church, which are proofs of the truth of his word and the kindness he bears to his people ... *"Behold, the former things have come to pass*; hitherto the

## Part II: Wisdom (Salvation)

Lord has helped his church, has supported her under former burdens, relieved her in former straits; and this in performance of the promises made to the fathers. *There has not failed one word,* 1 Kings 8:56. *And* now *new things do I declare.* Now I will make new promises, which shall as certainly be fulfilled in their season as the old ones were; now I will bestow new favours, such as have not been conferred formerly. Old-Testament blessings you have had abundantly; now I declare New-Testament blessings, not a fruitful country and dominion over your neighbours, but *spiritual blessings in heavenly things. Before they spring forth* in the preaching of the gospel, *I tell you of them,* under the type and figure of the former things." (Isaiah 42:8-9)

Those who have the word of God's promise to depend upon need not be afraid of any adverse powers or policies whatsoever. (Isaiah 44:8)

God's word of promise, being a firm foundation of hope, is a full fountain of joy to all believers. (Psalm 60:6)

The more we see events to be *the Lord's doing,* and see in them the product of a divine power and the conduct of a divine wisdom, the more marvelous they will appear in our eyes.... (Daniel 4:3)

God's compassions to his people infinitely exceed those of the tenderest parents towards their children. (Isaiah 49:15)

Those that have God for their god, have him for a crown of glory and a diadem of beauty; for they are made to him kings and priests. ... He will give them all the wisdom and grace necessary to the due discharge of the duty of their place. (Isaiah 28:1)

Thrones and crowns are tottering things, and are often laid in the dust; but there is a crown of glory reserved for Christ's spiritual seed which fadeth not away. (Psalm 89:38-39)

See how religion provides cordials, where irreligion administers corrosives. Heathenism aggravates that grief which Christianity studies to assuage. ... The loudest grief is not always the greatest; rivers are most noisy where they run shallow. (Matthew 9:23)

We tempt God if, in times of danger, we do not the best we can for ourselves. ... Whatever in nature is at any time serviceable to us, we must therein acknowledge the goodness of the God of nature, who, when he fashioned it long ago, fitted it to be so, and *according to whose ordinances it continues to this day.* Every creature is that to us which God makes it to be; and therefore, whatever use it is of to us, we must *look at him that fashioned it,* bless him for it, and use it for him. (Isaiah 22:9-11)

[H]e made them all after their kind, not only of divers shapes, but of divers natures, manners, food, and fashions—some to be tame about the house, others to be wild in the fields—some living upon grass and herbs, others upon flesh—some harmless,

## 9: Rewards and Blessings

and others ravenous—some bold, and others timorous—some for man's service, and not his sustenance, as the horse—others for his sustenance and not his service, as the sheep—others for both, as the ox—and some for neither, as the wild beasts. In all this appears the manifold wisdom of the Creator. (Genesis 1:24-25)

Good people sometimes, under the sense of their unworthiness, are ready to fly from the blessing and to conclude that it belongs not to them; but the blessing shall find them out and follow them notwithstanding. (Deuteronomy 28:2)

One instance of the honour and respect we owe to God, as our God, is rightly to possess that which he gives us to possess, receive it from him, use it for him, keep it for his sake, and part with it when he calls for it. He has given it to us to possess, not to enjoy. He himself only must be enjoyed. (Judges 11:24)

Those who *hunger and thirst* after spiritual blessings, *are blessed* in those desires, and *shall be filled* with those blessings. (Matthew 5:6)

Liberty of access to the throne of grace, and liberty of speech there, are the unspeakable privilege of the Lord's people at all times, especially in times of distress and danger. (Isaiah 37:13-14)

A privilege belonging to faith in Christ [is] namely, an audience in prayer. *This is the confidence that we have in him, that, if we ask any thing according to his will, he heareth us.* ... The Lord Christ emboldens us to come to God in all circumstances, with all our supplications and requests. Through him our petitions are admitted and accepted of God. The matter of our prayer must be agreeable to the declared will of God. (1 John 5:14)

... God has promised to give us what we ask of him. We have not only the goodness of nature to take comfort from, but the word which he has spoken ... "*Ask, and it shall be given you;* either the thing itself you shall ask or that which is equivalent; either the thorn in the flesh removed, or grace sufficient given in." (Luke 11:9-10)

Those that faithfully follow the pillar of cloud and fire shall find that though it may lead them about it leads them the right way and will bring them to Canaan at last. (Proverbs 3:5-6)

A believing hope and prospect of a blessed lot in the heavenly Canaan, at the end of days, will be an effectual support to us when we are going our way out of this world, and will furnish us with living comforts in dying moments. (Daniel 12:13)

Those, and those only, can with courage *see death,* and look it in the face without terror, that have had by faith a sight of Christ. (Luke 2:26)

The believing hopes of the soul's redemption from the grave, and reception to glory, are the great support and

## Part II: Wisdom (Salvation)

joy of the children of God in a dying hour. (Psalm 49:15)

Good Christians in a trying hour, particularly a dying hour, may thus plead: "*Now the hour is come,* stand by me, appear for me, now or never: now *the earthly tabernacle is to be dissolved, the hour is come that I should be glorified.*" 2 Cor. 5:1. (John 17:1-5)

Our being ready for death will make it come never the sooner, but much the easier: and those that are fit to die are most fit to live. (Isaiah 38:1)

Let old people be willing to rest themselves, though it look like burying themselves alive. (1 Samuel 25:1)

Those that are going to heaven themselves ought to be concerned for those they leave behind them on earth, and to leave with them their experiences, testimonies, counsels, and prayers, 2 Pet. 1:15. (2 Kings 2:4)

At death we must all *fail*…. Death eclipses us. A tradesman is said to *fail* when he becomes a *bankrupt*. We must all thus fail shortly; death shuts up the shop, seals up the hand. Our comforts and enjoyments on earth will *all fail* us; flesh and heart fail. …It ought to be our great concern to make it sure to ourselves, that *when* we *fail* at death we may be *received into everlasting habita-tions* in heaven. The *habitations* in heaven are *everlasting,* not *made with hands,* but *eternal,* 2 Cor. 5:1. Christ is gone before, to prepare a place for those that are his, and is there ready to *receive them*…. (Luke 16:9)

The most that death does to our Christian friends is to take them out of our sight, not out of being, not out of bliss, but out of all relation to us, only out of sight, and then not out of mind. (John 16:16)

The souls of believers, when they are delivered out of the prison of the body, come to the heavenly Zion with singing. (Isaiah 51:11)

It is the unspeakable comfort of all God's faithful subjects, not only that he does reign universally and with an incontestable sovereignty, but that he will reign eternally, and there shall be no end of his dominion. (Exodus 15:18)

When good men die they are transplanted from the land of the living on earth, the nursery of the plants of righteousness, to that in heaven, the garden of the Lord, where they shall take root for ever; but, when wicked men die, they are rooted out of the land of the living, to perish forever, as fuel to the fire of divine wrath. This will be the portion of those that contend with God. (Psalm 52:5)

… # -10-

## Service

Thanksgiving is good, but thanks-living is better.

It is better to be serving God in solitude, than serving sin with a multitude.

Matthew Henry
on Psalm 50:23 and Psalm 84:1-2

Thanksgiving is good, but thanks-living is better. (Psalm 50:23)

It is better to be serving God in solitude, than serving sin with a multitude. (Psalm 84:1-2)

It is better to be at liberty in a wilderness than bond-slaves in a land of plenty, to enjoy God and ourselves in solitude than to lose both in a crowd.... (Ezekiel 20:10)

The Spirit herein acts, (1.) As a spirit of judgment, enlightening the mind, convincing the conscience,—as a spirit of wisdom, guiding us to deal prudently, (Isa. 52:13), —as a discerning, distinguishing, Spirit, separating between the precious and the vile. (2.) As a Spirit of burning, quickening and invigorating the afflictions, and making men zealously affected in a good work. The Spirit works as fire, Matt. 3:11. An ardent love to Christ and souls, and a flaming zeal against sin, will carry men on with resolution in their endeavours to *turn away ungodliness*.... (Isaiah 4:4)

The security of sinners in their sinful way is just matter of lamentation and wonder to all serious people, who should think themselves concerned to pray for those that do not pray for themselves. (Isaiah 29:9)

It becomes us to give warning of the danger of sin, and the fatal consequences of it, with all seriousness and earnestness.... (Jeremiah 44:4)

Those that are themselves affected with the terrors of the Lord should endeavour to affect others with them. (Jeremiah 9:20)

Those that would affect others with the word of God should evidence that they are themselves affected with it. (Jeremiah 4:19)

Those who have themselves tasted the comforts of religion should do what they can to bring others to the taste of them. One cheerful Christian should make many. (Acts 16:33-34)

Those that have experienced the performance of God's promises themselves should encourage others to hope that he will be as good as his word to them also: *I will tell you what God has done for my soul.* (Luke 1:45)

We must always be ready and forward; [1.] To obey the commands of God, Ps. 119:60. [2.] To do good to our brethren, and to carry comfort to them, as those that felt from their afflictions; *Say not, Go, and come again, and to-morrow I will give;* but now quickly. (Matthew 28:7)

Our light *burns* in love to God, but it *shines* in love to our neighbour. (Matthew 19:19)

When we have heard some good word that has affected and edified us we should be ready to communicate it to others that did not hear it, for their edification. *Out of the abundance of the heart the mouth speaks.* (Jeremiah 36:12-13)

It is not so much the good *words* as the

## 10: Service

good *intention* of them that Christ looks at. (Mark 10:17-18)

God's people, wherever their lot is cast, should endeavour thus, by all the instances of an exemplary and winning conversation, to gain an interest in the affections of those about them, and recommend religion to their good opinion. (Isaiah 14:1)

It is the plain duty of those in so near a relation to seek the salvation of those to whom they are related. (1 Corinthians 7:16)

God expects vineyard-fruit from those that enjoy vineyard-privileges, not leaves only, as Mark 11:12. A bare profession, though ever so green, will not serve: there must be more than buds and blossoms. Good purposes and good beginnings are good things, but not enough; there must be fruit, a good heart and a good life, vineyard fruit, thoughts and affections, words and actions agreeable to the Spirit is the fatness of the vineyard ... acceptable to God, the Lord of the vineyard.... Such fruit as this God expects from us.... (Isaiah 5:1-2)

Man's heart is like soil, capable of improvement, of bearing good fruit; it is a pity it should lie fallow, or be like the field of the slothful, Prov. 24:30. (Matthew 13:3-8)

The soul of man stands ready to be hired into some service or other; it was (as all the creatures were) created to work, and is either a *servant to iniquity,* or a *servant to righteousness,* Rom. 6:19. The devil, by his temptations, is *hiring labourers* into his field, to *feed swine.* God, by his gospel, is *hiring labourers into his vineyard, to dress it, and keep it,* paradise-work. ... The work of religion is vineyard work, pruning, dressing, digging, watering, fencing, weeding. We have each of us our own vineyard to keep, our own soul; and it is God's and to be kept and dressed for him. ... A man may go idle to hell; but he that will go to heaven, must be busy. (Matthew 20:3-6)

*He* [Jesus] *comes, seeking fruit* and requires gospel-duty of all those that enjoy gospel privileges. (Song of Solomon 8:11)

God's usual method is to warn before he wounds. God ... [gave] warning to the Jews of the general desolation ... declared and published in all the cities of Judah and streets of Jerusalem, that all might hear and fear, and by this loud alarm be either brought to repentance or left inexcusable. (Jeremiah 4:5)

We may serve God and do good by writing to our friends at a distance pious letters of seasonable comforts and wholesome counsels. Those whom we cannot speak to we may write to; that which is written remains. (Jeremiah 29:1)

[T]he ages of Levi, Kohath, and Amran, the father, grandfather, and great grandfather, of Moses, are here recorded; they all lived to a great age, Levi to 137, Kohath to 133, and Amran to 137.

Moses himself came much short of them, and fixed seventy or eighty for the ordinary stretch of human life (Ps. 90:10); for now that God's Israel was multiplied and had become a great nation, and divine revelation was by the hand of Moses committed to writing and no longer trusted to tradition, the two great reasons for the long lives of the patriarchs had ceased, and therefore henceforward fewer years must serve men. (Exodus 6:16-26)

[T]he promises ... which God makes to the saints.... That they shall have a sufficiency of life in this world ... *With length of days will I satisfy him;* ... [T]hey shall be continued in this world till they have done the work they were sent into this world for and are ready for heaven, and that is long enough. (Psalm 91:16)

Every believer is a *living temple, building up himself in his most holy faith.* Much opposition is given to this work by Satan and our own corruptions. We trifle, and proceed in it with many stops and pauses; but he that has *begun the good work* will see it performed, and will *bring forth judgment unto victory. Spirits of just men* will be *made perfect.* (Ezra 6:14-15)

The devil has designed and endeavoured to ruin the work of God in this world. The Son of God has undertaken the holy war against him. He came into our world, and was manifested in our flesh, that he might conquer him and dissolve his works. Sin will he loosen and dissolve more and more, till he has quite destroyed it. Let not us serve or indulge what the Son of God came to destroy. (1 John 3:8)

*"Teach me to do Thy will,* not only show me what thy will is, but teach me how to do it, how to turn my hand dexterously to my duty." It is the desire and endeavour of all God's faithful servants to know and to do his will, and to stand complete in it. (Psalm 143:10)

That calling or condition of life is best for us, and to be chosen by us, which is best for our souls, that which least exposes us to sin and gives us most opportunity of serving and enjoying God. (Genesis 4:2)

[W]hat work God employs men in he does in some measure fit them for. (Isaiah 13:3)

What services God designs men for he will be sure in his providence to lead them to, though perhaps they themselves are not aware what guidance they are under. (Ezekiel 21:22)

Thus God, by hints of providence which seem casual, sometimes puts his people in mind of their duty, of which otherwise perhaps they would not have thought. (Acts 8:36)

When men are made use of as instruments of Providence in accomplishing its purposes it is very common for them to intend one thing and for God to intend quite the contrary. (Micah 4:12-13)

Many are serving God's purposes who are not aware of it. (2 Kings 24:3)

## 10: Service

When we are manifestly led by Providence to do things contrary to our own inclinations, and quite beyond our own intentions, it will be some satisfaction to us to be able to say, *Thou, O Lord! has done as it pleased thee*. And, if God please himself, we ought to be satisfied though he do not please us. (Jonah 1:14)

When God has work to do of any kind he will soon find those that are able to engage in it, and all the world cannot find those that are able to engage against it. ... God can bring to pass the greatest works by instruments least likely. (Jeremiah 49:19)

When the Spirit of the Lord comes upon men it will make them expert even without experience. (1 Samuel 11:6-7)

The God of nature can alter and control the powers of nature, which way he pleases, can turn waters into crystal rocks and rocks into crystal streams. ... The heavenly bodies, as well as earth and seas, are at God's command, and, when he pleases, at Israel's service too. (Habakkuk 3:15)

Common providence fetches waters from heaven, and bread out of the earth; but for Israel the divine power brings bread from the clouds and water from the rocks: so far is the God of nature from being tied to the laws and courses of nature. (Psalm 105:41)

If Providence calls us to solitude and retirement, it becomes us to acquiesce; when we cannot be useful we must be patient, and when we cannot work for God we must sit still quietly for him. (1 Kings 17:3)

Sometimes it is long before God calls his servants out of that work which of old he designed them for, and has been graciously preparing them for. Moses was born to be Israel's deliverer, and yet not a word is said of it to him till he is eighty years of age. (Exodus 3:1)

God delights to put honour upon the humble and diligent, to raise the poor out of the dust and to set them among princes; and sometimes he finds those most fit for public action that have spent the beginning of their time in solitude and contemplation. (Psalm 78:70)

See how God can raise up friends for his people in distress where they little thought of them, and animate men for his service even beyond expectation. (Jeremiah 38:9-10)

It is good to appear for God when we are called to it, though there be few or none to second us, because God can incline the hearts of those to stand by us from whom we little expect assistance. Let us do our duty, and then trust God with our safety. (Judges 6:31)

Many will consult God about their safety that would never consult him about their duty. (1 Samuel 14:18)

God herein encourages those that suffer for him to trust in him; for he can put it into the hearts of those to befriend them from whom they least expect it—can cause them to be pitied, nay, can cause them to be prized and valued, even in the eyes of those that carry them captive, Ps. 106:46. (Acts 27:3)

God has often raised up friends for his people, by making men know that it is at their peril if they hurt them. It is a dangerous thing to offend Christ's little ones. (Genesis 12:17)

Even great men and bad men are tools that God makes use of, and are *working for him* even when they are pursuing their own covetous and ambitious designs; so wonderfully does God overrule all to his own glory. (Ezekiel 29:20)

God can find out ways to make those serviceable to the kingdom of Christ who yet have no sincere affection for it and who have vigorously set themselves against it. Enemies are sometimes made a footstool, not only to be trodden upon, but to ascend by. (2 Samuel 3:12)

The scripture is often fulfilled by the agency of those who have not themselves an eye to the scripture in what they do, Isa. 45:4. (John 12:16)

God has the sovereign command of all the hosts of men, even of those that know him not, that own him not, and they are all made to serve his purposes. He directs their marches, their countermarches, their retreats, their returns, as it pleases him; and furious armies, like *stormy winds*, in all their motions are *fulfilling his word*. ... Whatever instruments God has determined to make use of in any service for him, whether of mercy or judgment, they shall accomplish that for which they are designed, whatever incapacity or disability they may lie under or be reduced to. Those by whom God has resolved to save or to destroy, saviours they shall be and destroyers they shall be.... (Jeremiah 37:7-10)

Those that have much to do in the world are in great danger of doing much amiss; and it is hard to deal with many without violence to some. (Ezekiel 28:16)

Great care must be taken in the government of our zeal, lest that which seemed supernatural in its causes prove unnatural in its effects. That is no good divinity which swallows up humanity. Many a war is ill ended which was well begun. (Judges 21:1)

Those mistake who think that a burning zeal for holy church, and the propagating of the faith, will serve to consecrate robberies and murders, massacres and depredations; no, Zion's walls owe those no thanks that build them up with blood and iniquity. The sin of man works not the righteousness of God. (Micah 3:10)

God makes use of wicked men, not only to smite, but to slay his people, for they are his sword, Ps.17:13. But, when the cup of trembling comes to be put into their hand, it will be much worse with them than ever it was with God's people in their greatest straits. ...

## 10: Service

Though God's persecuted people may be great losers, and great sufferers, for a while, yet those that oppress them will prove to be greater losers and greater sufferers at last, here or hereafter; for God will render double to them, Rev.18:6. (Isaiah 27:7)

He that is the God of nations will sooner or later assert the injured rights of nations against those that unjustly and violently invade them. The God of the whole earth will break *the hammer of the whole earth.* (Jeremiah 50:23)

Those that go on God's errands must rise and go, must stir themselves to the work cut out for them. (Jonah 1:1-3)

Those that sincerely design and endeavour to do their duty may in faith beg of God direction and strength for the doing of it. (Exodus 33:12-13)

Those enterprises which we undertake by a divine warrant, and prosecute by divine direction, we may expect to succeed in. If we take God's method, we shall have his blessing. (Deuteronomy 20:10-13)

Those that go where God sends them shall have him with them wherever they go and they need desire no more to make them easy and prosperous. (Joshua 1:9)

When God calls we must not plead any inability to come; for he that calls us will help us, will strengthen us. (Jeremiah 31:8)

Though our infirmities ought to humble us, yet they ought not to discourage us from doing our best in any service we have to do for God. His strength is made perfect in our weakness. (Exodus 6:10-13)

The more diligent we are in the services of religion the more we shall reap of the advantages of it. (Leviticus 7:7)

God saves us by strengthening us, and works out our happiness by working in us to do our duty. And thus we are engaged to the utmost diligence in using the strength God gives us; and yet, when all is done, God must have the glory of all. God is our strength, and so becomes our song and our salvation. (Zechariah 10:6)

It is best with us when our duty becomes in a manner natural to us. (Philippians 2:19-20)

Note, the increase and multitude of labourers in the Lord's work should be made not an excuse for our negligence, but an encouragement to our diligence. The more busy others are, the more busy we should be, and all little enough, so much work is there to be done. (Matthew 11:1-6)

The greater gifts of some do not *render* the labours of others, that come short of them, *needless* and *useless;* there is work enough for all hands. They are sullen that will sit down and do nothing when they see themselves out-shone. (John 3:23-24)

Great things may be brought to pass when the undertakers are numerous and unanimous, and stir up one another. Let us learn to provoke one another to love and to good works, as sinners stir up and encourage one another to wicked works. (Genesis 11:3-4)

If God strengthen us, we must bestir ourselves, must *walk up and down* in all the duties of the Christian life, must be active and busy in the work of God, must walk up and down as industrious men do, losing no time, and letting slip no opportunity. (Zechariah 10:12)

Delay in execution is as bad, on the one hand, as precipitancy in resolution is on the other hand; when we have taken time to consider, and then have determined, let it never be said, we left that to be done to-morrow, which we could do today. (Matthew 8:21-22)

Those that do the will of God heartily will do it speedily; while we delay, time is lost and the heart hardened. (Genesis 22:3)

When any work is to be done for God it is good to set about it quickly, while the sense of duty is strong and pressing. (Numbers 1:18)

Those that have lost time have need to redeem time; and the longer we have loitered in that which is good the more haste we should make when we are convinced of our folly. (Haggai 1:15)

The consideration of the time we unavoidably lost in our minority should quicken us, when we have come to years, to act with so much the more vigour in the service of God. Having begun late we have need to work hard. (2 Kings 21:3)

Those that are in the prime of their time ought to be busy in doing the work of life: for, as they go into years, they will find themselves less disposed to it and less able for it. (1 Samuel 8:1)

Those who can but do little, or have but little to do for the world, must do so much the more for their souls; as the rich, the aged, and the infirm. (Matthew 12:9-10)

Those whom God makes use of shall not lose by him; much more will he be found the bountiful rewarder of all those that designedly and sincerely serve him. (Jeremiah 27:7)

It is good when commendations thus quicken us to our duty, and when the more we are praised for doing well the more vigorous we are in well-doing. (2 Chronicles 19:4)

Those that are hearty in the service of God shall receive fresh encouragements from him to proceed in it, as their case calls for them. Set the wheels a going, and God will oil them. (Haggai 2:1)

Those who with courage and zeal break through difficulties in God's service, will perhaps find them not so apt to recur as they fear. Resist them, and they will flee. (Matthew 13:1)

## 10: Service

[E]ven when we act with the courage that becomes the faithful servants of God, yet we must conduct ourselves with the humility and modesty that become dutiful subjects to the government God has set over us. A lion in God's cause must be a lamb in his own. (Jeremiah 38:18-21)

[M]en may be truly devout though they do not abound in the shows and expressions of devotion, and therefore we must not judge nor despise our brethren. (Esther 9:20-21)

We must not judge of people's religion by that which falls under the eye and observation of the world. (Matthew 9:14)

[A]ll good people are not alike happy in their temper. (John 20:25)

There are many who are hearty in Christ's interests, how, though they do not make any show in their outward profession of it, yet will be more ready to do him a piece of real service, when there is occasion, than others who make a greater figure and noise. (Luke 23:50-52)

As secret acts of sin, so secret acts of faith, are known to the Lord Jesus, and are under his eye. If believers derive virtue from Christ ever so closely, he knows it, and is pleased with it. (Mark 5:32)

When we come to heaven, as we shall miss a great many there, that we thought had been going thither, so we shall meet a great many there, that we did not expect. (Matthew 8:11-12)

It becomes us to give honour to those whom our God puts honour upon. (Isaiah 39:1)

Those that are honourable should study to be serviceable.... (Numbers 1:16)

Those that are most humble and most serviceable are really most honourable. (Numbers 2:3)

In this world it is often hard to *discern between the righteous and the wicked*. They are mingled together, good fish and bad in the same net. The righteous are so distempered, and the wicked so disguised, that we are often deceived in our opinions concerning both the one and the other. There are many who, we think, serve God, who, having not their hearts right with him, will be found none of his servants; and on the other hand, many will be found his faithful servants, who, because they followed not with us, did not, as we thought, serve him. ... [Y]ou could not know wicked men by God's frowning upon them, for they commonly prospered in the world, nor righteous men by his smiling upon them, for they were involved with others in the same common calamity. None knows God's *love or hatred* by *all that is before him*, Eccl. 9:1. (Malachi 3:14)

Though the righteous be among the wicked, yet the righteous God will not, certainly he will not, destroy the right-

## Part II: Wisdom (Salvation)

eous with the wicked. Though in this world they may be involved in the same common calamities, yet in the great day a distinction will be made. (Genesis 18:23)

There are many, too many, who are our kinsfolk and acquaintance, that we cannot avoid conversing with, among whom we find little or nothing of Christ. (Luke 2:46)

*The good seed are the children of the kingdom,* true saints. ... *The tares are the children of the wicked one.* ... God has so ordered it, that good and bad should be mixed together in this world, that the good may be exercised, the bad left inexcusable, and a difference made between earth and heaven. (Matthew 13:38)

[T]hose that excel in any endowment should not only use it for the common good themselves, but teach others also, and not grudge to make others as wise as themselves. The way of praising God by musical instruments had not hitherto been in use. But David, being a prophet, instituted it by divine direction.... (1 Chronicles 15:22)

And let not the wisest of men think it any disparagement to them to pursue the good designs which those that went before them have laid, and to build upon their foundation. Every good piece is not an original. (2 Chronicles 6:7)

[R]ighteousness towards men is as much a branch of pure religion as religion towards God is a branch of universal righteousness. ... (1.) We must be doing, not merely cease to do evil and then stand idle. (2.) We must be doing good, the good which the Lord our God requires and which will turn to a good account. (Isaiah 1:16-17)

Idleness is an inlet to much sin. ... The standing waters gather filth and the sitting bird is the fowler's mark. (Ezekiel 16:49)

Idle people lie more open to the temptations of Satan than to the calls of God. (Matthew 4:18)

Though it may be charity to relieve sluggards, yet a man may, in justice, not relieve them; they deserve to be left to starve. Those that would not provide oil in their vessels begged when the bridegroom came, and were denied. (Proverbs 20:4)

The devil visits idle men with his temptations. God visits industrious men with his favours. (1 Samuel 6:13)

Freedom from service, and liberty to range at pleasure, are but the privileges of a wild ass. It is a pity that any of the children of men should covet such a liberty, or value themselves on it. It is better to labour and be good for something than ramble and be good for nothing. (Job 39:5)

An honest man may be made a beggar, but he is not honest that makes himself one. (Proverbs 27:13)

The confinement of business is a thousand times better than the liberty of idleness. (John 7:6)

It is the prudence of those who have ever so much of the world to keep an account of what they have. Some think that they *pass under the hand of him that telleth them* that they may be tithed, Lev. 27:32. (Jeremiah 33:12-13)

God, who is the first, must have the first; and, if it belongs to him, his priests must have it. We may *then* comfortably enjoy what we have, when a share of it has been first set apart for works of piety and charity. (Ezekiel 44:20)

[G]ive to God the first and best we have, as those that believe him to be the first and best of beings. (Deuteronomy 26:2)

Whatever our substance is we must honour God with it, by giving him his dues out of it. Not that God has need of or may be benefited by any thing we can give him, Ps. 50:9. No; it is but an *oblation*; we only *offer it* to him; the benefit of it returns back to ourselves, to his poor, who, as our neighbours, are ourselves, or to his ministers who serve continually for our good. (Ezekiel 45:13)

Whatever we give to God, it is but *of his own* that we *give him*, 1 Chron. 29:14. And it becomes us, who receive so much from him, to study what we shall render to him. (Deuteronomy 26:2)

Those that by reason of distance, or otherwise, cannot forward a good work by their persons, must, as they are able, forward it by their purses; if some find hands, let others fill them. (Zechariah 6:11)

Worldly wealth is but poor substance, yet, such as it is, we must honour God with it, and then, if ever, it becomes substantial. ... It is our duty to make our worldly estates serviceable to our religion, to use them and the interest we have by them for the promoting of religion, to do good to the poor with what we have and abound in all works of piety and charity.... (Proverbs 3:9-10)

We must *labour*, not *to be rich* (Prov. 23:4), but to be charitable, *that we may have to give* (Eph. 4:28), not to spend. (Job 20:15)

How much soever we have to do of business for ourselves and our families, we must not neglect nor omit what we have to do for the glory of God and the serving of his honour, for that is our best business. (Joshua 4:1-4)

Of the many that add to the numbers of the church, there are comparatively but few that contribute to the service of it. So it has been, and so it is; many have a place in the tabernacle that do but little of the work of the tabernacle.... (Numbers 4:34-36)

Men of estates, having more leisure than men of business, ought to employ their time in the service of the public, and by doing good they make them-

## Part II: Wisdom (Salvation)

selves truly great; the *messengers of the church* were the *glory of Christ*, 2 Cor. 8:23, (Zechariah 7:2-3)

Those that affect to ramble are many times out of their place when they are most needed. (Jeremiah 41:11-12)

It becomes the disciples of Christ to make the best of that which is, to abide by it, and not be for shifting upon every dislike or inconvenience. (Matthew 10:11-15)

There are a great many valuable men, and such as might be made very useful, that lie long buried in obscurity, and some that have done eminent services that live to be overlooked and taken no notice of; but, whatever men are, God is not unrighteous to forget the services done to his kingdom. (Daniel 5:12-13)

Many a man is buried alive in poverty and obscurity who, if he had but fit encouragement given him, might be a great blessing to the world; many a pearl is lost in its shell. (Ecclesiastes 9:16)

Privacy and obscurity are not always a protection and security. Many that affect to be strangers to the world may yet by unthought-of providences be forced into it; and those that live most retired may have the same lot with those that thrust themselves forth and lie most exposed. (Jeremiah 49:28-33)

What a shame it is that great men think the service of the true God below them and will not stoop to it, and yet will humble themselves to bow down to an idol. (Isaiah 2:9)

God keeps an account how long we have enjoyed the means of grace and how powerful those means have been, how often we have been not only spoken to, but protested to, concerning our duty. (Jeremiah 11:4)

As long as we see ourselves in the way of God and duty it is weakness and folly, when we meet with difficulties and discouragements in it, to wish we had never set out in it. (Jeremiah 20:7-8)

We often meet with hindrances and obstructions in our work, by our friends that are about us, and are taken off by civil respects from our spiritual concerns. Those who really wish well to us and to our work, may sometimes, by their indiscretion, prove our back-friends, and impediments to us in our duty; as *Peter* was offensive to Christ, with his, *"Master, spare thyself,"* when he thought himself very officious. (Matthew 12:46-47)

The courtesies of our friends often prove a snare to us, through a misguided affection. (John 18:16-17)

It is the subtlety of Satan, to send temptations to us by the unsuspected hands of our best and dearest friends. Thus he assaulted Adam by Eve, Job by his wife, and Christ by his beloved Peter. (Matthew 16:23)

It is hard to say which is worse between yoke-fellows and other rela-

## 10: Service

tions—a discord in good or concord in evil. (Acts 5:9)

It is the policy of Satan to tempt us by our nearest and dearest relations, or those friends we have an opinion of and an affection for. The temptation is most dangerous when it is sent by a hand that is least suspected: it is our wisdom therefore to consider, not so much who speaks as what is spoken. (Genesis 16:2)

If those that should be our helpers in the way of our duty prove hindrances to us, let not this drive us off from it. (Judges 8:4)

Those that undertake great and public services must not think it strange if they be discountenanced and opposed by those from whom they had reason to expect support and assistance; but must humbly go on with their work, in the face not only of their enemies' threats, but of their friends' slights and suspicions. (1 Samuel 17:29-30)

Though we may be jeered for well-doing, we must never be jeered out of it. Those can bear but little for God, and their confessing his name before men, that cannot bear a scoff and a hard word rather than quit their duty. (Psalm 69:13-14)

Let us never be driven from our duty by the fear of reproach; for to be steady and resolute in it will perhaps turn to our reputation more than we think it will. Piety will have its praise. Let us not then be indifferent in it, nor afraid or ashamed to own it. (2 Samuel 6:20-23)

We must never be driven off from our duty either by the malice of our foes, or the unkindness of our friends. (Matthew 21:18-19)

Christian fortitude will be sharpened by opposition. Every temptation to draw us from duty should quicken us so much the more to duty. (Nehemiah 6:9)

Though we must not be driven off from our duty by the malice of our enemies, yet we should order the circumstances of it so as to make it the least offensive. (Luke 14:4)

Though those who are employed for God may be driven off from their work by a storm, yet they must return to it as soon as the storm is over. (Haggai 1:3-4)

He that flies may fight again. It is no inglorious thing for Christ's soldiers to quit their ground, provided they do not quit their colours: they may go out of the way of *danger*, though they must not go out of the way of *duty*. (Matthew 10:23)

In imminent peril present opportunities may be waved, nay, we ought not to throw ourselves into the mouth of danger. Christ himself absconded often, till he knew that his hour had come. (1 Samuel 20:25)

It seems policy to shun trouble, but if

with that we shun duty, it is fleshly wisdom (2 Cor. 1:12), and it will be folly in the end. (Mark 8:31-32)

[I]n doing our duty, we ought to use all lawful means for our own preservation; even the apostles of Christ did so. (Jeremiah 38:15)

Even the Christian law of self-denial and suffering for Christ has not abrogated and repealed the natural law of self-preservation, and care for our own safety, as far as God gives an opportunity of providing for it by lawful means. (Acts 12:16-17)

Those that are in the way of God and their duty may expect that Providence will protect them, but this will not excuse them from taking all prudent methods for their own safety. God will keep us, but then we must not wilfully expose ourselves. Providence must be trusted, but not tempted. (Joshua 2:19-21)

In times of peril, when God opens a door of escape, it is lawful to flee for our own preservation, unless we have some special call to expose ourselves. (Matthew 14:13)

We may be called to lay down our lives, but not to throw away our lives. (Acts 19:31-32)

It becomes the people of God to lay to heart the dishonour done to God by the blasphemies of wicked men, though they do not think it prudent to reply to those blasphemies. (Isaiah 36:21)

The best way to baffle the malicious designs of our enemies against us is to be driven by them to God and to our duty and so fetch meat out of the eater. ... The wind, instead of forcing the traveller's coat from him, makes him wrap it the closer about him. (Isaiah 37:1)

When God, by an over-ruling providence, brings good out of evil to his church and people,—when that which threatened their ruin turns to their advantage,—when their enemies are made serviceable to them, and the wrath of men turns to God's praise— then comes *meat out of the eater* and *sweetness out of the strong*. (Judges 14:14)

The more impudent wicked people are in their opposition to religion the more openly and resolutely should God's people appear in the practice and defence of it. (Ezekiel 3:8-9)

The unwearied industry of wicked people in doing that which is evil, should shame us for our backwardness and slothfulness in that which is good. They that *war* against Christ and thy soul, are up early; *How long then wilt thou sleep, O sluggard?* (Mark 15:1)

A failure in good manners will easily be excused in those who follow Christ, if it be made up in a fulness of good affections. (Mark 6:33)

There is nothing lost in the long run by an unshaken resolution to go on with our work, neither courting the

## 10: Service

smiles, nor fearing the frowns of men. (Matthew 11:7-8)

The seals of the covenant, though they dignify us, and lay us under obligations, will not save us, unless the temper of our minds and the tenour of our lives agree with the covenant. That only is circumcision, and that baptism, which is *of the heart*, Rom 2:28-9. (Jeremiah 9:26)

It is the greatest honour of God's creatures to be in a capacity of answering the end of their creation; and the more ready we are to do every good work the nearer we approach to the dignity of angels. (Ezekiel 1:4-9)

Those that come to enquire of their duty must be willing first to be told of their faults. And those that seem zealous for the outside of a duty ought to examine themselves faithfully whether they have the regard they ought to have to the inside of it. (Zechariah 7:5)

Those that do their duty must not take it ill to be told their duty. (Jeremiah 15:19-21)

There are many that have much grace, but they have little courage, that are very honest, but withal very timorous. (Jeremiah 26:21)

We often frighten ourselves from our duty by foolish, groundless, fears, that are merely the creatures of our own fancy and imagination. (Jeremiah 38:19)

Many are diverted from real duties, and debarred from real comforts, by seeming difficulties. (Joshua 18:2-3)

We often perplex and ensnare ourselves with fears which soon appear to have been altogether groundless. We often fear where no fear is. (Genesis 12:19)

It pleases God sometimes to try those with great afflictions who are but young beginners in religion. (Genesis 12:10-13)

Young beginners in religion, like fresh-water soldiers, are apt to be discouraged with the little difficulties which they commonly meet with at first in the service of God. ... [T]heir faith is weak, and ... they are yet but babes, who cry for every hurt and every fright. (Jeremiah 45:3)

The righteous must be bold as a lion (Prov. 28:1); a cowardly Christian, who is afraid to profess the doctrines or practise the duties of the gospel, must expect that Christ will be ashamed of him another day. (2 Peter 1:5-11)

The warmest affections are not always accompanied with the boldest resolutions; many are swift to run religion's race that are not stout to fight her battles. (John 20:4-6)

It is good to acquaint children betimes with the delights of religion, and to make the services of it as pleasant as may be to them, that, learning betimes to rejoice in the Lord, they may with

## Part II: Wisdom (Salvation)

purpose of heart cleave to him. (Zechariah 10:7)

If those that are young do God's work as well as they can, they shall be accepted, though they cannot do it so well as those that are aged and experienced. (Leviticus 2:14-16)

Young beginners in religion must not be put upon the hardest duties at first, lest they be discouraged. ... There may be *over*-doing even in *well*-doing, a being *righteous over-much;* and such an *over*-doing as may prove an *un*doing through the subtlety of Satan. (Matthew 9:16-17)

Persons expose themselves to great danger by attempting to perform what is above their strength, and at the same time not bound upon them by any law of God. If they abstain from lawful enjoyments, they may be ensnared into unlawful ones. (1 Corinthians 7:5)

God graciously *considers the frame* of young Christians, that are *weak* and *tender,* and so must we.... Weak Christians must take heed of *overtasking* themselves, and of making the yoke of Christ otherwise than it is, easy, and sweet, and pleasant. (Mark 2:18-20)

Young beginners in religion are subject to mistakes, which time and the grace of God will rectify. (John 1:45)

Thus Christ used his disciples first to less difficulties, and then to greater, and so trains them up by degrees to live *by faith, and not by sense.* (Matthew 14:24-27)

Brief summaries of Christian doctrine are of great use to young beginners. The principles of the oracles of God brought into a little compass in creeds and catechisms have, like beams of the sun contracted in a burning glass, conveyed divine light and heat with a wonderful power. (John 16:28-33)

Those that have the greatest knowledge of divine things must remember the time when they were as babes, unskilful in the word of righteousness. *When I was a child I understood as a child.* Yet let us not despise the day of small things. (1 Samuel 3:6-9)

Christ reveals his mind to his people gradually, and lets in light as they can bear it, and are fit to receive it. (Matthew 16:21)

And it is sometimes the fault of old people to discourage the services of the present age by crying up too much the performances and attainments of the former age, with which others should be provoked to emulation, but not exposed to contempt. *Say not thou that the former days were better than these* (Eccl. 7:10), but thank God that there is any good in these, bad as they are. (Haggai 2:3)

When we see, and complain of, the wickedness of the present times, yet we do not *enquire wisely of that matter,* if we say that all *the former days were better than these....* The worst of hypocrites and evil doers have had their predecessors. (Mark 7:6-10)

Though the work of righteousness may be toilsome and costly, and expose us to contempt, yet it is peace, such peace as is sufficient to bear our charges. (Isaiah 32:17)

God's faithful servants must not think it at all strange if their foes be *those of their own house* (Matt. 10:36), and if those they expect kindness from prove such as they can put no confidence in…. (Jeremiah 12:6)

Temperance, self-denial, and mortification to the world, do very much befriend the exercises of piety, and help to transmit the observance of them to posterity. The more dead we are to the delights of sense the better we are disposed for the service of God; but nothing is more fatal to the entail of religion in a family than pride and luxury. (Jeremiah 35:18-19)

Despair of happiness in the creature, and of satisfaction in the service of sin, is the first step towards a well-grounded hope of happiness in God and a well-fixed resolution to keep to his service; and those are inexcusable who have had sensible convictions of the vanity of the creature, and yet will not be brought to say "There is no hope to be happy short of the Creator." (Isaiah 57:10)

Those that are employed in holy things are therein God's ministers, and on him they attend. (Joel 1:13)

# -11-

# Ministers
# (The Great Commission)

This is the work of ministers, by the word of God, to be as a lamp and a light, to expose the sin of men and expound the providences of God.

Matthew Henry
on 2 Chronicles 24:20

This is the work of ministers, by the word of God, to be as a lamp and a light, to expose the sin of men and expound the providences of God. (2 Chronicles 24:20)

This is the character of a good teacher, to preach the truth, the whole truth, and nothing but the truth, and not to suppress, pervert, or stretch, any truth, for favour or affection, hatred or good will, either out of a desire to please, or a fear to offend, any man. (Matthew 22:16)

Note, *First,* There are two great interests on foot in the world, with the one or the other of which all the children of men are siding. The interest of sin and wickedness is the devil's interest, and all wicked people side with that interest; the interest of truth and holiness is God's interest, with which all godly people side; and it is a case that will not admit a neutrality. *Secondly,* It concerns us to enquire whether we are on the Lord's side or not. *Thirdly,* Those who are on his side are comparatively few, and sometimes seem fewer than they really are. *Fourthly,* God sometimes calls out those that are on his side to appear for him as witnesses, as soldiers, as intercessors. (Ezekiel 32:26)

Those whom God calls to the ministry, as he furnishes their heads for it, so he bows their hearts to it. (Ezekiel 3:12-14)

Those whom God employs to speak for him ought to depend upon him for instructions, and *it shall be given them what they shall speak,* Matt. 10:19. (Exodus 4:12)

1. There are a people in the world that are God's people. 2. It is the will of God that his people should be a comforted people, even in the worst of times. 3. It is the work and business of ministers to do what they can for the comfort of God's people. 4. Words of conviction … must be followed with words of comfort … for he that has torn will heal us. (Isaiah 40:1-2)

Ministers must try both ways in dealing with people, must speak to them from Mount Sinai by the terrors of the law, and from Mount Sion by the comforts of the gospel, must set before them both life and death, good and evil, the blessing and the curse. (Job 22:1)

Our pleading with sinners must be to drive them to repentance, not to drive them to despair. (Hosea 2:2)

The hearts of sinners are not only as stone, but as rough stone, which requires a great deal of pains to bring it into shape, or as knotty timber, that is not squared without a great deal of difficulty; ministers' work is to hew them, and God by the minister hews them, *for with the froward will he show himself froward.* (Hosea 6:4)

The conversion of sinners from their evil courses is that which ministers should aim at in preaching; and people hear the word in vain if that point be not gained with them. To what

## 11: Ministers (The Great Commission)

purpose do we hear of the evil God will bring upon us for sin if we continue, notwithstanding, to do evil against him? (Jeremiah 36:3)

Custom in sin is a very great hindrance to conversion from sin. The disease that is inveterate is generally thought incurable. (Jeremiah 13:24-25)

Ministers are spiritual physicians.... (Acts 2:37-38)

If reformers will but put on resolution, more may be done towards the breaking of bad customs than they can imagine. Vice connived at is indeed a daring thing, and will bid defiance to counsel and reproof; but it may be made cowardly, and will be so when magistrates make themselves a terror to it. (Nehemiah 13:21)

We must not despair of the conversion of the worst; no, not of those who have been instrumental to pervert and debauch others; even they may be brought to repentance, and, if they be, shall find mercy. (Jeremiah 12:14-15)

We should think no pains too much to take for the recovering of a sinner to repentance. (Matthew 18:15-17)

Those that are converted need to be confirmed; those that are planted need to be rooted. Ministers' work is to establish saints as well as to awaken sinners ... *To retain is sometimes as difficult as to acquire.* (Acts 14:22-23)

Those we preach to we must pray for. (John 17:1-5)

Faithful ministers water their preaching with their prayers, because, whoever sows the seed, it is God that gives the increase. We can but speak to the ear; it is God's prerogative to speak to the heart. (Romans 15:5-6)

If ministers give warning, and people take it, it is well for both. Nothing is more beautiful than a *wise reprover upon an obedient ear*; the one *shall live because he is warned* and the other *has delivered his soul*. What can a good minister desire more than to *save himself and those that hear him?* 1 Tim. 4:16. (Ezekiel 3:21)

It is sad to think that, though divine revelation be one of the greatest blessings and honours that ever was bestowed upon the world, yet it has been turned very much to the reproach of the most zealous preachers and believers of it. (Jeremiah 20:8)

See what need those have to stand upon their guard who have made a great profession of religion, and shown themselves forward and zealous in devotion, because the devil will set upon them most violently, and, if they misbehave, the reproach is the greater. It is the evening that commends the day; let us therefore fear, lest, having run well, we seem to come short. (1 Kings 11:4)

If those that are in reputation for religion in any thing set a bad example, they know not what a deal of mischief they may do by it, particularly to their own children. One bad act of a good man may be of more pernicious consequence to others than twenty of a wicked man. (1 Kings 11:6-8)

Nothing brings a greater reproach upon religion than ministers' covetousness, sensuality, and imperiousness. (1 Samuel 2:17)

The more eyes we have upon us, and the greater our influence is, the more need we have to speak and act wisely and to govern our passions strictly. (2 Samuel 19:2-3)

Ministers must stand upon their guard, lest, under pretence of being advised with, they be ensnared. (Mark 10:2)

A man may be a preacher, may have gifts for the ministry, and an external call to it, and perhaps some success in it, and yet be a wicked man; may help others to heaven, and yet come short himself. (Matthew 7:22-23)

The case of those people is very pitiable, who either have no ministers at all, or those that are as bad as none; that seek their own things, not *the things of Christ* and souls. (Matthew 9:35-36)

The instruction of a gospel minister must be in the *kingdom of heaven*, that is it about which his business lies. A man may be a great philosopher and politician, and yet if not instructed to the kingdom of heaven, he will make but a bad minister. (Matthew 13:51-52)

We must take heed of over-valuing ministers, as well as of under-valuing them; they are not our lords, nor have they dominion over our faith, but ministers by whom we believe, stewards of our Lord's house. We must not give up ourselves by an implicit faith to their conduct, for they are not that light; but we must attend to, and receive, their testimony; for they are sent to bear witness of that light; so then let us esteem them, and not otherwise. (John 1:8)

It is a very great abuse of their power, and highly criminal in common ministers, to lord it over their fellow-servants, and challenge authority over their faith or practice. For even apostles were but servants of Christ.... (1 Corinthians 4:1-2)

Ministers, however instrumental they are of good to us, are not to be put in Christ's stead. They are not to usurp Christ's authority, nor encourage any thing in the people that looks like transferring his authority to them. (1 Corinthians 1:13)

The instruments of God's favour to us, though they must be respected, must not be idolized; we must take heed of reckoning that to be done by the instrument which God is the author of. (Acts 3:12)

God's ministers must expect to pass through *honour and dishonour, evil report and good report*, and must resolve in both to hold fast their integrity and keep close to their work. (Hosea 1:1)

## 11: Ministers (The Great Commission)

Those who are *reprovers in the gate*, reprovers by office, magistrates and ministers, are concerned to *walk circumspectly*, and to be very regular in their conversation: an *elder must have a good report*, 1 Tim. 3:2, 7. The snuffers of the sanctuary were to be of pure gold. (Matthew 7:1-6)

The ministry being a great trust, it is fit that men should be tried for a time, before they are entrusted with it. Let them *first be proved* ... because some men's sins go before, and other's follow…. (Matthew 10:1)

The ministers of Christ should not think it strange to be put upon the proof of their ministry by some who have had experimental evidence of the power of it and the presence of God with it. (1 Corinthians 9:1-2)

That should always grieve us most by which God's honour suffers and the interest of his kingdom is weakened. (Jeremiah 13:17)

As long as ministers keep closely to the instructions they have from heaven they need not fear the opposition they may meet with from hell or earth. (Jeremiah 26:12-15)

The enemies of God's people and ministers have been often very crafty themselves, and confederate with one another, to do them mischief. What they cannot act to the prejudice of religion separately they will try to do in concert. (Jeremiah 18:18)

It is no new thing for those that are at variance in other things, to join in a confederacy against Christ. (Mark 12:13)

It has often been the artifice of Satan, to turn that artillery against the church, which was originally planted in the defence of it. Brand the true prophets as seducers, and the true professors of religion as heretics and schismatics, and then it will be easy to persecute them. (Matthew 23:37)

It has been the artifice of Satan to make God's ministers and people odious to the commonality, by representing them as dangerous men, who aimed at the destruction of the constitution and the changing of the customs, when really there has been no ground for such an imputation. (Acts 16:22)

The greatest merits cannot secure men from the greatest indignities and affronts in this ungrateful world. (Exodus 32:1)

Neither the innocence of the dove, no, nor the prudence of the serpent to help it, can secure men from unjust censure and false accusation. (Jeremiah 20:10)

Thus the men that have been the greatest blessings of their age have been represented not only as the burdens of the earth, but the plague of their generation. (Acts 22:22-23)

It is common for wicked people to look upon God's faithful ministers as their enemies, only because they show them what enemies they are to themselves while they continue impenitent. (Jeremiah 38:4)

That man's condition is very miserable that has made the word of God his enemy, and his condition is very desperate that reckons the ministers of that word his enemies because they *tell him the truth,* Gal. 4:16 (1 Kings 21:20)

If Christ's ministers could cure bodily diseases as Christ did, there would be more flocking to them than there is; we are soon sensible of bodily pain and sickness, but few are concerned about their souls and their spiritual diseases. (Matthew 15:30)

Those are very unjust who complain of ministers for preaching hell and damnation, when it is only to keep them from that place of torment and to bring them to heaven and salvation. (Jeremiah 26:13)

The messengers of God's wrath will be sent against those that would not receive the messengers of his mercy. One way or other God will be heeded, and will make men know that *he is the Lord.* (Jeremiah 25:9)

It becomes God's ministers to be of a tender spirit, not to desire the woeful day, but to be like their master, who wept over Jerusalem even when he gave her up to ruin, like their God, *who desires not the death of sinners.* (Isaiah 15:5)

Those that put the evil day far from them will be the more terrified when it comes upon them; and those who before slighted God's ministers may then perhaps be glad to court an acquaintance with them. (Jeremiah 21:1-2)

The obstinacy of people, in refusing to hear the word of God, will be heartbreaking to the poor ministers, who know something of the terrors of the Lord and the worth of souls, and are so far from desiring that they tremble at the thoughts of the death of sinners. (Jeremiah 13:17)

It is a great vexation to the spirits of good ministers to see people deaf to all the fair warnings given them, and running headlong upon ruin, notwithstanding all the kind methods taken to prevent it. (Exodus 11:8)

The best and most powerful preachers of the gospel must expect to meet with some, that will not so much as give them the hearing, nor show them any token of respect. ... Contempt of the gospel, and contempt of gospel ministers, commonly go together, and they will either of them be construed into a contempt of Christ, and will be reckoned for accordingly. (Matthew 10:14)

Good men cannot but mourn to see how slowly the work of God goes on in the world and what opposition it meets with, how weak its friends are and how active its enemies. (Daniel 10:2)

It is a strong temptation to poor ministers to resolve that they will preach no more when they see their preaching

## 11: Ministers (The Great Commission)

slighted and wholly ineffectual. But let people dread putting their ministers into this temptation. (Jeremiah 20:9)

Ministers have little heart to speak to those who have long and often turned a deaf ear to them. (Jeremiah 38:15)

Their condition is sad who have the prayers of good ministers and good people against them. (Jeremiah 11:20)

It will be a comfort to God's ministers, when men despise them, if they have the testimony of their consciences for them that they have not by any vain foolish behaviour made themselves despicable, that they have been dead not only to the wealth of the world, but to the pleasures of it too.... (Jeremiah 15:17)

It is not enough that we do not delight in the sins of others, and that we have not fellowship with them, but we must mourn for them, and lay them to heart; we must grieve for that which we cannot help, as those that hate sin for its own sake, and have a tender concern for the souls of others.... (Ezekiel 9:4)

Ministers must with meekness instruct even those that oppose themselves, and render good for evil. (Jeremiah 38:15)

It is some comfort to poor ministers that, if men will not hear them, God will; and to him they have liberty of access at all times. Let them close their preaching with prayer, and then they shall have no reason to say that they have laboured in vain. (Jeremiah 10:22)

It ought not to discourage the ministers of Christ that some reject them, for they will meet with others that will welcome them and their message. (Luke 4:42-44)

It is an encouragement to a faithful minister to cast the net of the gospel where there are a great many fishes, in hope that some will be caught. (Matthew 5:1-2)

We must not abruptly quit the callings wherein we are called because we have not the success in them we promised ourselves. The ministers of the gospel must continue to *let down* that *net*, though they have perhaps *toiled long* and *caught nothing*; and this is thankworthy, to continue unwearied in our labours, though we see not the success of them. (Luke 5:5)

Let not ministers be discouraged, though they see not the fruit of their labours presently; the seed sown seems to be lost under the clods, but it shall come up again in a plentiful harvest in due time. (Acts 16:35-40)

Previous dispositions to that which is good, are both directions and encouragements to ministers, in dealing with people. ... They that entertain the gospel, must neither grudge the expense of it, nor promise themselves to get by it in this world. They must enquire, not who is rich, but who is worthy; not who is the best gentleman, but who is the best man. (Matthew 10:11-13)

The best men, the best ministers, cannot do the good they would do in the world. (Isaiah 1:1)

When we cannot do what we would in religion, we must do as we can, and God will accept us. (Matthew 18:19-20)

All that are separated to Christ as his ministers are separated to work; Christ keeps no servants to be idle. (Acts 13:2)

The ministry is not a matter of carnal ease nor pleasure, but of pains; if any are idle in it, they answer not their calling. Christ bids his disciples *pray the Lord of the harvest to send forth labourers*, not loiterers, *into his harvest*, Matt. 9:39. (Philemon 23-25)

Ministers are sometimes so bashful and timorous, and so much at a loss, that they must be put on to speak, and to speak boldly. (Ezekiel 11:4)

Persecution for religion is sometimes a correction and rebuke for the sins of professors of religion. Men persecute them because they are religious; God chastises them because they are not more so: men persecute them because they will not give up their profession; God chastises them because they have not lived up to their profession. (Hebrews 12:4-7)

[T]hose who have that power in their hands contract the guilt of sin themselves if they do not use their power for the preventing and restraining of sin in others. "You trespass if you do not keep them from trespassing." (2 Chronicles 19:10)

Those who do not what they can to keep others from sin do what they can to cut them off. (Numbers 4:18)

It bodes well to a people when God enlarges the liberties of his ministers and they are countenanced and encouraged in their work. (Ezekiel 29:20-21)

God goes along with those whom he sends, and is, by his powerful protection, at all times and in all places present with them; and with this they ought to animate themselves, Acts 18:10. (Jeremiah 1:8)

We must not only consult the written word (*to the law and to the testimony*), but must have recourse to God's messengers, and desire instruction and advice from them in the affairs of our souls as we do from physicians and lawyers concerning our bodies and estates. (Malachi 2:5)

See what need there is of the preaching of the word; people must hear the word preached because they will not make the use they ought to make of the word written. (Jeremiah 34:8-10)

[I]t is good to hear twice what God has spoken once (Ps. 62:11) and to review what had been delivered to us, or to have it repeated, that we may not let is slip. (Joshua 8:35)

People need to have good truths pressed again and again upon them, and if they be preached and heard with new affections, they are as if they were fresh to us. (Matthew 10:7)

## 11: Ministers (The Great Commission)

The ministry of the word is concerning matters of *life and death,* for those are the things it sets before us, *the blessing and the curse,* that we may escape the curse and inherit the blessing. (Ezekiel 3:18-19)

The writing and repeating of the sermons that have been preached may contribute very much towards the answering of the great ends of preaching. What we have heard and known it is good for us to hear again, that we may know it better. (Jeremiah 36:6)

Preaching is not designed to teach us something new in every sermon, somewhat that we knew nothing of before; but *to put us in remembrance,* to call to mind things forgotten, to affect our passions, and engage and fix our resolutions, that our lives may be answerable to our faith. *Though you know these things,* yet you still need to *know them better.* (Jude 5)

Ministers may be serving Christ, and promoting the great ends of their ministry, by writing good letters, as well as by preaching good sermons. (Acts 18:7-11)

The private compositions of good men, designed by them for their use, may be serviceable to the public, that others may not only borrow light from their candle, but heat from their fire. Examples sometimes teach better than rules. (Psalm 18 Title)

Ministers are the church's teeth; like nurses, they chew the meat for the babes of Christ. ... Faith, by which we feed upon Christ, meditation, by which we ruminate on the word and chew the cud upon what we have heard, in order to the digesting of it, are the teeth of the new man. (Song of Solomon 4:2)

That which is of universal concern ought to be of universal cognizance. It is fit that the word which concerns all the people, as the word of God does, the word of the gospel particularly, should be divulged to all in general, and, as far as may be, addressed to each in particular. (Jeremiah 25:2)

Ministers must not think it enough to preach before their hearers, but must preach to them, nor enough to preach to them all in general, but should address themselves to particular persons.... (Proverbs 22:17)

Ministers' doors should be open to such as desire to receive instruction from them, and they should be glad of an opportunity to advise those that are in care about their souls. (Acts 28:30-31)

Ministers should in their private visits, and as they go from house to house, discourse of those things which they have taught publicly, repeat them, inculcate them, and explain them, if it be needful, asking, *Have you understood all these things?* And, especially, they should help persons to apply the truth to themselves and their own case. (Acts 20:20)

Note, [1.] It is requisite that those who hear the word should understand it, else it is to them but an empty sound of words, Matt. 24:15. [2.] It is therefore required of those who are teachers by office that they explain the word and give the sense of it. (Nehemiah 8:7-8)

It is the duty of a faithful minister of Christ to consult the capacities of his hearers and teach them as they can bear. (1 Corinthians 3:1-2)

God's ministers must *become all things to all men, if by any means they may gain some*, must comply with them in circumstances, that they may secure the substance. St. Paul preached privately to those of reputation, Gal. 2:2. (Jeremiah 36:14-15)

It is as bad to God's faithful ministers to have their mouth stopped as to have their breath stopped. (Jeremiah 11:21)

Even silenced ministers may be doing a great deal of good by writing letters and making visits. (Ezekiel 33:21-22)

Those that are sent to discover sin ought to lay aside the enticing words of man's wisdom. Plain-dealing is best when we are dealing with sinners to bring them to repentance. (Jeremiah Introduction)

Private admonitions must always go before public censures; if gentler methods will do the work, those that are more rough and severe must not be used, Titus 3:10. Those that will be reasoned out of their sins, need not be shamed out of them. (Matthew 18:17) Reproofs are ordinarily *most profitable when they are least provoking*.

(John 4:17-18)

We must not be ashamed to own the secret transactions between Christ and our souls; but, when called to it, mention, to his praise, and the encouragement of others, what he has done for our souls, and the experience we have had of *healing virtue* derived from him. And the consideration of this, that nothing can be hid from Christ, should engage us to confess all to him. (Mark 5:33)

Ministers will make a good use of their converse with the business and affairs of this life if they learn thereby to speak more plainly and familiarly to people about the things of God, and to expound Scripture comparisons. For they ought to make all their knowledge some way or other serviceable to their profession. (Jeremiah 18:4)

Knowledge is given us to do good with, that others may light their candle at our lamp.... (Proverbs 22:21)

[L]et not ministers be ambitious of coining new expressions, nor people's ears itch for novelties; to write and speak the same things must not be grievous, for it is safe. (Matthew 7:19)

Those that would learn well, and teach well, in religion, must not affect new-found notions and new-coined phrases, so as to look with contempt upon the knowledge and language of their predecessors; if we must keep to the good old way, why should we scorn the good old words? Jer. 6:16. (Proverbs 4:3-4)

## 11: Ministers (The Great Commission)

It is sometimes a good help to memory to put much matter in few words, which serve as handles by which we take hold of more. (Isaiah 8:1)

A prudent pen may go far towards making up the deficiencies of the memory.... (Deuteronomy 17:18)

The duties of Christianity are more necessary to be known than the notions of it; and yet the notions of it are more necessary to be illustrated than the duties of it; which is that which parables are designed for. (Matthew 20:1)

And a weighty adage may sometimes do more service than a laboured discourse. (Hosea Introduction)

[O]ne observation built upon matter of fact is worth twenty notions framed by an hypothesis. (Job 12:6-11)

The power of imagination, if it be rightly used, and kept under the direction and correction of reason and faith, may be of good use to kindle and excite pious and devout affections.... (Ezekiel 4:7-8)

It concerns ministers to make it to appear in their whole conversation that they do themselves believe that which they preach to others; and in order that they may do so, and impress it the more deeply upon their hearers, they must many a time deny themselves.... (Jeremiah 32:14-15)

We must deny ourselves sometimes in our ease, pleasure, and convenience, rather than give offence even to those who causelessly take it; but we must not deny ourselves the satisfaction of serving God, and doing good, though offence may unjustly be taken at it. (Mark 3:5)

The most active servants of Christ cannot be always upon the stretch of business, but have bodies that require some relaxation, some breathing-time; we shall not be able to serve God without ceasing, day and night, till we come to heaven, where they *never rest* in praising him, Rev. 4:8. (Mark 6:31)

Those in the most public stations, and that are most publicly useful, must sometimes go aside privately, both for the repose of their bodies, to recruit them, and for the furnishing of their minds by meditation for further public work. (Luke 9:10)

Good men that are very active sometimes need to be dissuaded from overworking themselves, and good men that are very bold need to be dissuaded from exposing themselves too far. (Acts 21:12)

Those that are called to preach must find time to study, and a great deal of time too, must often shut themselves up in their houses, that they may give attendance to reading and meditation, and so their profiting may appear to all. (Ezekiel 3:24-25)

Ministers must not think that their public performances will excuse them from their family-worship; but when they have, with their instructions and prayers, blessed the solemn assemblies, they must return in the same manner to bless their households, for with them they are in a particular manner charged. (2 Samuel 6:20)

Young scholars may gain a great deal by converse with old Christians, as young students in the law may by old practitioners. (Acts 18:24-26)

Enquire for the old way, the wells which our fathers digged, which the adversaries of truth have stopped up: *Ask thy elders, and they shall teach thee.* (Genesis 26:18)

It concerns God's prophets and ministers to treasure up the things of God in their minds, and there to digest them well. If we would have God's word ready in our mouths when we have occasion for it, we must keep it in our hearts at all times. (Daniel 7:28)

Words of direction and comfort are often out of the way when we have occasion to use them, till the blessed Spirit brings them to our remembrance, and then we wonder how we overlooked them. (Song of Solomon 6:1-3)

There is many a good truth that we thought was well laid up when we heard it, which yet is out of the way when we have occasion to use it. (Matthew 12:46-47)

Those who are appointed to be teachers have need to be very diligent careful learners, that they may neither forget any of the things they are entrusted with nor mistake concerning them. (Ezekiel 44:5)

The mistakes of preachers often give rise to the prejudices of hearers. (John 1:46)

Even those whom Christ hath taught, have need to be taught *again.* Such is the fulness of the Christian doctrine, that there is still more to be learned; and such our forgetfulness, that we need to be reminded of what we do know. (Mark 10:1)

Ministers have lessons to learn as well as lessons to teach, and must themselves hear God's voice and preach to themselves. (Jeremiah 12:5-6)

It is worth while to change our quarters, that we may be near to Christ, and have opportunities of converse with him. (Matthew 8:14-17)

It becomes God's ministers, that are warm in preaching, to be calm in suffering and to behave submissively to the powers that are over them, though they be persecuting powers. (Jeremiah 26:14)

Note, [1.] It is the lot of faithful ministers often to be reduced to great difficulties, and to stand in need of much patience. [2.] Those who approve themselves to God must approve themselves faithful in trouble as well as in peace, not only doing the work of God diligently, but also in bearing the will of God patiently. (2 Corinthians 6:4-5)

## 11: Ministers (The Great Commission)

Christ's witnesses are under his special care, and, though they may fall into the hands of the enemies, yet he will take care to deliver them out of their hands, and he knows how to do it. (Acts 26:17)

God will not only deliver his people out of their troubles in due time, but he will sustain them and bear them up under their troubles in the mean time. (Psalm 18:18)

If God do not deliver his ministers from trouble, it is to the same effect if he support them under their trouble. (Jeremiah 1:8)

Ministers must spend, and be spent, for the good of souls. (Jeremiah 13:9-11)

Dying saints may be justly envied, while living sinners are justly pitied. (Jeremiah 22:10)

The happiness of saints is the envy of sinners. Whom heaven blesses, hell curses. (Genesis 27:41)

God's ministers have work to do which they need not be either ashamed or afraid to go on in, but they do need to be helped by the divine grace to go on in it without shame or fear. (Jeremiah 17:18)

We need the constant and continual waterings of the divine grace; for, if that be at any time withdrawn, we wither, and come to nothing. God waters his vineyard by the ministry of the word by his servants the prophets, whose doctrine shall drop as the dew.

Paul plants, and Apollos waters, but God gives the increase; for without him the watchman wakes and the husbandman waters in vain. (Isaiah 27:2-3)

Our souls are never valuable as gardens but when they are watered with the dews of God's Spirit and grace. (Jeremiah 31:12)

It is sometimes so; when good preaching is most scarce it does most good, whereas the manna that is rained in plenty is loathed as *light bread*. (Haggai 1:12)

Ministers are God's gifts to the church; their ministry, and their ability for it, are God's gifts to them. (Matthew 9:9)

Souls are first drawn to Christ with the *cords of a man*, and kept to him by the *bands of love*, Hos. 11:4. (Matthew 10:5-15)

It is our duty earnestly to desire and pray for the prosperity and success of Christ's kingdom in the world. (Matthew 21:9)

We must not think that Christ's church and cause are lost because not always alike visible and prevailing. (Luke 17:21-22)

There has been, and shall be, a succession of God's ministers to the end of the world, by whom he will speak; and though contempt may be put upon them, that shall not put a period to their ministration: *In your days, O rebellious house! will I say the word.* (Ezekiel 12:25)

As Christ's faithful ministers are not taken out of the world, so they are not removed from any place, till they have finished their testimony in that place, Rev. 11:7. (Matthew 19:1)

It is a comfort to useful men, when they are going off the stage, to see those rising up who are likely to fill up their place. (John 3:23-24)

Ministers may be silenced, and imprisoned, and banished, and slain, but the word of God cannot be run down. The prophets *live not forever, but the word takes hold*, Zech. 1:5, 6. (Matthew 14:1-12)

Those that follow Christ must be dealt plainly with, and warned not to expect great things in this world. (Matthew 16:21-23)

The apostles were so far from flattering people with an expectation of worldly prosperity in religion that, on the contrary, they told them plainly they must count upon trouble in the flesh. (1 Thessalonians 3:4)

[W]hat there is of trouble and danger in the service of Christ, he tells us of it before, tells us we shall *suffer*, perhaps we shall *die*, in the cause; and represents the discouragements not *less*, but *greater*, than commonly they prove, that it may appear he *deals fairly* with us, and is not afraid that we should know the worst; because the *advantages* of his service abundantly suffice to *balance* the *discouragements*, if we will but impartially set the one over against the other. (Mark 8:34-35)

Those that follow Christ, in expectation of great things in this world by him, and by the profession of his religion, may probably live to see themselves sadly disappointed. (Mark 15:33-41)

There is a proneness in good men to expect the crown without the cross. (Matthew 17:4)

Great sufferings are reconcilable to the promise of the deliverance of God's people, for it is not promised that they shall be kept from trouble, but kept through it; and sometimes God delivers them into the hands of their persecutors that he may have the honour of delivering them out of their hands. (Acts 26:17)

A natural state is a dark state, and those who continue in that state meet with no disturbance from Satan and the world; but a state of grace is a state of light, and therefore the powers of darkness will violently oppose it. Those who will live godly in Christ Jesus must suffer persecution. (Hebrews 10:32)

[T]hose who inherit the blessing must expect persecution; those who have peace in Christ shall have tribulation in the world, John 16:33. Being told of this before, we must not think it strange, and, being assured of a recompense hereafter, we must not think it hard. (Genesis 28:1)

The Lord Jesus Christ, being consecrated and perfected through suffer-

## 11: Ministers (The Great Commission)

ing, has consecrated the way of suffering for all his followers to pass through unto glory; and hereby their sufferings are made necessary and unavoidable, they are hereby made honourable, useful, and profitable. (Hebrews 2:10-13)

*They* shall not share with him in his glory then, that were not willing to share with him in his disgrace now. (Mark 8:38)

They mistake the design of the gospel, who think their profession of it will secure them from, for it will certainly expose them to, trouble in this world. … Christ has dealt fairly and faithfully with us, in telling us the worst we can meet with in his service; and he would have us deal so with ourselves, in sitting down and counting the cost. (Matthew 10:34-42)

# -12-

# Prophecy

It is God's prerogative to foretell things to come, Isa. 46:10.

Matthew Henry
on Genesis 40:8

(Paragraphs rendered in **bold typeface** in this section are quotations from the Bible as cited by Matthew Henry.)

It is God's prerogative to foretell things to come, Isa. 46:10. (Genesis 40:8)

The learned Dr. Grew ... describes prophecy in this sense to be, "A declaration of the divine prescience, looking at any distance through a train of infinite causes, known and unknown to us, upon a sure and certain effect." ... So Tully argues ... *He who knows the causes of future events must necessarily know the events themselves; this is the prerogative of God alone.* ... And therefore we find that by *this*, the God of Israel proves himself to be God, that by his prophets he foretold things to come, which came to pass according to the prediction, Isa. 46:9-10. (Isaiah Preface).

God always foresees, and has sometimes foretold as certain, that which yet to us seems most contingent. (2 Kings 23:20)

Where God has a mouth to speak we must have an ear to hear; we all must, for we are all concerned in what is delivered. (Micah 1:2)

God, by the prophet, speaks as if he thought the time long till men would be men, and show themselves so by understanding and considering: *"You fools, when will you be wise,* so wise as to know that God sees and regards all you say and do, and to speak and act accordingly, as those that must give account?" (Psalm 94:8)

In all the providences of God concerning his church it is good to take notice of the fulfilling of his word; for there is an exact agreement between the judgments of God's hand and the judgment of his mouth, and when they are compared they will mutually explain and illustrate each other. (Lamentations 2:17)

God's word and his works mutually illustrate each other. The performance makes the promise appear very true and the promise makes the performance appear very kind. (Joshua 21:43)

[F]rom what *has been* we conjecture what *will be.* See the benefit of experience; by *taking notice* we may come to *give notice.* Whose is wise will *observe* and *learn.* (Luke 12:54-55)

There is an amiable admirable harmony and agreement between the Lord's prophets, though they lived in several ages, for they were all guided by one and the same Spirit. (Ezekiel 39:17)

Such an admirable harmony there is between the word and the works of God that the remembrance of what is written will enable us to understand what is done, and the observation of what is done will help us to understand what is written. *As we have heard, so have we seen.* The scripture is every day fulfilling. (John 12:16)

From the earliest period of time, for 4,000 years, a great number of men have predicted the advent of Christ, and presented a harmonious statement of his birth, life, character, actions, and death, and of that economy which he came to establish. (Isaiah Preface)

## 12. Prophecy

It is the folly of many curious enquirers concerning the times to come that they look for that *before them* which is already *among them*. (Luke 17:20-21)

Prophecies should not be too plain, and yet intelligible to those that search them; and they are best understood by comparing them first with one another, and at last with the event. (Mark 13:14)

Those who would know the mind of God in the scripture must compare one part of the scripture with another, and put those parts together that have reference to the same thing, for the latter discoveries of divine light explain what was dark and supply what was defective in the former, *that the man of God may be perfect*. (Numbers 29:1)

These future events are shown, not in the clearest light in which God could have set them, but in such a light as he saw most proper, and which would best answer his wise and holy purposes. Had they been as clearly foretold in all their circumstances as God could have revealed them, the prediction might have prevented the accomplishment; but they are foretold more darkly, to beget in us a veneration for the scripture, and to engage our attention and excite our enquiry. (Revelation 2:1)

[Prophecy] is ... foretold in somewhat obscure expressions, as it is fit that such particular prophecies should be delivered, lest otherwise the plainness of the prophecy might prevent the accomplishment of it. (Zechariah 11:12)

**Seventy weeks are determined upon thy people and upon thy holy city, to finish the transgression, and to make an end of sins, and to make reconciliation for iniquity, and to bring in everlasting righteousness, and to seal up the vision and prophecy, and to anoint the most Holy.**

In general, it is *seventy weeks*, that is, *seventy times seven years*, which makes just 490 years. The great affairs that are yet to come concerning the people of Israel, and the city of Jerusalem, will lie within the compass of these years.
(1.) These years are thus described by weeks, [1.] In conformity with the prophetic style, which is, for the most part, abstruse, and out of the common road of speaking, that the things foretold might not lie too obvious. [2.] To put an honour upon the division of time into weeks, which is made purely by the sabbath day, and to signify that that should be perpetual. [3.] With reference to the seventy years of captivity; as they had been so long kept out of the possession of their own land, so, being restored to it they should seven times as long be kept in the possession of it. ... Some make them to end at the death of Christ, and think the express words of this famous prophecy will warrant us to conclude that from this very hour when Gabriel spoke to Daniel, at the time of the evening oblation, to the hour when Christ died, which was towards evening too, it was exactly 490 years; and I am willing enough to be of that opinion. (Daniel 9:24)

**5 Behold, I will send you Elijah the prophet before the coming of the great**

**and dreadful day of the LORD: 6 And he shall turn the heart of the fathers to the children, and the heart of the children to their fathers, lest I come and smite the earth with a curse.**
Prophecy was now to cease in the church for some ages, and the Spirit of prophecy not to return till the *beginning of the gospel,* ... But we Christians know very well that John Baptist was the Elias that was to come, Matt. 17:10-13; and very expressly, Matt. 11:14, *This is Elias that was to come;* and *v.* 10, the same of whom it is written, *Behold, I send my messenger....* (Malachi 4:5-6)

For above three hundred years the church had been without prophets; those lights had been long put out, that *he* might be the more desired, who was to be the great prophet. After Malachi there was no prophet, nor any pretender to prophecy, till John the Baptist, to whom therefore the prophet Malachi points more directly than any of the Old Testament prophets had done (Mal. 3:1); *I send my messenger.* (Matthew 3:1-3)

**But thou, Beth-lehem Ephratah,** *though* **thou be little among the thousands of Judah,** *yet* **out of thee shall come forth unto me** *that is* **to be ruler in Israel; Whose goings forth** *have been* **from of old, from everlasting.**
*... of old, from everlasting* ... can be applied to no other than to him who was able to say, *Before Abraham was, I am,* John 8:58. ... The Jews object that our Lord Jesus could not be the Messiah, for he was so far from being ruler in Israel that Israel ruled over him, and put him to death, and would not have him to reign over them; but he answered that himself when he said, *My kingdom is not of this world.* John 18:36. (Micah 5:2)

**Therefore the LORD himself shall give you a sign; Behold, a virgin shall conceive, and bear a son, and shall call his name Immanuel.**
"In a glorious manner; for, whereas you have been often told that he should be born among you, I am now further to tell you that he shall be born of a virgin, which will signify both the divine power and the divine purity with which he shall be brought into the world,—that he shall be an extraordinary person, for he shall not be born by ordinary generation,—and that he shall be a holy thing, not stained with the common pollutions of the human nature...." They *shall call his name Immanuel—God with us,* God in our nature, God at peace with us, in covenant with us. This was fulfilled in their calling him *Jesus—a Saviour* (Matt. 1:21-25), for, if he had not been *Immanuel—God with us,* he could not have been *Jesus—a Saviour.* (Isaiah 7:14)

**Rejoice greatly, O daughter of Zion; shout, O daughter of Jerusalem: behold thy King cometh unto thee: He** *is* **just, and having salvation; lowly, and riding upon an ass, and upon a colt the foal of an ass.**
That here begins a prophecy of the Messiah and his kingdom is plain from the literal accomplishment of the ninth verse in, and its express application to, Christ's riding in triumph into *Jerusa-*

# 12. Prophecy

*lem,* Matt. 21:5, John 12:15. (Zechariah 9:9)

**12 And I said unto them, if ye think good, give *me* my price; and if not, forbear. So they weighed for my price thirty *pieces* of silver. 13 And the LORD said unto me, Cast it unto the potter: a goodly price that I was prised at of them. And I took the thirty *pieces* of silver, and cast them to the potter in the house of the LORD.**

Now we find a particular accomplishment of this in the history of Christ's sufferings, and reference is had to this prophecy, Matt. 27:9, 10. *Thirty pieces of silver* was the very sum for which Christ was sold to the chief priests; the money, when Judas would not keep it, and the chief priests would not take it back was laid out in the purchase of *the potter's field.* Even that sudden resolve of the chief priests was according to an ancient prophecy and the more ancient counsel and foreknowledge of God. (Zechariah 11:12-13)

**My God, my God, why hast thou forsaken me?**

But it must be applied to Christ: for, in the first words of this complaint, he poured out his soul before God when he was upon the cross. (Matt. 27:46).... (Psalm 22:1)

**16 For dogs have compassed me: the assembly of the wicked have enclosed me: they pierced my hands and my feet.... 18 They part my garments among them, and cast lots upon my vesture.**

The very manner of his death is described, though never in use among the Jews.... [I]t is such an eminent prediction of the death of Christ and was so exactly fulfilled. ... *They parted my garments among them,* to every soldier a part, and *upon my vesture,* the seamless coat, *do they cast lots.* This very circumstance was exactly fulfilled, John 19:23,24. (Psalm 22:16-18)

**And I will pour upon the house of David, and upon the inhabitants of Jerusalem, the spirit of grace and of supplications: and they shall look upon me whom they have pierced, and they shall mourn for him, as one mourneth for *his* only *son,* and shall be in bitterness for him, as one that is in bitterness for *his* firstborn.**

It is foretold that Christ should be pierced, and this scripture is quoted as that which was fulfilled when Christ's side was pierced upon the cross; see John 19:37. (Zechariah 12:10)

**4 Surely he hath borne our griefs, and carried our sorrows: yet we did not esteem him stricken, smitten of God, and afflicted. 5 But he *was* wounded for our transgressions, he *was* bruised for our iniquities: the chastisement of our peace *was* upon him; and with his stripes we are healed. 6 All we like sheep have gone astray; we have turned every one to his own way; and the LORD hath laid on him the iniquity of us all. 7 He was oppressed, and he was afflicted, yet he opened not his mouth: he is brought as a lamb to the slaughter, and as a sheep before her shearers is dumb, so he openeth not his mouth. 8 He was taken from**

prison and from judgment: and who shall declare his generation? for he was cut off out of the land of the living: for the transgression of my people was he stricken. 9 And he made his grave with the wicked, and with the rich in his death: because he had done no violence, neither *was any* deceit in his mouth.

In these verses we have, 1. A further account of the sufferings of Christ. ... He had wounds and stripes. He was scourged,... He was stricken to death, to the grave which he made *with the wicked* (for he was crucified between two thieves, as if he had been the worst of the three) and yet *with the rich*, for he was buried in a sepulchre that belonged to Joseph, an honourable counsellor. (Isaiah 53:4-9)

**And *one* shall say unto him, What *are* these wounds in thine hands? Then he shall answer, *Those* with which I was wounded *in* the house of my friends.**

Christ was wounded in his hands, when they were nailed to the cross, and, after his resurrection, he had the marks of these wounds; and here he tells how he came by them; he received them as a false prophet, for the chief priests called him a deceiver, and upon that account would have him crucified; but he received them in the house of his friends—the Jews, who should have been his friends; for *he came to his own*.... (Zechariah 13:6)

**20 This gate of the LORD, into which the righteous shall enter. 21 I will praise thee: for thou hast heard me, and art become my salvation. 22 The stone *which* the builders refused is become the head *stone* of the corner. 23 This is the LORD's doing; it is marvellous in our eyes.**

We have here an illustrious prophecy of the humiliation and exaltation of our Lord Jesus.... Some by this gate understand Christ, by whom we are taken into fellowship with God and our praises are accepted; he is *the way;* there is no coming to the Father but by him (John 14:6).... [H]ere we have, 1. His humiliation. He is *the stone which the builders refused....* This stone was *rejected by the builders,* by the rulers and people of the Jews (Acts 4:8, 10, 11).... 2. His exaltation. He *has become the headstone of the corner....* He is the chief cornerstone in the foundation, in whom Jew and Gentile are united, that they may be built up one holy house. ... *This is the Lord's doing....* He sent him, sealed him; his hand went with him throughout his whole undertaking, and from first to last he did his Father's will; and this ought to be *marvellous in our eyes.* (Psalm 118:20-23)

It was not only determined in the secret counsel of God, but declared to the world many ages before, *by the mouth* and pen *of the prophets, that Christ should suffer,* in order to the accomplishment of his undertaking; and it was God himself that *showed* it by them, who will see that his words be made good; what he showed he fulfilled, he so fulfilled as he had shown, punctually and exactly, without any variation. (Acts 3:18)

## 12. Prophecy

We call the prophets the *pen-men* of scripture, whereas they really were but the pen. The tongue of the most subtle disputant, and the most eloquent orator, is but the pen with which God writes what he pleases. (Psalm 45:1)

Those that are prophets must first be seers; those who undertake to speak to others of the things of God must have an insight into those things themselves. (1 Samuel 9:9-10)

God's prophets saw what they spoke of, knew what they said, and require our belief of nothing but what they themselves believed and were sure of.... (Isaiah 1:1)

God's ambassadors must keep closely to their instructions, and not in the least vary from them, either to please men or to save themselves from harm. They must neither *add* nor *diminish*, Deut. 4:2. (Jeremiah 26:2)

*Rebuke a sinner* and *he will hate thee*, and do thee a mischief if he can; yet God's prophets must rather expose themselves than betray their trust: he that employs them will protect them, and restrain the wrath of man.... (1 Kings 13:4)

Those that have messages to deliver from God must not be *afraid of the face of man*.... (Jeremiah 1:8)

See what care God takes of his prophets: He *suffers no man to do them wrong;* all the rage of their enemies cannot prevail to take them off till they have finished their testimony. (Jeremiah 12:18-23)

Those that are employed for God, though their success answer not their expectations, must not therefore throw off their commission, but continue to follow God, though the storm be in their faces. ... If what we say and do be right before God, we may easily despise the reproaches and censures of man. *It is a small thing to be judged of their judgment.* (Jeremiah 17:14-16)

In transmitting divine revelation to the children of men it has been God's usual way to make use of the *weak and foolish things* and persons *of the world*, and such as were *despised* and despaired of, *to confound the wise and mighty,* that the excellency of the power might be of him. (Daniel 2:26-27)

The Spirit of God sometimes served his own purpose by the particular genius of the prophet; for prophets were not speaking trumpets, *through* which the Spirit spoke, but speaking men *by* whom the Spirit spoke, making use of their natural powers, in respect both of light and flame, and advancing them above themselves. (Isaiah Introduction)

[The prophets] ... all aimed at one and the same thing, which was to bring people to repent of their sins and to return to God and to do their duty to him. ...[T]hey make it their business to press the great and *weighty matters of the law, judgment, mercy, and truth.* (Isaiah Preface)

## Part II: Wisdom (Salvation)

[T]he Spirit of prophecy never rests upon any but a holy and wise man, and one whose passions are allayed ... a humble man and a man of fortitude, that is, one that has power to keep his sensual animal part in due subjection to religion and right reason. (Isaiah Preface)

Those that begin low are likely to rise high, and it is good for those that are designed for prophets to have their education under prophets and to be serviceable to them. Baruch wrote what Jeremiah dictated.... (Jeremiah 36:4)

[A]ll prophecy makes itself known to the prophet that it is prophecy indeed ... (which Jeremiah intimates when he says, *The Word of the Lord was as a fire in my bones*, Jer. 20:9), and therefore they always spoke with great assurance, knowing they should be justified, Isa. 1:7. ... "The prophetical Spirit, seating itself in the rational powers as well as in the imagination, did never alienate the mind, but inform and enlighten it; and those that were actuated by it always maintained a clearness and consistency of reason, with strength and solidity of judgment. ...God did not make use of idiots or fools to reveal his will." ... [T]he pretenders to prophecy ... underwent alienations of mind ... tearing their hair, foaming at the mouth. (Isaiah Preface)

Wicked prophets are the worst of men; their sins against God are most heinous, and their plots against religion most dangerous. (Hosea 9:8)

The great thing Satan aims at is to make people forget God, and all that whereby he has made himself known; and he has many subtle methods to bring them to this. Sometimes he does it by setting up false gods (bring men in love with Baal, and they soon forget the name of God), sometimes by misrepresenting the true God, as if he were altogether such a one as ourselves. Pretenses to new revelation may prove as dangerous to religion as the denying of all revelation; and false prophets in God's name may perhaps do more mischief to the power of godliness than false prophets in Baal's name, as being less guarded against. ... He that pretends to have a message from God, whether by dream or voice, let him declare it, and it will easily appear which is of God and which is not. Those that have spiritual senses exercised will be able to distinguish; for *what is the chaff to the wheat?* (Jeremiah 23:26-28)

"Take heed of those who pretend to revelation, and admit them not without sufficient proof, lest that one absurdity being admitted, a thousand follow." ... Satan turns himself *into an angel of light*.... (Matthew 7:15-20)

Let us not therefore desire visions and apparitions, nor seek to the dead, but *to the law and to the testimony* (Isa. 8:19, 20), for that is *the sure word of prophecy*, upon which we may depend. (Luke 16:30-31)

God is pleased often-times to single out some sinners, and to make them monuments of his justice, for warning to others of what is coming; and some

## 12. Prophecy

that thought themselves very safe are snatched away suddenly, and drop down dead in an instant, as Ananias and Sapphira at Peter's feet when he prophesied. (Ezekiel 11:8-13)

[W]hen God speaks to you by his prophets do not think yourselves too good to be taught; be not scornful, be not wilful, let not your hearts rise against the word, nor slight the messengers that bring it to you. (Jeremiah 13:15)

[T]hose that will not hear of their faults from God's prophets, that are reprovers in the gate, shall be made to hear of them from conscience, which is a reprover in their own bosoms that will not be daunted nor silenced. And miserable is the man that is thus made a terror to himself. (Jeremiah 20:4)

Those who will not consider that a prophet is among them, and who improve not the day of their visitation while it is continued, will be made to remember that a prophet has been among them when the things that belong to their peace are *hidden from their eyes*. (Ezekiel 33:33)

Those that misuse God's prophets justly lose them. (Lamentations 2:9)

The death of good men is a thing to be laid to heart and considered more than common deaths. ... Little children, when they are little, least lament the death of their parents, because they know not what a loss it is to them. ...[T]he righteous in their removal ... *are taken away from the evil to come*, then when it is just coming. ... When the deluge is coming they are called into the ark, and have a hiding-place and rest in heaven when there was none for them under heaven. ... In wrath to the world, to punish them for all the injuries they have done to the righteous and merciful ones; those are taken away that stood in the gap to turn away the judgments of God, and then what can be expected but a deluge of them? It is a sign that God intends war when he calls home his ambassadors. (Isaiah 57:1-2)

God usually warns sinners before he strikes; and, where his warnings are slighted, the blow will fall the heavier. (Hebrews 11:7)

The work of God's prophets is to give us warning; if, being warned, we do not save ourselves, it is our own fault, and our blood will be upon our own head. (2 Kings 6:9-10)

The voice of the prophets is *the Lord's voice*, and that *cries to the city*, cries to the country. ... When the sin of a city cries to God his voice cries against the city; and, when the judgments of God are coming upon a city, his voice first *cries unto it*. He warns before he wounds, because he is *not willing that any should perish*. (Micah 6:9)

The church of God is like Moses's bush, burning, yet *not consumed;* whatever hardship it has met with, or may meet with, it shall have a being in the world to the end of time. It is *persecut-*

ed of men, *but not forsaken* of God, and therefore, though it is *cast down*, it is *not destroyed* (2 Cor. 4:9), corrected, yet *not consumed*, refined in the furnace as silver, but *not consumed* as dross. (Lamentations 3:22)

The word of God is like fire. ... Fire has different effects, according as the matter is on which it works; it hardens clay, but softens wax; it consumes the dross, but purifies the gold. So the word of God is to some *a savour of life unto life, to others of death unto death*. (Jeremiah 23:29)

It well becomes God's prophets to acquaint themselves with grief; the great prophet did so. The afflictions of the world, as well as those of the church, should be afflictions to us. (Isaiah 16:11)

It is the unspeakable comfort of the people of God that, though they have hosts against them, they have *the Lord of hosts* for them and *he shall thoroughly plead their cause*, pleading he shall plead it, plead it with jealousy, plead it effectually, plead it and carry it, *that he may give rest to the land*, and to his people's land, rest from all their enemies round about. This is applicable to all believers, who complain of the dominion of sin and corruption, and of their own weakness and manifold infirmities. ... [H]e will *make them free*, and they shall be *free indeed*; he will give them *rest, that rest which remains for the people of God*. (Jeremiah 50:34)

God will be justified when he speaks, and both heaven and earth shall declare his righteousness.... (Isaiah 1:2)

Jews and Gentiles shall become *one sheep-fold*; and they shall all, as far as they are sanctified, have a disposition to love one another, the gospel they profess having in it the strongest inducements to mutual love, and the Spirit that dwells in them being the Spirit of love. Though they may have different apprehensions about minor things, they shall be all one in the great things of God, being renewed after the same image. Though they may have many paths, they have but *one way*, that of serious godliness. (Jeremiah 32:40)

Note, the spirit of life is from God; he at first in the creation breathed into man the breath of life, and so he will at last in the resurrection. (Ezekiel 37:10)

What comes from heaven in a promise should be sent back to heaven in a prayer, "Come, Lord Jesus, put an end to this state of sin, sorrow, and temptation; gather thy people out of this present evil world, and take them up to heaven, that state of perfect purity, peace, and joy, and so finish thy great design, and fulfil all that word in which thou hast caused thy people to hope." (Revelation 22:20-21)

The kingdom of Satan will certainly fall before the kingdom of Christ, error before truth, profaneness before godliness, and corruption before grace in the hearts of the faithful. When the interests of religion seem to be run down and ready to sink, yet even then we may be confident that the day of their

## 12. Prophecy

triumph will come. Great is the truth, and will prevail. (1 Samuel 5:2-3)

When we take a view of the affairs of this world, and of the church of God in it, we cannot but think, What will be the end of these things? We see things move as if they would end in the utter ruin of God's kingdom among men. When we observe the prevalence of vice and impiety, the decay of religion, the sufferings of the righteous, and the triumphs of the ungodly over them, we may well ask, *O my Lord! what will be the end of these things?* But this may satisfy us in general, that all will end well at last. Great is the truth, and will prevail at long-run. All opposing rule, principality, and power, will be put down, and holiness and love will triumph, and be in honour, to eternity. The end, this end, will come. (Daniel 12:8)

# Thematic Subtopic Index

A select index to help readers navigate the wisdom of Matthew Henry in sub-categories

| | |
|---|---|
| Adultery | 110, 116 |
| Afflictions | 134, 190, 221, 222, 224, 236, 243, 244, 245, 246, 247, 249, 276 |
| Alcohol (Drunkenness) | 98, 113, 114 |
| Apostasy | 21, 58, 86, 93, 99, 118, 231, 241 |
| Applause (Worldly Praise) | 90, 102, 121, 122, 215, 229, 234, 238 |
| Atheists | 22, 50, 53, 59, 64 |
| Baptism | 161, 162 |
| Beauty | 67, 68, 253 |
| Beginners (in Religion) | 182, 276, 277 |
| Business (Industry) | 27, 28, 77, 109, 119, 128, 218, 258, 272, 290 |
| Censures | 43, 206, 207, 233, 247, 284, 289, 302 |
| Charity | 49, 79, 150, 151, 158, 206, 207, 271 |
| Cheating | 70, 119, 127, 128, 232 |
| Children | 60, 61, 179, 222, 226, 248, 249, 276, 283 |
| Communion of Saints | 201, 221 |
| Conscience | 25, 27, 34, 35, 57, 58, 59, 79, 100, 103, 105, 109, 118, 140, 154, 155, 202 |
| Conversion | 20, 59, 129, 150, 154, 157, 161, 162, 163, 165, 166, 281, 282 |
| Conviction | 20, 21, 22, 23, 100, 101, 154, 155, 163, 179, 281 |
| Covenant | 37, 43, 110, 156, 161, 163, 165, 170, 175, 203, 217, 242, 243, 276, 299 |
| Coveting | 44, 53, 58, 68, 69, 90, 105, 113, 115, 117, 118, 238 |
| Death | 25, 27, 68, 136, 139, 141, 169, 170, 171, 175, 222, 261, 304 |
| Delays | 153, 162, 177, 187, 188, 190, 192, 193, 269 |
| Deliverance | 83, 159, 161, 168, 169, 173, 175, 177, 181, 195, 225, 252, 292, 293 |
| Delusion | 59, 115, 123, 125 |
| Depression (Melancholy) | 27, 220, 251 |
| Desire | 54, 109, 110, 111, 119, 124, 136, 178, 182, 208 |
| Direction | 23, 204, 223, 224, 225, 268 |
| Discontent | 25, 26, 135 |
| Disease | 45, 55, 63, 82, 93, 114, 124, 138, 139, 169, 241, 246, 285 |
| Divination | 123, 124, 187, 237 |
| Duty | 150, 163, 209, 218, 237, 264, 268, 273, 274, 275, 276 |
| Envy | 44, 74, 86, 136, 253, 254 |
| Estates | 68, 79, 119, 139, 230, 231, 257, 272 |
| Evil | 37, 144, 150, 151, 152, 205 |

## Thematic Subtopic Index

Expectations .................................................................. 69, 77, 113, 197, 203, 293, 302
False Doctrine ............................................................... 24, 86, 87, 88, 91, 124, 212
Family ........................................................................ 60, 61, 226, 227, 248, 257, 278, 291
Fear ............................................................. 21, 25, 26, 191, 192, 193, 194, 204, 210, 274, 276
Forewarning ............................... 20, 45, 56, 98, 141, 234, 235, 241, 247, 297, 298, 300
Fretfulness ............................................................................... 25, 26, 47, 100, 136
Gentiles ................................................................................................... 163, 183
Glory ........................................ 217, 219, 222, 225, 226, 229, 238, 246, 252, 253, 294
Gospel .................... 17, 19, 21, 22, 23, 24, 46, 85, 86, 91, 99, 161, 166, 211, 213, 264
Grief (Sorrow) ............... 42, 82, 102, 110, 111, 115, 141, 178, 221, 222, 236, 259, 305
Guilt ............................................... 27, 57, 82, 127, 151, 163, 164, 166, 167, 168, 170
Hatred ........................... 18, 33, 41, 42, 43, 44, 48, 49, 59, 91, 116, 121, 137, 191, 302
Health ................................................................. 113, 150, 158, 166, 169, 175, 246
Heaven ............. 47, 48, 49, 133, 140, 152, 153, 166, 197, 204, 236, 252, 253, 261, 283
Hell ........................ 36, 47, 64, 82, 89, 103, 104, 123, 130, 133, 134, 140, 141, 142, 285
Holy Spirit ...................... 22, 23, 64, 105, 154, 162, 165, 168, 181, 183, 202, 204, 212,
..................................................................................... 213, 217, 255, 257, 263, 302
Honesty ....................... 43, 69, 70, 73, 74, 127, 128, 202, 209, 218, 239, 242, 271, 276
Husbands and Wives ............................................................................................ 256
Idleness ............................................................................. 31, 154, 264, 271, 272, 287
Ignorance ............ 17, 18, 24, 31, 32, 37, 39, 42, 46, 49, 53, 85, 126, 135, 212, 233, 246
Illness ............................................................................ 79, 135, 139, 169, 175, 246, 285
Impenitence ......................... 20, 33, 34, 35, 36, 37, 38, 41, 57, 104, 133, 138, 144, 145
.................................................................................................................. 149, 153, 285
Instruments ....................... 46, 49, 59, 63, 68, 76, 220, 243, 265, 266, 267, 283
Knowledge ...................... 18, 19, 45, 64, 85, 124, 180, 182, 208, 212, 215, 231, 255,
........................................................................................................................ 258, 277, 289
Lust .................. 54, 98, 109, 110, 111, 112, 113, 149, 153, 156, 201, 207, 211, 241, 248
Malice ............................................... 44, 46, 47, 49, 50, 59, 73, 74, 86, 88, 122, 247, 274
Martyrdom ................................................................................ 170, 209, 274, 275
Miracles ............................................. 17, 106, 167, 175, 177, 197, 225, 234, 255, 299
Mirth .......................................................................... 41, 111, 114, 129, 138, 190, 202
Misery ......... 17, 55, 75, 93, 102, 109, 111, 112, 123, 130, 138, 139, 140, 174, 177, 285
Mourning ...................... 18, 81, 82, 115, 134, 138, 156, 222, 236, 285, 286, 300
Original Sin ................................................................................ 35, 53, 54, 55, 60, 242
Parents ......................................................................... 38, 60, 61, 226, 248, 249, 259, 304
Passion .................. 25, 27, 45, 48, 97, 109, 110, 114, 117, 209, 230, 249, 283, 288, 303
Peace ................. 23, 50, 104, 105, 121, 126, 152, 155, 157, 163, 170, 181, 198, 251, 304
Persecutors (Enemies) ..................... 44, 45, 46, 48, 49, 50, 58, 59, 75, 79, 80, 91, 103,
.................................................................................................... 122, 137, 268, 284, 287, 293

# Thematic Subtopic Index

Piety .................. 44, 58, 64, 65, 81, 90, 97, 100, 129, 145, 166, 206, 219, 253, 272, 274
Posterity ............................................................................................... 177, 179, 278
Poverty ........................................... 31, 61, 66, 71, 118, 133, 154, 189, 233, 266, 273
Prejudices ................................... 18, 22, 44, 47, 53, 59, 88, 91, 122, 284, 291
Prosperity ............. 55, 64, 66, 68, 75, 117, 118, 119, 128, 129, 130, 136, 137, 139,
  ............................................. 168, 173, 189, 221, 231, 233, 234, 253, 292, 293
Providence ............ 55, 134, 138, 142, 169, 176, 179, 187, 188, 189, 190, 193, 201,
  .......................... 215, 225, 244, 245, 246, 247, 252, 265, 266, 275, 281, 297
Reformation ............ 32, 42, 56, 58, 79, 80, 83, 86, 105, 126, 134, 149, 152, 155,
  ................................................................................................ 181, 243, 282
Relations (Family) ......................... 48, 55, 100, 164, 169, 170, 246, 261, 264, 274
Reservations (for Sin) ..................................................................... 137, 156
Rest ............... 127, 130, 150, 155, 169, 187, 218, 219, 258, 261, 286, 290, 304, 305
Revenge .............. 39, 41, 49, 60, 73, 74, 78, 87, 112, 128, 133, 137, 142, 143, 144,
  ................................................................................ 158, 193, 232, 236
Righteousness ............... 17, 61, 79, 127, 137, 165, 168, 187, 249, 264, 267, 270, 271,
  .................................................................. 276, 277, 278, 298, 301, 304
Sabbath ................................................................................. 155, 218, 219, 298
Saints .................. 34, 42, 45, 47, 68, 85, 90, 97, 100, 134, 140, 161, 162, 166, 170, 176
  .............................................. 179, 190, 196, 232, 236, 238, 253, 257, 292,
Sanctification..... 21, 60, 64, 68, 103, 105, 140, 163, 165, 166, 175, 180, 189, 215, 305
Satan ... 27, 36, 45, 46, 53, 56, 57, 75, 102, 103, 110, 113, 114, 125, 126, 128, 129, 130,
  ..... 137, 164, 167, 168, 188, 190, 193, 199, 204, 208, 241, 252, 271, 273, 274, 284, 303
Scripture .................... 23, 24, 35, 36, 53, 85, 87, 88, 91, 212, 213, 224, 233, 267, 289,
  ................................................................................................ 297, 298, 302
Security ........................... 23, 119, 130, 137, 142, 178, 188, 231, 234, 251, 263, 273
Sermons .......................................................................................... 20, 36, 288
Shame ................. 18, 21, 35, 38, 41, 42, 48, 56, 61, 67, 73, 77, 82, 103, 114, 116, 138,
  ................................................................ 141, 149, 158, 215, 233, 276, 289, 292
Sin ........................ 53, 54, 55, 56, 57, 58, 60, 61, 125, 126, 127, 129, 130, 161, 162,
  .................................................................................... 163, 165, 166, 167
Slander ........................................................................................ 47, 92, 121, 204
Solitude .............................................................. 201, 216, 217, 222, 232, 263, 266
Soul ............... 18, 19, 23, 27, 54, 55, 139, 140, 161, 165, 166, 167, 169, 170, 171, 178,
  ............................................................................................ 181, 182, 208, 211, 292
Speech .......... 35, 45, 46, 66, 92, 114, 118, 121, 123, 165, 204, 205, 206, 216, 260, 302
Study (Meditation) ............. 23, 99, 119, 176, 205, 206, 210, 215, 216, 221, 224, 231,
  ........................................................................................ 258, 270, 272, 288, 290
Suffering ............... 45, 49, 55, 58, 81, 82, 134, 141, 169, 192, 195, 196, 209, 221, 235,
  ................................................................ 239, 243, 246, 247, 253, 266, 291, 293

## Thematic Subtopic Index

Suicide ............................................................................................. 27, 33, 34
Talents ............... 19, 31, 32, 37, 55, 77, 97, 117, 163, 174, 229, 231, 254, 255, 256, 268
Tears ................................................................. 69, 81, 140, 191, 196, 221, 235, 236
Temptation ............... 27, 41, 44, 47, 55, 56, 57, 67, 70, 102, 113, 115, 117, 118, 119
..... 123, 126, 128, 129, 130, 179, 190, 193, 201, 204, 208, 241, 242, 271, 273, 274, 285
Time ................ 25, 27, 42, 54, 93, 118, 119, 123, 124, 135, 136, 142, 153, 162, 163
..................................................................................... 177, 184, 266, 269, 272, 290
Tithing ................................................................................................................. 272
Trials (Tribulation) ..................... 25, 171, 178, 179, 189, 190, 191, 236, 244, 251, 293
Trinity .......................................................................................................... 17, 167,
Tyranny ............................................................................. 49, 76, 78, 85, 154, 208,
Vineyard ............................................................................. 19, 101, 257, 264, 292,
Vows ....................................................................................................... 89, 203,
Wealth ........ 55, 66, 67, 68, 70, 73, 78, 90, 117, 118, 180, 189, 208, 213, 230, 253, 254,
............................................................................................. 255, 258, 272, 286
Wheat and Tares ............................ 58, 61, 98, 104, 125, 126, 176, 243, 247, 271, 303
Wickedness ........... 19, 34, 37, 38, 45, 54, 57, 61, 64, 74, 75, 81, 82, 89, 93, 94, 97, 98,
..................... 109, 113, 115, 123, 127, 136, 137, 141, 143, 144, 145, 235, 249, 277, 281
Wicked People ................... 32, 36, 59, 78, 133, 136, 137, 141, 157, 174, 176, 201, 202
................................................................................................. 275, 281, 284,
Wrath ............................................................... 135, 136, 137, 138, 139, 140, 141, 144
Writing ................................................................................... 264, 265, 288, 289
Zeal .......................... 36, 44, 81, 85, 87, 88, 162, 182, 207, 226, 263, 267, 269, 276, 282

www.ingramcontent.com/pod-product-compliance
Lightning Source LLC
Chambersburg PA
CBHW050528300426
44113CB00012B/2005